ADM-7492

up

WITHDRAWN

D0389044

The
Blueberry Years

ALSO BY JIM MINICK

•

Finding a Clear Path

Her Secret Song

Burning Heaven

The Blueberry Years

A Memoir of Farm
and Family

Jim Minick

THOMAS DUNNE BOOKS
St. Martin's Press
New York

THOMAS DUNNE BOOKS.
An imprint of St. Martin's Press.

THE BLUEBERRY YEARS. Copyright © 2010 by Jim Minick. All rights
reserved. Printed in the United States of America. For information, address St. Martin's Press, 175 Fifth Avenue, New York, N.Y.
10010.

www.thomasdunnebooks.com
www.stmartins.com

Design by Kathryn Parise

LIBRARY OF CONGRESS CATALOGING-IN-PUBLICATION DATA

Minick, Jim, 1964–
    The blueberry years : a memoir of farm and family /
Jim Minick.—1st ed.
                p. cm.
    Includes bibliographical references.
    ISBN 978-0-312-57142-9 (alk. paper)
    1. Minick, Jim, 1964-—Homes and haunts.   2. Minick,
Jim, 1964-—Family.   3. Fruit growers—United States—
Biography.   4. Farm life—Virginia—Floyd County.   5. Fruit
culture—Virginia—Floyd County.   6. Blueberries—Virginia—
Floyd County.   I. Title.

    SB63.M64A3 2010
    634'.7370922755712—dc22
    [B]   2010021687

10   9   8   7   6   5   4   3   2

For our families and all the pickers
who supported our farm,

for all the blueberries
that bore so much,

for John M. Sutherland, 1919–2007,

and for Sarah,
who picked me.

CONTENTS

Contents

PART II
Grow (1995–1996)

PART IV
Prune (2000)

Contents

AUTHOR'S NOTE

I have kept to the truth as much as possible as I perceived it in telling this story, but I admit that memory often creates its own world.

Much of the information in the Interludes came from other sources, and I'm extremely grateful for the generosity of so many experts. Any errors, however, are all my own. Likewise, I've tried to provide accurate Internet addresses and contact information, but these often change. The publisher and I cannot be responsible for these changes. Nor can the publisher or I be responsible for third-party Web sites or their content.

Names have been changed for the usual reasons. And an occasional composite character walks across the page.

A note about that slippery companion we call time: We bought our blueberry farm in 1991, planted the blueberries in 1995, and left in 2002. In the service of art and good storytelling, I've compressed this twelve-year span of time: Part I occurs from 1991–1995, Part II is 1995–1996, Part III is 1997–1999, Part IV is 2000, and Part V is 2001–2002.

Finally, the recipes in this book. Please follow them exactly and be responsible. The author and publisher cannot be held accountable for any readers' specific health or allergy needs that may require medical supervision. Likewise, the author and publisher are not responsible for any adverse reactions to the recipes contained in this book.

They [berries] seem offered to us not so much for food as for sociality,
inviting us to pic-nic with Nature. We pluck and eat in remembrance of her.
It is a sort of sacrament—a communion—the not forbidden fruits,
which no serpent tempts us to eat.
—*Henry David Thoreau,* "Huckleberries"

In physical perfectness of form and texture and color,
there is nothing in all the world that exceeds a well-grown fruit.
—*Liberty Hyde Bailey,* The Holy Earth

Prologue

❀❀❀

a globe, all ocean, with swirling clouds,
on top a crater—
each one hit by a falling star

The Pickers

❧

They come to fill buckets and pans, canning jars, freezer bags, pie crusts, and always, the ever-waiting tongue. They come to visit and eat, to sate the hungers of loneliness and body. Though we offer only blueberries, they come wanting more.

They come from the American Dream—CEOs and wealthy realtors, two kids piling out of just-washed SUVs, wives stylish in their special picking outfits.

They come from communes named Left Bank, Abundant Dawn, and A Light Morning. *They* come tie-dyed, shoeless, braless, bathless.

On a good day, thirty cars of pickers fill our one-acre field, strangers and friends all picking side by side. Most come from a distance, driving twenty miles or more just because we're organic. They negotiate the winding dirt road into these Virginia hills, the directions taped to the steering wheel, their vehicles grinding the last half mile of steep lane. Often they step out of their cars and ask, "How did you ever find this place?"

They bring their children, wild or well behaved, all fascinated for a little while by a bush with a sweet berry. The toddlers hide in the maze of canes while six-year-olds sneak fruit from their mother's buckets. When scolded,

they sit and fill their pails with leaves and green berries. The infants go home
pooping blue.

One picker travels with her daughter all the way from North Carolina,
three hours away. They are reading *Blueberries for Sal*, the mother tells me as
she pulls up, and "We just have to see a blueberry bush." The wide-eyed
daughter strains in her baby seat and points to the field.

Many pickers come five times a season, year after year. Others come
only once. Some come in Cadillacs and Land Rovers, their cars pitching and
scraping on our lane, the hubcaps sparkling like newly minted coins. Some
drive twenty-year-old Dodges and Fords, the rust as hungry as the driver.

They come from France and Germany, Korea and South Africa, Ecua-
dor, Costa Rica, and Japan. Once a writing group of Japanese women spill
out of three cars to cover the field with quick voices and beautiful smiles.
Because it is the last day of the season, they find only two or three pounds
apiece, but still they laugh and sing. One shares a blueberry haiku and says
we should open a restaurant here, sell hot dogs.

Before any foreigners leave, I ask them to pronounce "blueberry" in their
tongue, and then write in our notebook: *paran dalgi, fresa azules, blaw beeren.*

Most people harvest for themselves, but some pick for us on shares, a
bucket for us, a bucket for them. We'll sell these at market and be glad for
the help. Others harvest for restaurants, markets, or CSAs, community-
supported agriculture farms. These pickers come the same day every week,
rain or shine. I pick with them through soaking rains, our slickers and wool
sweaters useless. After a while our fingers wrinkle and numb, too cold to
pluck even the biggest berry.

Others come to barter, with chickens and eggs, lettuce and tomatoes,
fresh milk and goat cheese. With one, I trade berries for massages; with
another, a year's supply of berries for our Web site. Once I even barter berries for a truckload of fleeces. I want to try wool as a mulch for the bushes,
as if to warm them, as if to make socks for these baby blues.

They come bringing recipes and gifts of homemade soap, a blueberry
cookie jar, a straw hat from Hawaii. Sometimes they bring us lunch or a bag
of cookies, water or a jar of just-canned jam. One time they even bring sushi. They offer us homemade blueberry beer, or a Mason jar of moonshine
filled with blueberries. We call it "Blue Shine" and sip it behind the shed.

Usually they come early in the morning, but some come in the middle of
the hottest afternoon, the picked berries baking in their cars. Most use our

buckets, but some come with their own cut-off milk jugs or special berry baskets. A few bring their own stools.

One dowdy picker carries her purse into the field where she inspects her one-pound harvest berry by berry. Her lanky husband waits by the check-out and cleans his pistol. Thankfully, they never return, and everyone else comes unarmed.

Previous owners of our farm come, like Jesse Moore, surprised by a new road and pond. Or Mary Lewis, a spry woman in her seventies, who tells of her honeymoon working in this same field sixty years ago. She is amazed to pick berries where once she hoed corn. Older neighbors come, like Daniel Hughes, who drilled oats here in the early 1960s. He is the last farmer to work this land before the field was abandoned to pines.

Some come wearing T-shirts proclaiming GOD IS DEAD, and others hand us leaflets of doom. Sometimes they invite us to their houses of worship or swimming holes or geodesic domes.

They come single or divorced, widow or bachelor, coupled, gay and straight, married and not; they come celebrating their sixtieth anniversary or their honeymoon, feeding each other gentle pinches of blue. On the day before their wedding, one couple picks for their reception, their eyes shining like each berry.

They come crawling behind their parents or walking with canes or rolling in wheelchairs, a companion dog helping over the bumps. Some who came regularly will never come again, like Greta, killed in a car wreck, or Tim, at forty sucked away by skin cancer, or Ruby, whose generous heart laughs no more.

At the end of the season, they come as gleaners for local soup kitchens, beating the blue jays for the last berries. We let them pick for free, and then close the gate, hanging a sign that reads SEASON'S OVER. SEE YOU NEXT YEAR.

And every day in every season, Sarah and I, we, too, come to this field—as pickers, as pilgrims, as gleaners of whatever we find.

Part I

Root and Seed

(1991-1995)

a small clutch of seeds
in a green-white nest
what blue dreams will you hatch?

Chapter 1

❄❄❄

Meeting the Berries

Two hours before sunset, I pick up the jarring phone to hear this: "Uh, Mr. Minick? I got your blueberries on my rig." In the background, I hear the huge engine idling. "I'm sitting here in Riner and I can't see your farm. Been driving back and forth for the past hour trying to find it. Where *are* you?"

This from an eighteen-wheel truck driver hauling our precious bushes all the way from Michigan to Virginia; this from Riner, the town that happens to be our mailing address, a one-street village twelve miles away; this from an order we placed six months earlier, sending in a whopper check from our wimpy bank account. The canceled check is the only proof that we might receive plants. Without any confirmation call, we have no idea if the shipment of 1,000 bushes will come on our preferred date of April 1, 1995. When April 1 arrives, we answer this call and feel like fools.

I tell the driver to park at the Riner convenience store, where Sarah and I meet him twenty minutes later. A round, balding man climbs down from the silver rig chewing on a toothpick. He seems friendly enough, but his shoulders sag a little when I tell him we have another 12 miles to go, away from the interstate. He explains that he has an order waiting for pickup in Atlanta, 400 miles away, by the next day.

His teenage son, along for company, scoots back into the sleeping compartment. I grab the chrome and climb the three steps into the leather-upholstered cab where I ride shotgun. In the mirror I watch Sarah in our compact red car get in behind this monster—no one told us it would be a big rig. So far below this rolling giant, Sarah looks even tinier than she is. *What* are *we in for?* I keep wondering to myself. I can't see the furrow between her brows, but I know it's there, know she is wondering the same.

I direct the driver through the maze of country roads, traveling several miles on Route 8, the main artery into Floyd County, and then turning right onto Alum Ridge. We lean into the long curves on these two highways, the driver downshifting on the steep inclines, the back of the long rig crossing the yellow lines on the sharpest curves. These roads, at least, have yellow lines.

"This sure is pretty country," the driver muses, but I also hear a hint of worry in his voice, his Michigan eyes used to straight roads, few hills, no mountains. All the while, between the small talk, I keep speculating where I'm going to get him and his rig to turn around. I know where I want to unload the berries, down by the stream below the house where we can water them until I finish getting the field ready. But we're talking skinny roads, graveled when the county can afford it, traveled by the mailman and school bus, nothing bigger. And after we unload, where *would* we get this huge tractor trailer turned to face the other way?

Another five miles and I tell him to slow for the next right onto Lester Road. This one is paved, but has no lines. He makes the wide arcing turn and I sense his worry intensify. "How far back in here do you live?" he asks. Three more miles, I tell him, hoping he'll hear the nonchalance in my voice. He is driving slowly now, his arms hugging the wide steering wheel. Too slowly.

We're heading directly into a mountain-framed sunset, but the driver doesn't notice. Then a mile down Lester, two miles from our new farm, the hardtop ends. The driver brakes hard, stopping in the loose gravel. He rolls down his window, looks around, and spits out his toothpick. He glances across the gear shift to me, then stares out the windshield before saying, "This is as far as we go." I try to convince him to drive on, knowing from our brief conversation that he's maneuvered this rig through the tight alleys of New York City. I explain that our neighbor sometimes drives his logging equipment down this dirt road, but I can tell from his steady stare that he won't budge.

At the fork in the road where Lost Bent Creek turns off, where we should be heading, the driver backs his trailer, jimmying the hind end around. In less than two minutes, he has faced the still-loaded rig the wrong way, back toward Riner. He pulls over by a wide spot on the side, looks at a grassy shoulder next to a pasture fence, and says, "Can we unload here?" It is not really a question. I tell him I don't know, but will have to check with the neighbor who lives across the road. I get out, leaving the door open to let him feel some of the cold April air. Sarah waits beside the car where I tell her the predicament. Together, we open the white picket gate to a small, neatly kept bungalow.

We've never met Mrs. Allen, but were told that her late husband plumbed our house fifteen years before we bought it. She greets us at the door, a little startled to find a tractor trailer parked in front of her house. We introduce ourselves and tell her why the truck sits there blocking her view. She nods, slowly smiles, and says that unloading there would be fine. The seeds of our dream farm, now waiting in the cavern of a trailer, will sit precariously by the side of the road, all $2,500 of them free for someone else's taking. It is our only choice.

Mr. Friendly Driver has turned more businesslike; he wants to move on. His son has already opened the trailer doors, and the driver puts on his gloves, ready to grab plants and get them off. By the dimness of overhead lights, I climb in and begin to unload.

Our plants are tucked against the front end of the trailer, all neatly stacked three high, the last small part of his load. With a flashlight, I try to inspect these babies we are about to adopt, try to get a sense of their number and kind, but all I see are six-inch twigs in gallon pots of dirt. *This is what I paid so much money for?* In her yellow ball cap, Sarah has climbed in behind me. She takes off a glove and scratches the stem of one of these twigs. Her thumbnail fills with inner bark, the green tissue affirming the dormant life within.

Then we begin searching for labels, finding a few bushes with NELSON and BLUECROP on them, but only a few. To save money, it looks like the company has only attached the plastic bands on a fourth of the 1,000 plants, stringing together all of the unlabeled to the labeled. And given how these potted sticks are all stacked on top of each other, there is no way to count them, really, until we've unloaded. I cuss under my breath.

This initial greeting between soon-to-be "parents" and twiggy "children" lasts less than two minutes. The trucker and his son already have started hauling the pots to the back of the truck, and we realize if we want to keep any order to this chaos, we'd better start hauling and organizing. Now.

So we walk the fifty feet of the bed again and again, pinching the edges of black pots three in each hand, carrying all we can. On the ground, Sarah and the son carry the pots from truck bed to road bank, scurrying in the dimming light. In all of this, we call out what labels we can read, what labels exist.

We've ordered six varieties, and because of their different ripening times (early, midseason, and late), we want to keep like with like. Otherwise, we'll roam the field with our pickers, never sure of the next ready bush. I call out "Berkeley" or "Spartan" every time I can, and Sarah tries to steer the helper to the right group. The driver mentions again his next load in Georgia, so we finish quickly, try to double-check our numbers, and sign his sheet. Then we watch his rear lights glow around the bend.

What possessed two young schoolteachers to buy ninety acres of woodland and sink all of their capital, and a lot of the bank's, into digging dirt? We ask ourselves this as we water bushes, grub tree roots, fork wet mulch. We have stellar grade point averages and degrees from respected institutions— didn't they teach us better? Not really, though what we want to learn, we realize later, isn't what they teach. And after college graduation, we work enough in our "career" fields (business and education) to know we want something more, something else.

We pursue that something else by moving to Floyd County, Virginia. Really, we move so that I can escape a job I hate, teaching high-school English in suburban Maryland. I enroll in the master's program at Radford University while Sarah begins her teaching career in a small, country elementary. When I graduate with my MA in 1991, Radford hires me on, so we decide to stay. Sarah likes her job well enough, and we both love the mountains and valleys, the rural nature of land and people, the fertile possibilities.

Eventually we realize that something else we want is to stay home and pursue "the good life" like Helen and Scott Nearing, our new heroes and "preachers" of this lifestyle in their 1954 classic *Living the Good Life: How to Live Sanely and Simply in a Troubled World*. We want to write and make baskets, grow most of our own food, and follow a dream we call homesteading. The farm, we hope, will allow this, and the berries will be our cash crop, our money-maker to pay taxes and other expenses. In the long run we hope our art will bring in some money as well.

In the meantime, teaching will have to fund the homesteading dream. Every morning we drive our separate ways: Sarah to teach kindergarten-ers, and I to struggle with college freshmen and sophomores; she to wade through the sniffles and first discoveries of words, me to wade through stacks of grading and moments of insight and clarity. Our summers off give us enough nibbles of freedom to want the whole year to ourselves, to be our own bosses. And why not? The stress we carry home from school makes us realize that this homesteading life will probably be a lot healthier, too. We hope.

The next day, a Sunday, we journey in our pickup past the Mennonite church at the end of our road to travel on to our new house of worship, the church of *Vaccinium corymbosum*, the high order of the highbush, with Berke-ley and Nelson serving as deacons, Blueray and Bluecrop members of the choir, and Spartan and Patriot the ushers for the day. In the bright clear light of spring we pause from the immense work before us to greet these new friends. And in this light, I begin to see that they are much more than just sticks in pots of dirt; the stems fill with bright colors, some vibrant yellow and red, some pea green. I kneel among the pots and realize each variety has its own peculiar shape, the Berkeley tall and stout, the Bluecrop tall and skinny, the others differing in size with the Nelson the shortest and roundest of the six varieties.

Last night as we unloaded, Sarah had kept like with like, and this morn-ing, as we inspect the clustered varieties more closely, we find a few unla-beled pots that don't seem to fit their cluster, but only a handful out of a thousand. We pick up pots and compare them with labeled ones, asking each other's opinions. The more I look and touch each plant, the more I also see each is different from the others in the same variety, a bending branch on a Blueray peculiarly unique, a V-shaped notch on the next bush its own signature.

But the detailed differences vanish when I stand in the bed of the truck and look at the mass from a distance. This is a congregation of individuals, for sure, but they are all only one or two years old, children really, waiting to root and grow into adulthood. Blueberries can live for over fifty years. What kind of chorus will this choir raise in 2045? And will we be here to join in, to lift our own voice in this song of blue?

What took four people an hour to unload takes Sarah and me a full day to haul the two more miles to our farm. What filled only a minute portion of the tractor trailer fills our pickup five times as we haul and drive, load and unload. We pinch pots again, cramping our fingers and heaving the weight onto the truck bed. Then on the bank of Lost Bent Creek, we unload and sort into clusters by variety, 167 Patriot here, 168 Spartan there. We've picked a small space to waylay them for now, a narrow strip of land between the stream and our new farm road. I soak my feet and pull up five-gallon buckets of cold water while Sarah dips quart containers from bucket to plant, soaking the roots and soil, the dripping water sparkling in the sun.

The best time to plant blueberries is late spring, right before they break dormancy. It is April 2, the ideal time, but the bushes sit here by the stream where we water them once a week. They have to wait because the field, that vast opening in the woods a half mile farther up our lane, that center of our homesteading dream, isn't ready yet.

And we both have to return to our day jobs tomorrow.

Chapter 2

❦

Meeting the Field

We first journeyed down this road that the trucker refused to travel in the fall of 1991, four years before we planted blueberries. And that's how our life seemed to define itself now: before berries and after berries. Before we had these wild ideas, after we had these 1,000 wild realities. Before we could travel as we saw fit, after we could only travel on the farm road between house and field, back and forth, back and forth. We didn't have kids, just 2 mutts and 1,000 young blueberries.

In 1991, we first encountered the field and the farm that it centered, and that would eventually center us. To call it a field then would be to speak of its history, for when we walked it with Jesse Moore, the owner's son, we really walked *around* it looking in. The field wasn't a pasture of grass full of grazing bovines, nor was it a plowed, fallow cropland waiting for spring planting. No, this field was full of pine trees, mostly spindly leaning bull pine, many bent and crossed, damaged by ice and wind. Some farmer last worked this field forty years ago, and in those intervening four decades the surrounding forest had filled the void, taken over, converting three-inch grass blades to thirty-foot timber. So instead of wading through thick green meadow, we skirted the dense thicket of scaly brown trees. We hiked along the rotted remains of a split-rail fence that once separated cows from corn, which now kept the bull pines from charging into the mature stands of oak and hickory.

But we still fell in love, despite these faults. Like infatuated lovers, we overlooked the flaws of this new partner. Sure, we acknowledged that no good road existed to the field and that we didn't know how we'd clear these scrub trees or what we'd do with them once down. We saw these things out of the sides of our eyes, only looking directly at what we wanted to. Which was plenty.

The field itself seemed to lay well, with a steep grade at the lower side, but the top was flat enough for tilling or building. We just had to figure out how to drive there. With an old survey plat, we estimated that the original field held eight to ten acres of tillable land, plenty for us to begin.

The farm came with a spring and three small creeks, some good timber, and some other abandoned fields that could be cleared in the future. And it came with a long history, like an ancient book filled with the remnants of earlier homesteaders. On one ridge, we found the rotted remains of a log cabin next to gnarled apple trees. In the valley, we tiptoed on stepping stones across Lost Bent Creek, a stream named after a Mr. Bent. Sometime in the 1800s, Bent lay down to drink from its cold water, and for some reason died there; he wasn't found for several months. Though we never knew him, we remembered his lostness every time we mentioned this creek.

By this brook, a barn and four sheds—some useable, some too rotted— circled a small, beautiful, hundred-year-old house. We looked in each building, checked foundations, and wondered about ghosts. The house, like most old dwellings, needed work, but Sarah and I had a place to live while we focused our energies on blueberries.

A month after walking around the field and through the house, we signed the papers, took on our largest debt ever, and moved into our new home the first of the year 1992. Of the ninety acres, only the garden was cleared and tillable, but still we owned land and the makings of a farm.

Chapter 3

❧

Blue Blood

I think I bleed blue. Not the blue blood of snobby aristocrats or the long rich, nor even the blue of fanatic sports fans. Genetically, it seems, blueberries have flowed in my family's blood for several generations. And this, for the longest time, helped Sarah believe I knew what I was doing.

Long before my birth, my grandparents and great-grandparents picked huckleberries on Blue and Kittatinny Mountains in Pennsylvania. I've heard stories of the long wagon rides up rough roads, the empty lard pails slowly filling from a secret patch, and the sweet voices singing hymns through the long afternoon. I'm guessing this tradition happened every summer even before my grandfather, Arthur, the only child, was born in 1907. And at some point, the huckleberry patch high in the mountains disappeared or my grandfather tired of the journey.

But Arthur had that blue streak in his blood, too; he still loved the taste of these berries. So in the 1950s, my grandfather planted 300 domesticated blueberry bushes on the homeplace. This Pennsylvania farm that my great-grandparents bought in the early 1900s produced my grandfather, raised my father and his three brothers, and eventually me. The fields and pastures, the pond and woodlot, sit above the town of Newburg on Minick's Hill where Grandpa fenced off a quarter acre behind the barn and next to the orchard for his patch. If you look north from the patch, Blue Mountain sweeps the horizon, the same mountain where he first picked huckleberries as a child.

Grandpa didn't like farming very much; the miscreant cows and groundhog-riddled hayfields always sparked his short temper. But he wanted to diversify the dairy farm and bring in a little extra income, and he enjoyed coming home from his electrician's job and walking the six long rows up and over the hill. I imagine him at dusk sitting among the blueberries, out of sight of the house and barns, where he would smoke his cigar, scan Blue Mountain, and watch a pair of wood ducks fly into the pond a quarter mile away.

I don't remember the first time I visited the hilltop patch, the first time I looked across the small valley to the village of Newburg where I lived, the first time I plucked a blue fruit and ate. All of these moments happened before memory even existed. My parents carried me there before I could walk, still an infant swaddled in a baby-blue blanket. And I'm sure I gobbled whatever sweetness they fed. It was, and still is, a sweetness flavored by my family's love.

Early on, before we married, during the summer of 1987, I wanted Sarah to also experience this blue-flavored love. Our farm dream hadn't even been conceived, yet I wished for her to know somehow my long-gone grandpa and grandma, a woman also named Sarah. I wanted my Sarah to know this soil, to remember this view of Blue Mountain, to become part of this family tradition, to taste this sweet fruit.

So one July evening, after supper, she and I and my parents walked through the patch, plucking and tasting a ripe dessert. "Oh, this is a good bush," my mother called, her small body hidden by the wide green mass. My dad, as tall as the six-foot plants, grazed his way to the middle of the patch where he stopped by what he proclaimed his favorite bush. In his huge hand, he cupped a mass of blue jewels and called for Sarah to "come try these, the sweetest in the patch."

I glanced at Sarah as she tasted from Dad's collection, then she wandered on and sampled others, disappearing into the greenery. But I was too caught up in filling my bucket to really watch Sarah. Not until twenty years later, long after we had walked out of Grandpa's patch with our buckets and bellies full, did Sarah confess that she had never tasted a ripe, raw blueberry until that evening. She had eaten fresh strawberries and peaches, indulged in Duncan Hines's blueberry muffins with their tiny blue dots, but never a fresh-off-the-bush, nickel-sized berry the color of night.

Admitting this in front of my parents would have caused great alarm. Sarah had already learned to stay quiet when possible. My new girlfriend was from the South, from a place that, as my dad pointed out on her first visit, was ignorant about winter coats. ("Where's your winter coat?" he asked as he hung her jacket. "That *is* my winter coat," she replied.) In the same way, Sarah, the city girl, didn't know how to use a paring knife, according to my mother. The first time Sarah offered to help in the kitchen, Mom gave her a knife and a stack of apples to peel for a pie. Halfway into paring the first, she felt my mother's eyes, then heard, "Didn't your mother ever teach you how to peel an apple?" Which, for Sarah, translated to: "And *what else* did she not teach you?" Then: "And you're marrying *my* son!?" Sarah never offered to help again.

Understandably, as we moved among Grandpa's bushes, shy Sarah kept quiet about this new venture into the unknown. She knew my parents' reactions would have been great gasps of disbelief, even if they already loved her. It was just their way. So, twenty years later, she finally confessed to me what really happened that first time in the Minick berry patch. Hidden behind a bush, she watched in amazement as we plucked and gobbled handfuls of berries right off the bush. She didn't know you *ate the skin* and she wondered *why we didn't wash them*, but this worry disappeared with the first bite. She gingerly placed a berry in her mouth and felt the rush of surprise as it exploded against her cheeks. Standing there in the dense greenery, Sarah realized she had never before tasted a color, never experienced and enjoyed the elemental, unrefined, sun-water-earth-and-air-created color of blue.

So in the winter of 1992, the year after we bought our Virginia farm, Sarah and I returned to Pennsylvania to visit the blueberry patch of Arthur Minick, to learn what we could from this place. We walked the windy ridge this time to consider the future as much as the past. The patch was dormant, leafless, and had dwindled to about half its original size. We passed holes where dead bushes had never been replaced, and on the living bushes, we peered through the mass of branches to lichen-covered trunks, stout stems, some thick as my wrist.

But at forty years old, these blueberries looked healthy, despite some of their early tending. Grandpa, as my uncles told me, didn't know what to do when it came to pruning. Instead of annually cutting some of the old growth along with new, he cut back only new canes. Without any new growth to replace the old, the bushes would eventually have died. Since Grandpa's passing, Uncle Pete and Aunt Kim have tended the patch. They read that a little of the new *and* the old was to come out every year. Their decades of pruning slowly righted Grandpa's wrong.

One other slight on Grandpa's part was his lack of records about the field. As a result, no one in the family remembered the names of all of the varieties. Like my dad, each could take you to his or her favorite bush, but they only knew one variety, Berkeley, and no one was sure where it ended and others began. When I asked Pete and Kim why they didn't plant more, fill in the holes, expand the field, they looked at me incredulously. Later, when I told them we planned on planting a space four times bigger, an acre of over 1,000 bushes, they just laughed, and said, simply, "Don't." Their love of this place had little nostalgia and a lot of calluses.

So even Grandpa fumbled his way down the blueberry path, pruning the wrong stems, never fertilizing, never knowing for sure what he was doing. Early on in our venture, neither Sarah nor I understood this. Sarah believed that with this family history, this blue blood swishing through my veins, surely I must know everything about blueberries. And we both witnessed the productivity of Grandpa's patch, these bushes older than ourselves. We shrugged off my aunt and uncle's advice, their years of experience. We were going to do things differently, prune correctly from the start, fertilize the bushes, and become certified-organic. Crowds of people, not birds, would flock to the field. We would succeed at both this family tradition and the business of blues.

Long before my birth, my family immersed itself in the language of blueberries. My great-grandparents knew the verbs *pick* and *eat* and *preserve*. And my grandfather learned the verbs *plant* and *tend*. All my relatives, even the youngest children, understood the nouns of *berry* and *bush*, the adjectives of *blue* and *ripe* and *sweet*. I grew up in this language, learned to love these words, and shared this love with Sarah. And despite my uncle's and aunt's warnings, I wanted to speak its poetry fully and often on our own farm in Virginia.

❧ BLUE INTERLUDE ❧
Our Hero

Our hero, *Vaccinium corymbosum*, is a humble fellow. Nothing too flashy, unless maybe the bark in winter, which turns a bright fire of yellows and reds. No towering height or great girth like an oak tree. Just a bush, in our case, a highbush, that at maturity usually stands about five or six feet tall.

No showy blooms, either, like a rose or a magnolia—just delicate white flowers shaded with pink. These hang shyly downward like a string of bells to ring the sky of bees because oh, do they smell sweet. But not an overpowering sweet—simply a fleeting breeze of a delicate thought that you want to hold but can't.

In the height of summer, our hero has a shiny green mane of oval leaves, smooth to the touch. These sprout from lichen-covered stems that grow from a huge mat of shallow roots. And, of course, this humble fellow has the bluest eyes.

The highbush's wild cousin, the lowbush, *Vaccinium angustifolium*, is even humbler. It only grows to a height of two feet, if that. It, too, has the delicate, bell-like blooms but its fruit, of course, is harder on the back to pick.

The highbush calls the East Coast and upper Midwest of the United States home; the lowbush hails from farther north, especially in Maine and eastern Canada. But their ranges overlap, and these cousins do hybridize, and—with apologies to my antianthropomorphizing scientist friends—this gives us a whole new insight into the term "kissing cousins."

In the southern parts of the United States, the rabbiteye blueberry, *Vaccinium virgatum*, can grow to nine feet in height. I know of a fellow who has to use a stepladder to pick his patch. Also in southern states, researchers have developed the southern highbush, *Vaccinium darrowii*, that grows like the regular highbush, but tolerates the heat and longer days better.

A blueberry is not a huckleberry, though they in many ways have similar appearances and flavors. The huckleberry, *Gaylussacia baccata*, ranges throughout the eastern half of North America, so the two berries often share similar habitat. Seeds and flesh mark the main differences between these two. A blueberry's seeds are minute, many in number, yet hardly noticeable, and they're surrounded by a greenish-white flesh. A huckleberry's seeds are larger, fewer in number (ten), and definitely noticeable. And this fruit's flesh is purple through and through.

Both blueberries and huckleberries share a sweetness, a long history, and both humble fruits are unique to our continent. In *Wild Fruits*, Thoreau comments on how our word for "berry" comes from the Saxon *beria*, meaning grape. He continues:

It is evident that the word "berry" has a new significance in America. We do not realize how rich our country is in berries. The ancient Greeks and Romans appear not to have made much account of strawberries, huckleberries, melons, and so on because they had not got them.

And thankfully we have got them here in rich abundance.

Chapter 4

❀∧❀

Test Plot

I n the years before we bought our 1,000 bushes, we researched everything. If a book had "blueberry" in its title, we bought it, even if we couldn't afford it. But we also bought tomes on garlic and raspberries, attended seminars on Christmas trees and asparagus, visited growers of heritage turkeys, ginseng, and shiitake mushrooms. We wanted to know all options, needed to weed out all potential cash crops, before we could fully say yes to blues.

Our growing library of berry manuals all advised to start small and put in a test plot. Sample different varieties, see if the soil is right, they cautioned, if the crop is suitable. And by implication, see if the grower is worthy of tending the crop. Kind of like foster care, it seemed, before adopting a child.

Sarah thought this was sound advice, especially before plunging into clearing land for such a commitment. "We can put them behind the house, next to the pines," she cajoled my reluctance. "And besides," she said, pointing to the catalogs, "all of these descriptions sound the same. They're all 'good.' At least this will give us a chance to sample a few."

She was right, of course, and as usual, her hazel eyes pierced any of my doubts. So we hiked up the steep backyard, turned to look down on the house's green tin roof, and wondered if the plants would get enough sun.

The huge pines might shade them some, but we had no other space to squeeze in even six bushes. We needed that field cleared.

I reread the soils sections of our manuals, all of them saying to dig deep and add peat moss and fertilizer to create a rich humus. We paced off the row, and I set shovel to soil. The first thrust of my foot drove the blade an inch, maybe two, the *ting* of steel on rock jarring my whole body. "Great," I thought aloud, "this will be easy going." I scraped off the sod over an area roughly hundred square feet to find shale underneath, sheets of inch-thick rocks. They would loosen and pry up, but all very slowly.

An hour later, bright-eyed Sarah came to inspect. Her blond hair glistened in the sun, her ponytail bobbing as she hiked up the hill. She had a nursery catalog, and she wanted to discuss the six varieties she had chosen, to share that moment of anticipation before the final deciding. Her round face glowed like an expectant mother. But as soon as she sat in the grass beside my growing rock pile, I said, "Whatever, just choose." My back already ached, and my reservoir of patience had emptied. I doubted any dirt would remain for the roots after I pried out all of these rocks, and I worried that I'd have to wheelbarrow soil uphill from the garden 150 yards. Sarah didn't stay long.

Luckily, I didn't have to use the wheelbarrow. Once I added a bale of peat moss and chopped in the thin layer of sod, the trench filled, enough anyway. The next month, when the six test-plot bushes arrived in the mail, we parted the loosened dirt, laid in the roots, and gently tamped out the air pockets. We raked pine needles from the nearby woods to mulch our new babies, and I fenced out the rabbits with heavy wire. I even used up the piles of slate to build below the bushes a rock wall—pretty, but useless. The new patch looked good, even if it might get shaded to death by the nearby pine trees.

Now all we had to do was wait. But long-lived blueberries are also long to mature, and I soon learned we were testing more than just varieties. It takes two years for blueberries to begin to bear, five before they fully mature. I didn't tell Sarah, but that long I doubted I could wait.

❧ BLUE INTERLUDE ❧
Latin Laurel Hells

To the common person, a blueberry is a blueberry is a blueberry. But in the Latin-loving world of science, a highbush blueberry is really *Vaccinium corymbosum*, belonging to the Ericaceae Family and the *Cyanococcus* Section of the *Vaccinium* genus.

Ericaceae is the botanical name for the Heath Family, a large, diverse group of plants, which one expert calls "cosmopolitan" because of its wide distribution. Blueberries, it seems, have cousins all over the world that share some similar flower structures. In North America, this family includes Indian pipe, which grows to five inches; mountain laurel, which reaches five feet; and the sourwood tree, which can push fifty feet.

As to the root of this family name, another expert explains that the *eric* comes from the Greek *ereike*, which means "to break, since some ericas were supposed to break bladder stones." This particular health benefit for blueberries hasn't yet been documented, but maybe some poor stone-stuck sufferer needs to drink gallons of blueberry juice to find out.

The genus *Vaccinium* includes cranberries and a few other berry-bearing plants, "possibly 150 species in the northern hemisphere," according to scientist Henry Gleason. And though scientists know how to classify plants into or out of this genus, the origin of the word *Vaccinium* offers some puzzles. On other family and genus names, Gleason often gives a brief explanation of the word's roots. But for *Vaccinium*, he says little, only that it comes from the ancient Latin name for *Vaccinium myrtillus*, a European blueberry. *Gray's Manual of Botany* claims it is an "ancient name, presumably from the Latin *vaccinus*, of cows," and Gledhill in his *The Names of Plants* also explains that *Vaccaria*, a similarly rooted word, means "cow-fodder (an old generic name from 'vacca,' a cow)."

So what do blueberries have to do with cows?

Eventually I stumble onto two experts and their opinions of this nomenclature problem. In *Wild Fruits*, Thoreau is "inclined to think that [*Vaccinium*] is properly derived from *bacca*, a berry . . . though the etymology of this word is in dispute." He also conjectures that "[i]f the first botanists had been American this might have been called the Huckleberry Family, including the heaths," instead of the *Ericaceae* family of heaths, including huckleberries.

A more contemporary view is offered by Sam Vander Kloet and his authoritative article "On the Etymology of *Vaccinium L.*" Vander Kloet is *the* taxonomic expert on all things *Vaccinium*, and he traces the first recorded uses of *Vaccinium* back to Virgil and Ovid. Early translators interpreted this word as hyacinths, but the context of the Virgil line takes place in a swamp, and the Ovid line is about natural dyes. Blueberries, not hyacinths, fit both of these contexts.

Vander Kloet explains that during both authors' time, "'B' and 'V' were moving toward a common pronunciation and could be confused." He then concludes that "this interpretation resolves a dichotomy in meaning and unifies ancient usage with current usage. . . . Nonetheless the etymology *bacca* → *Vaccinium* is the most likely, although admittedly decisive textual proof is wanting." Meaning, even the most authoritative expert will never know for sure.

Anyway, back to the Latin sleuthing of the rest of blueberry's long name. The section name *Cyanococcus*, according to my biologist colleague Gary Coté, comes from the Greek for blue (*cyano-*) and berry (*coccus*). Gledhill defines cyaneus "Prussian-blue" and *coccus* as "-berried." Finally, a little sense in this naming game.

And then the species names usually make sense as well. Highbush blueberries, what fills our field, is *corymbosum*, which refers to how the plant flowers in a corymb, a flat-topped cluster. The lowbush blueberry has the species name of *angustifolium*, referring to its narrow leaves. And the tall rabbiteye blueberry is *Vaccinium virgatum*, which refers to its growth habit, "wand-like," according to *Gray's Manual*, and "twiggy," according to Gledhill's *Names of Plants*.

So there you have it, a brief, Latin-thick account of blueberries.

But one more blue note. Another blueberry cousin is the rhododendron, which grows in dense tangles on our farm, so thick that walking through them is impossible, crawling difficult. Old-timers call these thickets "laurel hells" and that, to me, seems like a fitting description for this brief descent into the Latin hell of blueberries.

Chapter 5

❦❦

Not to Bee

Long before we bought the farm or any blueberry bush, we knew we needed bees. How else could you insure a well-pollinated crop of any kind without a hive or two of honeybees? Plus, all that free honey!

Sarah's sweet parents lived in Charlotte and had little experience growing anything, but even they supported this idea. Her mother, a preacher's daughter who got behind any of our outlandish ideas, had great faith in this blueberry-honey dream. Her father, a soft-spoken engineer, held back his doubts and together they bought us the Bee Bible, a massively thick volume titled *The Hive and the Honeybee*. With this kind of backing, we figured we needed to act, so shortly after we invested in the land, we also invested in bee equipment and two hives full of black and yellow buzzers.

The equipment came via mail order. Two veils with drawstrings at the throat; heavy leather gloves that covered forearms as well as hands; a hive tool for prying apart the supers; and a smoker, a tin cylinder with a snout and bellows used to puff smoke into the hive. When bees sensed smoke, they instinctively gorged on honey for a quick escape rather than attack a honey robber.

We put on the veils and paraded around the house and Sarah pretended she was a new bride again waiting to be kissed. Outside, I fiddled with the smoker, trying paper and twigs to get a slow smoldering burn that wouldn't go out, but when I pumped the bellows, I usually ended with ash. Finally, I tried burlap and it worked, the little tool sending up smoke signals, if only for a minute.

The hives came from a few miles away. We answered an ad in the local paper and drove to find a bearded young man with two extras to sell. After the bees had returned to the hives the previous night, he had stuffed burlap into their entries, trapping them for the haul to our farm. He and I gingerly lifted each white wooden box onto our pickup truck, listening to the angry buzz inside. "They don't like being moved," he said, smiling, "but they'll settle into the new place right quick."

The "new place," though, was a hike from our house, from *any* house *or* road for that matter. Our Bee Bible preached that honeybees like to rise to the morning sun, that this will wake them early enough to work a few hours more than if they slept in the shade. Heaven forbid we didn't want lazy bees. Any location near our house soaked in the morning shade until noon on most days, the tree shadows covering even the garden. The field itself would've been ideal and close to the crop, but it wasn't even cleared yet, and we didn't want a falling tree to bust open a box and release an angry swarm. We could only imagine the bulldozer operator jumping from his machine to run away, arms thrashing.

So the best place for the beehives on all of our ninety acres was on another hill, what we soon called the Bee Hill. This small mountain sat opposite of both the house and the field, and on top of it were the remains of a fallen-in log cabin. We picked a high spot facing east and a half mile from our house, so we didn't need to worry about getting stung too much, we hoped. But this half mile was just a trail on an old roadbed, completely undrivable, and all uphill. Parts of the road had become swamp, other parts had grown thick with rhododendron, trees, and briars. I had cut a walking path, but access to all of it consisted of a six-inch-wide board across Lost Bent Creek. Not even our four-wheel-drive truck could begin to drive this.

Back home with the buzzing boxes, we first had to unload them, not an easy job for petite Sarah and clumsy me. We quarreled about wearing our new veils and gloves. ("We don't need them, the bees are sealed in. Plus I can't see with that damn veil on." And Sarah replying, "If I put money into that veil, I'm going to use it. And besides, what are you going to do if they escape?") I donned the veil and gloves.

In the truck, I slid one hive to the tailgate, jumped down, and then we both grabbed the white bottom and rested our chins on the top. Our noisy heaves only increased the inner roar. The wheelbarrow held one hive at a time, so I manned the handles, pushing the weight of wood, wax, and wings down through the yard to pause at the footbridge. I couldn't see it. Even without a veil, my vision was blocked by the wide wheelbarrow; I could only *feel* the two-by-six plank and hear the water below. I centered the wheel, and with Sarah shouting directions from the opposite bank, the bees and I inched across to safety.

Up the long road we traveled. In the marsh, I wobbled, tripping on a small stump, but then caught myself. Farther on, briars snagged my pants, leaves slapped my face, and sweat stained my shirt. We rested at the switchback but the perspiration kept coming even in the coolness of the March morning. I knew a false step meant a fast run and a major mess.

Sarah scooted alongside the whole time, hand resting on top of the hive, holding down the lid. I figured this might help if a bump jarred the top loose or, worse, if I lost my balance and started to tilt. I asked her to do this, and she gave me that questioning look, but then said nothing and joined in. As we made our way up the mountain, I realized the foolishness. Sarah's a mighty woman in many ways, but her 110 pounds could not stop the fall of an 80-pound hive. But just in case, she hiked along.

When we reached the hilltop, we carefully unloaded the hive and walked back down to do it all again. Two hours later, with both hives in place, I pulled the burlap and ran back into the pines, where Sarah and I watched the first bees fly out. They circled the maple tree and the log cabin's still-standing chimney, getting a bearing on this, their new home.

A few months after the bees' inaugural flight, we figured it was time to try our new equipment. If we really wanted to become beekeepers, we needed to learn how to open a hive, find the queen, and harvest some honey. We rubber-banded our outfits at our wrists and ankles, slid on the veils, and checked one another, bee-proofing any openings to flesh. Sarah carried a bucket for a frame or two of honey, while in the wheelbarrow, I hauled the smoker and empty supers to add to the hives, to give the bees room to make more honey. We tried to get to the hilltop before the day heated up (bees are less irksome in the early morning), but it was a Saturday, and we had unintentionally slept in. Sweat soaked our rubber-cuffed sleeves long before we reached the top.

Sarah's job was to operate the smoker, to "smoke'm and run," as she kept repeating on the hike up. I'd get the tinder smoldering, hand it over to her, and then begin prying open the hive. We donned our gloves, lit the smoker, and approached our first hive from behind. The worker bees were returning with pollen covering their bodies, while the guard bees checked each one. Then the guards noticed us, two hooded monsters lurking nearby. They flew to our heads and inspected, veering this way and that, stingers ready to penetrate thin fabric. *Just stay calm,* I kept thinking to myself. They sense your fear, I had read, and the more agitated you are, the more agitated they will be. "Easy does it now," I spoke to all of us—Sarah, me, and the bees. "Easy does it."

Sarah crouched behind me, leaned around the corner of the hive, and puffed the bellows into the hive entry. Nothing happened. The fire had stopped smoldering. So back to the pines we stumbled, a few agitated bees already following us. I took off my gloves, stuffed in more paper and burlap, and fired up the smoker. This time it stayed lit, and we repeated the slow approach, the long reach around to the front, the puff of smoke. It worked. The bees instantly changed their behavior, becoming less hostile. Now it was my turn.

Bees seal their hives with propolis, a hard waxy substance that keeps out moisture, bugs, and robbers, like me. I had read about this, learned about this word's roots (Greek, *pro*—before, *polis*—city; *before entering their city, any robber has to overcome this barrier,* I thought in the quiet coolness of our living room). But still the difficulty surprised me—I had to learn how to use the hive tool to cut and pry open the box. My rough knocking did nothing to please the bees, but slowly the wax released its hold, and we soon looked into a dark mass of swarming bodies. Or rather, I looked and shouted to Sarah, who sat in the grass and waited, twenty feet away, smoker ever ready. I called for her, and in she came, *puff, puff, puffing,* taking a quick glance and then making a quicker escape.

As with the lid, the bees had sealed each frame in place with propolis, so I cut and pried, the mass getting angrier. Many bees by now had landed on my veil, crawling over the hat, speaking their anger into my ear. "Easy does it now," I kept muttering, unable to rub the sweat burning my eyes. One frame came loose at last, and I slid it into the bucket, and replaced it with an empty one. We still had another hive to open, and my patience with flying stingers was disappearing, so I abandoned the idea of finding the queen. I lifted the new super into place and snugged the lid. One down, one to go.

The next hive proved no easier. Again, the fire in the smoker went out, twice; the more anxious Sarah became, the harder she worked the bellows, extinguishing the embers with too much air. Again we had to retreat to re-stoke and light it. Again we tried to approach slowly and calmly, but the heat of the day rained on us in full force, and each bee had already picked up the hot anger of the first hive. No matter how much Sarah puffed that smoker, the bees became more agitated as I awkwardly jarred open the lid and cut loose a frame.

Finally I slid another honey-filled frame into the bucket, but just as I did, Sarah let out a scream. Ten minutes earlier, she had given up the smoker, set it at my feet, and retreated to the pines, but the bees had followed. And not only had they followed, they had found an entry into her veil. She slapped her face and neck and head, but the bees kept coming, kept getting stuck in her hair, kept stinging. I dropped my tools and ran to her, but she was already racing down the hill, panicked and screaming, "Jim, Jim, get these things off of me!" I slammed the lid on the hive and sprinted after her.

Halfway down the hill, the living bees had given up the chase, and the dead ones Sarah had squished against the useless veil. I hugged her sobbing body, and then slowly untied and pulled off the thin gauze. She pointed and I counted, one on her cheek, two on her neck, then more on her chin and forehead. I parted her fine hair to remove the dead bees and found more stings on her scalp. Seven total. She was not allergic, but even so, she would swell and hurt for a long time. We slumped our way home where she got into bed for a recovery nap, ice packs on each sting. In the kitchen I made a mess cutting open the sealed frames, the honey draining into pans and jars, the sticky sweetness covering my hands and perfuming the air. Before she slipped off to sleep, I took her a spoonful of amber, hoping its sweetness might lessen the pain.

It didn't. Soon after she woke, Sarah began scratching and the welts began to rise. But these weren't the seven stings on her head, these were a kazillion welts all around her rubber-banded ankles and her tightly belted waist. The red lumps even began to rise in the dark private recesses. And they burned and itched more ferociously than any bee sting.

Chiggers. While she sat and waited through my inept handling of each hive, the chiggers found her tender body. They must have loved her smooth flesh and that one grassy spot where she sat, because these unseeably minute bugs ignored my hide. Instead the parasites drilled into Sarah's skin, buried themselves in flesh and left a constellation of long-burning stars. They flamed and itched for a month, long after the bee stings disappeared.

We never opened a hive again. After that first venture, we occasionally hiked up the bee hill road to watch the two hives, but only from a distance, and only in the cool months when the chiggers weren't out. A short time later, the untended bees left the hives, swarming to find a larger space, to rear a new brood, to start over.

The sweetener for any homestead dream would have to come from elsewhere, and the berries, it seemed, would have to get pollinated some other way.

For as long as we could, we savored that honey made even sweeter by the cost. But eventually the last Mason jar turned from amber full back to empty clear, and though I tried scraping its bottom, my knife clinking against glass, there was no more.

Chapter 6

❦

Meeting Joe

Joe Southard lived on the next farm down the road and he grew strawberries. That's all we had heard about our new neighbor when we moved in on January 1, 1992. But starting mid-May of that first year, we sat on our porch and watched the traffic dramatically increase from five cars a day to fifty. And even though we were a mile from his fields, we witnessed the great abundance of his crop. Every morning, starting around 6:00, the cars would slowly journey down the hill, usually with one or two people in the front and stacks of empty dishpans in the back. Then a few hours later, as the late pickers kicked up dust in their hurry to get started, the early birds would slip back out, the backseats aglow in red as the strawberries overflowed the blue dishpans. This heavy traffic went on for a month. Joe was onto a good thing, it seemed.

One Sunday afternoon, I headed down that road to meet this strawberry-growing legend. Before I even made it to his house, his driveway overwhelmed me. Across his lane he had dug several water bars, speed-bump affairs that traversed the road in huge mounding strips to funnel the water off and to prevent erosion. If a driver wasn't careful, she could easily scrape the bottom of her car. And the road had hairpin switchbacks, hungry-looking potholes, and overhanging laurels and pines, making it narrow and dark. "People *drive* this?" I wondered aloud.

Once on top of his small mountain, the pines gave way to sky and open field. Hand-painted signs hung on fence posts and shed doors—BERRIES AHEAD, WATCH FOR DOGS, and TURN AROUND AND PARK IN FIELD—all of them pointing to the field beyond the house. I stopped at the white-clapboard and was greeted by a chorus of yapping Chihuahuas. Soon, Joe in his ball cap and overalls followed them. He was tall, round in the middle, and looked to be in his early sixties. Later I learned he was actually in his early seventies. As I introduced myself, he held on to my hand, even grabbing my shoulder with his other hand. "Glad to meet you!" he repeated, and then, "I heard we had new neighbors. 'Bout time you came." His blue eyes sparkled with what looked like earnest friendliness mixed in with mischief.

Behind him hanging back on the porch, stood another man, smaller and younger, about my age, a black mustache unable to cover his shyness. Joe introduced him as Jerry, an orphan he had taken in twenty years ago, who now helped with the berry field.

Together, the three of us hiked around the corner of the house, through his orchard and well-tended garden, and toward the strawberries. All the while Joe kept talking, punctuating his sentences with questions: "What do you think of that, Jim?" or "Are you with me?" We swapped histories, he from the coalfields moving here to escape mining, me from Pennsylvania to go to school. He appreciated our common farming history, our shared German and Scots Irish roots, saying, "There're two kinds of Germans, Jim—the talkers and the sulkers. Which do you think I am?" I said I couldn't tell, and he appreciated the wit.

Standing by the field gate, Joe pointed in every direction as he named all the owners of the neighboring properties, and then he started on the long history of our place. He had known Ira Lester, the man who built our house in 1917, and Joe could even rattle off the price our land sold for at auction, when Lester died in 1953: $1,600 for ninety acres. He remembered when our fields grew buckwheat and corn, the hilltops clear of pines, the soil tended and fertile.

Joe looked me in the eye and commented on how he appreciated our honeybees visiting his field, helping his berries. "How did you know we had bees?" I asked, and he said they showed up shortly after we did, so he figured we brought them along. Then he asked how the bees were doing, embarrassing me into admitting I had no idea because these, our first hives, had swarmed and escaped. "Oh, I wondered. I saw a swarm down by our road last month." Joe, I realized, missed little.

In the patch, Jerry and Joe gave a tasting tour. The "droppers" (the hired planters) had mixed up the varieties, so now the two men had to identify each berry by shape and taste, rather than by row. They made a game of it, impressing me with their knowledge, or bluffing anyway. I believed, saw the weedless patch and worn hoes hanging on the fence, and recognized genius in this man who had grown strawberries for forty years, raising five kids on this hilly farm.

The patch was vibrant, the ribbed, green leaves hiding a plethora of red fruit. "You know how to pick, don't you, Professor?" And before I could say yes, he bent over and demonstrated, parting the leaves, plucking the berries. He handed me different ones, saying, "Here, try this Sparkle." Or "Here's a Red Chief, my favorite." I hesitated, like Sarah in my family's blueberry patch, wondering about the dirt. "A little dirt won't hurt you," he bantered after seeing me pause. I bit in, not wanting to offend this new friend. It tasted supremely sweet.

As I picked, we kept talking, especially about farming. When I shared my organic aspirations, he guffawed, and really drilled in: "No way can you grow tomatoes or strawberries without chemical fungicides." But other farmers do, I replied meekly, knowing I didn't know enough. He called me an environmentalist, asked what I was going to do when groundhogs dug in our field and deer ate the bushes. Then Joe proclaimed, "You gotta do something or they'll eat you up." I had no answer, so I just shrugged. But he recognized my stubbornness, my "faith" in the "organic religion," to use his word. And I saw the same hard-edged belief in him. Even then on that first meeting we agreed we'd try to convert each other, but both knew the futility of such efforts. It was, however, a peaceable treaty.

When he learned we were considering blueberries, he urged, "Why wait? Do it now." Then he told of visiting a huge, twelve-acre pick-your-own blueberry patch two counties away. He liked the idea, wished he had planted some years ago, but said he was too old to tackle that now. "But why wait, Jim? You're young. Go do it."

Sarah and I had wondered about pick-your-own (PYO) problems: the insurance, the access, and especially the location dilemma. We lived "way back" and "down in," even if you weren't a truck driver from Michigan. Only three households of six other folks lived beyond us on Berry Hill Road. Our main markets were towns anywhere from thirty to ninety minutes away. All the manuals advised to not even consider PYO if you didn't have an adequate market within a fifteen-mile radius; customers just wouldn't travel that far to harvest their own fruit.

But Joe proved the books wrong every year. If he could get this many people to labor for their own fruit in his hard-to-get-to field *for forty years*, why wait indeed.

Chapter 7

A Cleared Field

July 15, 1994, 95 degrees.
Debris of slapped-downed trees.
Clatter of dozer tracks.
The furnace door of the sun wide open.
And choking clouds of dust
mixed with sweat caked on skin
to become clay.
Not Garden of Eden here
but Desert of Hell.
That we created.
And it was not good.

I stood in the middle of chaos. Toppled white pines surrounded me, massive trunks packed and jumbled on top of roots now unrooted. The bulldozer heaped them here, the fiery power of diesel making an opening to the heavens, an opening we ordered, a contradiction we decreed.

And suddenly I felt very small beneath a newly revealed arch of sky.

. . .

For two years, Sarah and I hiked the perimeter of this used-to-be field, the broken-down fence a labyrinth we tried to unravel. With each walk-around, we admired the ancient oaks on one side and hated the muddled mass of scaly barked pine on the other. They were bull pines, named for their quick charge onto abandoned land, colonizers that grew so thickly, they often toppled into immense piles of Pick-up sticks. The only way through was to crawl.

So we walked in circles around our wannabe field and this question: How do we clear the land to make it a field again, and how do we do this with the least amount of harm? How do we create our own garden under the firmament and say at the end, this was good?

The task broke into two parts: How do we cut all the trees, and then what do we do with them afterward? Hand labor with a chain saw and a chipper seemed the best answer, converting the gangly trunks into much-needed mulch. We explored buying chippers, enormous commercial wood eaters as well as smaller backyard versions, all of them exceedingly noisy and foul smelling. For a time, we even considered a chain saw just for Sarah, but the smallest gas-powered one still weighed down her arms. How could she control its teeth without it biting into her legs? We didn't buy the saw.

One weekend, I set to cutting a wide path from one side of the field to the other. What I thought would be an afternoon chore swallowed two full days, and we knew the silliness of our thinking. In our lifetime, how would we ever cut the thousands of trees that covered this acreage? If we wanted any crop soon, we needed hired labor and big machines.

The summer of 1994, we employed the Cox cousins. In two weeks' time, Isaiah and Mike built a half mile of new road to give us access to the field, fashioned a pond as part of that road, and cleared the field. The clearing, what we had pondered for over two years, took Mike and his dozer all of two and a half days.

From the heap of white pines, I rested, peering through roots and needle-heavy limbs. On the other side of the field, the droning bulldozer mauled the bull pines, clobbering each clump one bite at a time.

Mike's method was simple: back up to field edge, lower the blade, and grind forward, slamming thirty-foot toothpicks to the ground. Sometimes trees hung on to others, refused to fall, and even started to fall backward onto the machine. In his open cab, the operator watched and backed off for a better angle. Always he breathed in the fine powdery dust.

The bull pines had no value as lumber or firewood, only for pulp, but the nearest pulp mill was too far away, and no logger would haul these holes-in-the-moneybag. So we did what our forbearers did, the antiquated practice of previous homesteaders: we chose the sinfully quick method of slash and burn. Under our directions, Mike crumpled all the trees into a huge pile that stretched like a beached whale across the middle of the two and a half acres.

The year before we cleared this land, I sought a way out of the pines' constant darkness. I wanted to see, really see this space, to understand the dimensions of this field, to fathom how it already was shaped by someone else's hands, to know, if possible, its history and the limits that history placed on our future. Would these boundaries be big enough, or too big? What were the limits of this place that we inherited, and that we created?

Aerial photographs in the county forestry office gave me access to a little of this, allowed me to observe the field as a bird would, as a bird flying over every ten or fifteen years. The forester opened his cabinet, pulled out files of yellowed black-and-whites, and we sorted through the stacks. He let me photocopy the prints of our place and I left with a pile I studied for hours back home.

The patterns and shapes slowly became familiar. Even on the more recent shots taken at a much higher elevation, I could find Lost Bent Creek and the peculiar outline of our land. I traced our boundaries on each copy and laughed when I discovered a silhouette shaped liked a person's head and armless torso. Our house sat at the neck like a brooch and the main field covered the heart. Or was it the heart?

The oldest photograph from the fall of 1937 revealed the dots of orchard trees and rows of corn shocks, the drying pyramids polka dots across the field. Even in the midst of the Depression, Ira and Dellie Lester, the homesteaders who built our house, supported their family of four from this soil. They, too, had slashed-and-burned the land to make it farmable. Of the ninety acres, they cleared sixty, using the steep hillsides for vegetables and pasture, the ridge tops for hay and grain. When I looked from these photos out our living room window, I saw nothing but hills and ridges of woodland, the fifty-plus years replacing corn and wheat with poplar and pine.

The 1953 photograph documented the slow change of land and neighborhood. In the sixteen years since the last flyover, one field, what the neighbors called the LeFew place, had already become dark with trees. Now when I visited Ms. Lefew's homestead, I sat on a pile of rocks where the dogs sniffed for rabbits. These fieldstones once taken from plowed ground also once were cemented up to form her chimney. Nothing else remained, no logs, no fence, no rusted door latch. Seventy-foot pines crowded the rock pile and squirrels hid in an ancient walnut tree probably planted by Ms. Lefew before she died in the late 1800s.

Back with my imaginary bird wings, I flew over the land again in 1962. Our property in these aerial photographs looked much like it did in 1953 with shades of gray squared into still worked fields, but not tilled by Ira Lester's hands—those hands were buried in the early 1950s. And these were not working fields for much longer.

Once abandoned, once left alone, the field became a not-field, and the photograph from 1974 showed this, the squares transformed to dark swaths of trees. The bull pine jumped the still-good fences and seeded the fallow earth, claiming all of the open land. This confirmed what a neighbor, Daniel Hughes, told me. He rented this farm in the 1950s and '60s, remembered its odd contours, and asked if the old orchard still remained. He was the last to make hay and drill oats on this place.

Fifteen years after Daniel drove his tractor across the ridges for the final time, the reforestation was complete. The 1980 aerial shot still had the same odd outline of an armless torso, the same slash of gravel road across the neckline, but none of the gray squares of nearby farms. The land was all wooded, the split-rail fence, like Robert Frost's useless wall, kept pines from oaks.

Among the worthless bull pines stood a scattering of valuable white pines, trees that we could convert into boards. I asked Mike to knock these down and push them aside. I wanted to save what I could.

With a chain saw, I climbed into the mass of needles and smooth bark. Every pine had to be limbed, severed from the stump, and cut to length. I had over seventy-five trees, each yielding two or three logs. I also had only two days because I wanted the dozer to push the leftover stumps and tops into the burn pile.

The burn pile . . . God, I felt like I was already in a burn pile, the flames of the sun reaching down to torch my body. Sweat-soaked jeans cooled nothing, nor did the drained gallons of water, or the pine pitch gluing gloves to saw. Chaps protected my legs from an errant cut, but they didn't protect my body from sunstroke; they only aided that problem. So I drank more than any belly could hold to fend off any immolation of the body. But the spirit still burned.

Usually the chain saw sliced right through the wood, the limbs falling away easily, but some branches bent under the trunk's weight to whack and bruise my thighs. Other trees shifted and pinched the chain before I could react. Once, I wedged the tip so tightly it wouldn't move no matter how hard I pried and pulled and swore. I had to trek across the field to fetch the ax and then return to chop loose the saw. Afterward, I pissed out my anger and took a break.

Every time I returned to the aerial photographs I saw again that familiar torso, but also I found something different, another piece of the history or geography, like the acute lines of Joe Southard's switched-back lane or the shiny roofs of a once well-kept homestead. One time, I realized how much each snapshot captured not only the forest's progressive in-migration, but also the human inhabitants' steady out-migration. This community had changed dramatically in sixty years.

In 1937, within a square mile of our house, there were ten other homesteads, the Akers and Alley families along with the Dulaneys, the Reeds, and others. When we bought our farm in 1991, of these ten homesteads, only five still existed, two as summer homes. We had wanted both solitude and community when we set down roots, but it looked like we'd only find the first in our immediate neighborhood.

The comparison between the 1991 and the 1937 photo illustrated an even more striking fact: only one property, Joe's, was still a working farm. In my rambles through the surrounding wooded properties, I stumbled over the broken remains of houses and barns, wagons and plows, china and canning jars. All that I found of one homestead was a hole in the ground, a cellar once full of winter food, now a dimple full of leaves. Why did these farmers disappear?

I looked out our front window at the hillside across from our house and understood the answer. As the land on all of the surrounding homesteads

filled in with trees, this one hill stayed mostly open. The soil, it seemed, had
played out more than elsewhere, had gotten lost in Lost Bent Creek. A scattering of bull pine and locust punctuated the broomsage and brambles, but
even these trees crooked into stunted forms. Ira Lester plowed this steep
slope for as long as he could, planting it to corn and tomatoes. I couldn't
imagine a horse dragging a moldboard across the face of this incline, it was
that steep.

Like with our own field-clearing, economic hardship dictated how the
Lesters farmed. As a result, the soil migrated downstream and most of the
people washed to the city.

After the bulldozer's rumble finally faded, we were left with an expanse we
couldn't have imagined, an opening, a hole, a blue-sky kingdom, a sunshine
pit, a naked-earth mess. One moment joy overwhelmed (We have actually
done this!) the next moment, regret (We have actually done *this?*). For the first
time, I could see as well as hear the broad-wing hawk circling above, but it
gave little joy. The bare earth, the twisted roots, the massive pile of trees
threw a bewildering sorrow. This was not the Eden we planned. We could
not step back like God to say, This was good. Not yet, at least.

We could now walk through this dreamed place, the field; no longer did
we have to skirt its borders. But the land only looked cleared from the
edges. When we kicked the crumbly dirt, inspected the rawness, we realized it wasn't really clear yet. The dozer had pushed together the bulk, but
not the finer mess. For the next week we hunched over and grubbed, backs
burning in the sun, pick ax and hoe connecting blistered hands to dusty
earth. At least we had the summer off from our school jobs to labor here in
our new field.

The work amounted to this: Drive truck to a parcel of new ground, swallow a quart of water, and take empty buckets, two to each hand, to head out
to a new section. Fill buckets with the rocks and roots and leftover remains
of a reluctantly gone forest. Haul mounded buckets back to truck and heave
them empty. When truck bed overflows, back it to the burn pile to unload,
again, by hand, one rock and root at a time. And in all of this, watch the
clouds and hurry. The faster you work, the sooner you beat any approach-
ing thunderstorm and the more exposed soil you save.

But how can you work quickly in such humid heat? Often I had to chop loose strands of roots with the ax, hacking into the ground to release the ghosts of bull pines. The rocks, too, pulled back when we hefted, wouldn't release to our tugs. Back to the pickup for a shovel and pry bar to break the ancient cement of another time. These rocks boomed when dropped into the truck bed, the echo a new sound in this new space.

We ate cold leftovers for supper, went to bed before the sun set, and tried to rattle out of the house before it rose. This work it seemed was a penance, a trial by dust and fire, and for what? Blueberries? They were worth this?

That question got buried in the burn pile like another worthless root. If I burned it, maybe I wouldn't ever think it again.

❧ BLUE INTERLUDE ❧
New Farmers and Failure

"Exit" is the word experts use when a farmer leaves farming.

As if you can just find a certain door with an arrow and big red letters, grasp a knob, and step through a threshold, and then suddenly,
you are a non-farmer. That easy.

The United States Department of Agriculture (USDA) estimates
that roughly 4–5 percent of all farmers—around 100,000—walk
through this door every year. Understandably, the highest number of
exits occurs in the oldest age groups as farmers park their tractors one
last time and retire. That leaves roughly 45,000 growers who, for
whatever reason, quit. They might have health problems, they might
take a better-paying off-farm job where weather isn't a factor, or they
might just get tired of the daily grind, of milking 75 cows, two times a
day, every day.

Like with any start-up business, new farmers have the greatest risk.
They have little equity, a short credit record, and less experience than
older growers. Banks shy away and the government programs created
to help these new tillers of the soil have had limited effect. The highest
concentration of failures occurs with new farmers on small farms. As
the USDA report, "Farmer Bankruptcies and Farm Exits in the United
States, 1899–2002," explains, "Farms with sales of less than $10,000
annually and operating smaller acreages have higher exit (and entry)
rates than larger, traditional farms." Of the 100,000 total annual farm
exits, roughly 20,000 file for bankruptcy.

So in 1991 when we bought our farm, we had a slew of slippery planks
to cross—any misstep would slide us through the exit door. We were
in our late twenties, new and inexperienced to agriculture. We planned
on tilling a small acreage, so our annual sales would probably be less
than $10,000, for a while at least. Our off-farm jobs as teachers se-
cured our financial future, in the bank's eyes, so it loaned us the
money. But would we make it as farmers, or would we become one of
those 100,000 exits a year?

We didn't know any of these figures at the time, but had we understood this high risk, would we have changed our course, never bought land, never planted ourselves and these bushes?

Probably not. There was a dream to chase, after all, and when you're dreaming, you never look for the exit doors, the red letters, the arrow. You just stay focused on that movie called *Your Ideal Life*, the colorful images capturing your smiles and good times. You never think about that flickering flash of blinding white, you never notice that background hum of the projector's spindles, you never anticipate the total blackness when the light is turned off.

Chapter 8

❦

Joe's Holey Spreader

O nce a month I hiked the half-mile hill to visit our neighbor Joe. Usually I found him in the evening sitting in slippers and overalls, commanding the TV remote from an upholstered recliner. Fox traps hung behind the woodstove, relics of his youth when he won an award for the best red pelt.

Happy for the company, he hollered over the racket of Chihuahuas that clambered out to greet me, their high yips muzzling even Dan Rather's voice on the evening news. Joe always shook my hand with a "Come on in, come on in, sit down," almost singing this welcome. And then he followed with, "I thought you were dead, it's been so long since you came to see me." He killed the TV, spat clean his tobacco, and told the dogs to "hush up, hush up now."

Joe didn't drive off the farm much—maybe once a month to buy groceries—so when he had company, the words avalanched. Usually he started with, "You know, I never give advice," his sly grin skewed. Then he would tell me how to grow tomatoes, interpret the Bible, or deal with women, despite his two failed marriages.

Cricket, Bluey, Lulu, and Puff, his Chihuahuas, surrounded him. In his stuffed chair, Cricket reigned queen, squeezed between armrest and Joe's denim belly. Bluey, her daughter, sat on top of her, and Lulu perched on his other leg. The outcast, Puff, curled on my lap. They all growled and yapped at each other and at me and at any noise outside, which every ten minutes they had to investigate. Down from the throne they scampered to scratch at the screen door, which Joe would dutifully lean around from his chair to open, and out they went barking. The whole routine didn't slow Joe one nip as he continued talking about the latest political scandal or his own education, where he graduated at the top of a class of twelve in a one-room school.

Every visit, our conversations ranged from religion to history, pornography to fertilizer, always fertilizer. Joe would quote St. Paul next to Julius Caesar, then Shakespeare next to the *Cornell University Berry Bulletin*. Often he followed the quote with a "He's full of crap" and a black slip of spit into the coffee-can spittoon. When he pouched his lip for a new dip, the tiny plastic spoon silenced his banter for a moment, but his next words came out veiled by a brown dust-cloud of snuff. I always sneezed.

Joe's "advice" usually focused on farming. He commiserated about the deer and coons and identified weeds for us. ("That's Korean lespedeza, introduced by our very own government, and now look at it. Deer won't even touch it.") When we broached our nutrient-belief differences, he'd shout, "You want to farm just like my grandmother, Jim: no spraying, no fertilizer, no nothing." He praised the modern chemicals that had kept him in red fields of strawberries for over forty years. ("Just a little Roundup won't hurt.") Several times he told me about using DDT in the 1950s, following the directions, fogging the whole kitchen—dishes, cabinets, and sink—to kill the flies. He now knew the danger, wondered why he never got sick, questioned why a neighbor, who in his words was "100 percent organic," died in her late thirties to cancer.

Always we talked about blueberries and strawberries, about our fields. I used his counsel often, like on where to place our new road to ease a steep grade, or what grass to seed between the blueberries.

We both laughed when I took Joe's advice on buying a fertilizer spreader—his. ("Why don't you just buy mine?" he suggested.) Of course, he thought he made a good deal, fifty dollars for a badly rusting machine, but I made a good deal, too, acquiring his advice on how to use it and avoiding the cost of a new one at five times more. We walked out to his barn and he pointed to the spreader in the dark corner, tongue up, tires flat, twenty years of cobwebs hanging from its sides.

"You sure it'll work?" I doubted.

"Of course it will, Jim. It might leak just a little here and there."

We dragged it out and filled the tires. The spreader was a primitive-looking machine probably from the 1950s. It amounted to a large tin pan riding on top of two tires. The gears beneath the pan rotated at whatever speed the whole contraption was pulled, and as the axle rotated, flanges flung out the fertilizer that some poor fool kept pouring into the pan.

Even as I signed the check to Joe, I knew we'd probably only use this old spreader one time, here at the beginning of our berry enterprise, when the field was wide open. Eventually I'd need to find some other, smaller contraption to spread fertilizer between the bushes. But this battered machine suited our present needs, so I attached it to the back of the pickup truck and trundled it home where it sat in our barn until we were ready.

After the bulldozer rattled down the road and we spent a week rock and root grubbing, I called Joe and told him it was time to use his spreader. I had already bought over three tons of organic fertilizer, black rock phosphate, Sul-Po-Mag, cottonseed meal, and others freighted all the way from Pennsylvania, special order, four pallets of fifty-pound bags.

At our old barn, I loaded the bags into the pickup as Joe inspected. I could tell what he was thinking and braced myself: "What's this, Jim? Black Rock Phosphate . . . never heard of that." Pause. Read the label more. "Why Jim, 0-3-0! Only 3 percent phosphorous!? Good God, my 10-10-10 has 10 percent phosphorous. Now that has punch. Sure you don't want to try it?"

At first I tried to explain how organic fertilizers lasted longer and worked differently than petroleum-based fertilizers, but this didn't quiet his skepticism. "These are just magic powders, aren't they, Jim? Why waste your time and money on 0-3-0? Good Lord Almighty, I swear, I never saw the likes of this." I stopped talking, threw the rest of the fifty-pounders into the bed, and pretended not to hear.

With the truck full, Joe, Sarah, and I drove up our new road to the newly cleared field. Even though he lived two ridges away, it was the first time Joe had seen this land since the 1960s. He admired the road ("You got that grade good." Or as we rolled over a hump, "Ah, that water bar will save your road washing out, good to see."). At the top, he praised the cleared field and remembered when Ira Lester last grew beans here.

Then we set to the task. Joe explained that the spreader worked best only at a steady speed of twenty miles per hour; if you went any slower the fertilizer wouldn't broadcast evenly or far enough, and it might clog up as well. Sarah climbed into the driver's seat, her eyes just peering over the steering wheel of our huge white Ford. Even with the seat adjusted all the way forward, Sarah's feet barely touched the pedals, especially the brake.

I looked at the back edge of the pickup bed where I was to work. The truck, like the spreader, had its share of rust, and I could peer through one fender to read the labels of fertilizer bags weighing down the whole hind end. Worse, the tailgate had fallen off the year before. This meant I had no platform to work from when I needed to fill the machine, only the skinny bumper, with Joe's holey spreader tagging along behind.

My job was to cut open a bag of fertilizer, turn and step down onto the six-inch bumper, heave-ho into the spreader, and then turn back to rip open the next, all at twenty miles per hour over bumpy ground. Sarah and I both eyed the three feet of empty space between truck and spreader; we both knew a false step would get me run over by the rolling contraption. Joe didn't seem to worry. He hoisted himself into the truck bed, climbed over the mounds of bags, and perched on the bed rail next to Sarah's window. There he could watch my progress and shout commands both forward to Sarah and backward to me.

I climbed on after him and braced my legs like a sailor. Sarah and I briefly made eye contact in the mirror; we both knew we wouldn't be able to hear each other over the engine. Then she yelled, "Here we go," slowly letting out the clutch. I threw the first bag of rock phosphate and watched as the black powder whipped out underneath the pan in a fine spray. It looked and felt like sand, expensive sand, and it whirred like wind against the spreader's metal sides.

Immediately Joe began yelling. He turned to the front and hollered into the cab, "Faster, Sarah, faster. This isn't fast enough!" And then back at me, "Come on, Jim, keep it going." After a moment, he leaned over the side and hawked a brown trail of tobacco. "Add a little nitrogen to this soil," he grinned to me, referring to the spit. "God knows it needs it."

At the first field corner, Sarah slowed for the turn, and this made Joe yell even more. "Don't touch that brake, Sarah. Speed it up a bit." She couldn't tell if he was serious or joking; neither could I. But at the next turn, she managed to wing our whole rig around without toppling me or slowing down too much. "That's the way," Joe said, nodding in approval as we both hung on.

On the straight stretch, Joe refilled his lip with snuff, smiled, and cheered, "You're getting the hang of it, Professor." Pause. Then, "You ain't tired yet, are you, Jim?" I just sliced open the next bag, lifted its bulky fifty pounds, stepped on the bumper, and dumped, watching the bare dirt zoom beneath my feet. Each fifty-pounder felt heavier than the last. Joe knew best how the spreader worked, but I could tell he relished this ride, grinned as the sweat dripped from my nose. I wondered silently how many ounces his little spoon of tobacco weighed.

When we finished, my legs wobbled, unsteady on solid ground, and my ears hurt from too much Joe. He jabbed one last time about "magic powders": "I sure hope these work, Jim. Are you sure you know what you're doing?"

No, Joe, I wanted to say, *I have no idea what I'm doing, but I'll be damned if I admit that to you.* Instead, I just shrugged as he climbed into his car and drove away.

We parked the spreader in the barn and later found another way to fertilize the bushes. And we never used that machine again.

Chapter 9

❧❦

Homestead Hint Number 1: Forget the Rope

Long before we ever bought the farm, maybe before we even moved to Virginia, I discovered on the back shelves of some library a little book titled *Homestead Hints: A Compendium of Useful Information from the Past*. The cover, a deep blue, shiny laminate, had a simple drawing, but I mainly remember the gold-embossed title. The spine was so skinny it easily disappeared among the larger hardbound *Back to Basics* or *How to Prune*. Somehow I found this book and fell in love with it.

The editor, Donald Berg, had gleaned from farm bulletins and almanacs of the 1800s bits of wisdom that might prove useful today, or at least quaint. To me, though, every page seemed full of hard-found intelligence, for I was already living this homestead life in my mind, and yes, I would need to know this recipe for homemade insecticide, or that "when gnats bite vigorously . . . rain may be expected."

I must confess something about this book. With apologies to Mr. Berg and to my former employer who unwittingly supplied paper and machine, I admit I copied the whole book, all 125 pages. I had no money for books then and rationalized the act as being educational and frugal, two homesteader commandments. I still have those copies, and obviously, the guilt.

So as a way to ease a portion of this angst, and in the spirit of those nineteenth-century writers, I now add my own Homestead Hint.

Sarah and I knew if we really wanted to homestead, we had to burn our ties to the utilities, at least metaphorically. A semblance of independence came only if we heated with wood, so our move into the old farmhouse seemed like the ideal time to start. But, to put it bluntly, we had no stove, no wood, and no saw.

Sarah's brother, Matt, bartered with us for his stove, an "Earthstove" from the 1970s. It sat under a tarp in his North Carolina woods, a front-loader with a wide door that opened like a mouth. He no longer needed the metal cavern and gladly traded it for a day of our labor on his new house.

The wood we had in enormous quantities now that we owned ninety acres, but none of it fit into our stove without a little work, so I bought a chain saw, a Stihl 026, a smaller version of the orange-and-white behemoths my dad and uncles always used. I grew up in a family that burned firewood and so inherited the fondness for wood smoke, but I never learned the how-tos of selecting a good tree, felling it the right direction, bucking it into manageable pieces. As a teen, I split the rounds into pie-shaped wedges or muscled the wood into the truck. Dad always ran the saw.

The day I carried home the shiny Stihl, I read the manual twice, then for safety's sake, Sarah made me read it a third time. A week later, when Matt helped lug the heavy stove into our house, I asked him for a lesson on using the chain saw. He illustrated what the manual couldn't get through my wooden head, how to cut through the pressure side of a bowed log, fell a tree with a notch cut, and avoid the snap of released branches.

We practiced on an already-downed apple tree, the heartwood fragrant, red and heavy. Sarah watched, fingers in ears, waiting to help. The large rounds she rolled on end for me to split, the smaller limbs she stacked. Out of the corners of our eyes, we checked each other, aware of the danger, but also of the fuel we were gathering to hold us through the winter.

By my sophomore year of cutting firewood, I had grown confident with the saw. I knew how to open an alley for the tree to fall into, and about half of the time, I could get the tree to land there. The other times when the top caught high up in another, I cut swatches from the base, backpedaling before the oak shifted and gravity pulled with an amazing speed. A couple of cut-and-runs and finally the whole weight of wood unhooked and thumped to the forest floor.

Over the course of the first year, we had cut and split and hauled ten pick-up loads, filled the woodshed, and then carried it armload by armload into the house to feed the stove's hungry mouth. Each cold morning, we bent to blow into the coals, to break winter's iciness with a whisper of air and a single stick of wood.

Passing by those five cords stacked neat and tight every day gave me a shallow confidence, and I knew, yes indeed, I was ready to cut the walnut tree.

It stood behind the house, taller than the two stories and ten feet away from the back window that it shaded so nicely. It filled a small, otherwise useless corner of steep bank between house and root cellar. And this walnut had bothered me for all of the few short months we had lived here. In its leaves, its hulls and sap, even from its roots, this walnut like all of its brethren emitted an allelopathic substance that few other plants can survive. Only raspberries and periwinkle thrived under this tree, nothing else, not even our new house paint. The previous owners had painted the metal roof and wooden siding a year before we arrived, and already, the roof coat in this one section had peeled into long shanks to reveal the ugly blue of the original tin. If I waited much longer, that blue would turn brown as the acidic rain rusted our hundred-year-old roof. The walnut, straight and healthy, beautiful in its expression of walnut-ness, had to go.

Of course, it leaned toward the house. I needed to fell it the opposite direction, uphill. I read the manual again on making tricky cuts and then geared up. I tied some rope as high as I could and positioned Sarah uphill at a 90-degree angle from where I wanted it to fall. I figured she could pull the skinny rope and guide the tree into the right spot. She said nothing, but I could read the "and you think this will work?" look on her face. She climbed the bank, rope in hand, thinking she'd do her part, or at least stand by to witness.

The wood sliced easily, the notch of deep brown dropping onto the ground in less than a minute. Then the difficult back cut. The idea was to score a narrow groove and stick a wedge into the leaning side, and then drive this wedge and push the tree away from where it naturally wanted to fall. The idea, anyway.

I checked Sarah, uphill and holding the rope tight, but smart enough to be well away from any danger. Then I cut what was to be a shallow slip, a few inches deep, enough to start the wedge. At four inches, I pulled out the blade and grabbed for the plastic wedge in my back pocket. But even as my arms moved, I could tell this wouldn't work. I had cut too deeply, the four-inch slice on one side, the notch on the other. The tree began to fulfill what gravity demanded. It leaned at first, then began its slow fall toward the roof of our house below. I tried to force the wedge into the closing slice, but too late and too close. I ran backward and yelled, "Nooooo!" while I heard Sarah screaming my name. That structure I was trying to save from further damage now was about to be pounded by my good intentions. Steady as a pendulum, the tall walnut swung right onto the house, hitting the crown of the roof directly above the kitchen.

The temper that I inherited from my grandfather flared and I heard him in my voice yelling at Sarah, "Why didn't you pull on the damn rope?"

She dropped the rope, held up her hands, and said, "I tried." She did not yell.

I ran to the garage to fetch the ladder, simmering down the anger, venting the frustration but also realizing she could have done nothing to steer the force of that falling tree. Then back with the ladder against the side of the house, I climbed to the flat porch roof with Sarah right behind. As she stepped from ladder to tin, I turned to give a hand, but she clambered up on her own and didn't even consider my offered hand.

Okay, I thought, and knew more was coming. We stood on the red roof, the pungent smell of crushed walnut leaves clouding the air, and she made eye contact, finally, to say, "Way to go, Lumber Jim."

I let that sink in, then replied, "Guess that makes us even."

She only nodded.

We turned then to our battered roof and fallen headache. The peeled bark of broken branches shone a bright yellow in the sun, and the new leaves made the metal under our feet even slicker. We both scrambled up the steep section of roof to straddle the peak and inspect. Ten feet of top stuck out over the other side of the roof, and a dent the size of a meat platter dimpled the ridge, but it looked like no cracks, no holes, and a little luck had saved us from seeing sunlight, or rain, filtering down on our kitchen sink.

As we examined the dented roof more closely, looking for cracks, we heard a car dusting down the state road right below the house. "Quick, duck, someone's coming." And we both slid partway down the roof to crouch, holding onto the ridge top and peaking over. It was Joe in his little red car, and like always, he beeped, but didn't stop. And hopefully, he didn't look up high enough to see this odd tree where it shouldn't be. I didn't need his memory and tongue to help me remember this day.

Before anyone else passed by, I scrambled down the ladder, grabbed the saw, and climbed back up to cut the walnut. The top-most section clanked onto the other side of the roof and rolled down to fall in the flower beds, but all else fell where hoped and soon, with Sarah's help, we had the log cut for firewood and the branches gathered in a heap on top of the stump. The dimple in the roof's ridgeline still remained. But no one else ever noticed this, the legacy of Lumber Jim.

So, Homestead Hint: Forget the saw, forget the manual, and definitely forget the rope. If a tree by your house must come down, call an expert, someone not named Jim.

Chapter 10

❧❧❧

Spying

"Vhat do you vant?" came the gruff German answer to our knock. He didn't open the screen door.

"We came to pick your blueberries. We talked on the phone, remember?" I asked, thinking he was a whole lot nicer two hours ago.

"Ya, but I just sat down to supper," and he started to turn away.

His wife came up behind him then and prodded him, "But dese are your customers! You should go. I'll keep your food varm."

The screen door opened.

Mr. German dumped his round body into an open, rusty army Jeep, the plate of warm sauerbraten still sitting before him in his mind. We piled back into our car, a VW Jetta, and tried to follow. The mad farmer zipped around some pines and disappeared down a steep farm road that we slid through, the gouged, muddy tire tracks steering the car more than my hands. "Are we going to get back up this?" Sarah voiced what we all wondered. Ruby was with us, a friend from Sarah's school we had dragged along. She chimed in, "Didn't know you needed your four-wheel-drive truck to go berry picking, did you, Jim?" I only shook my head.

The road emptied onto a small bottom, a meadow our friendly escort had lined with rows of blueberry and raspberry bushes. "Now this is pretty,"

Sarah commented. "And imagine the rich soil by this stream." We slowed to eye the canes and fruit, thinking we'd park and pick right here. But Mr. German didn't stop.

Laurel Fork divided the bottomland, a big stream for these parts, twenty feet across at least with cliffs for banks on both sides. A kingfisher cruised by, rattling its discontent at our interruption of his feeding. But it wasn't the only one to rattle or be rattled.

Sitting in our car, the three of us watched as the farmer in his 4WD Jeep steered down a cut in the stream bank, forded the wide stream, and drove up the other side.

"He wants us to go over there?" Sarah managed to say, her eyes as wide as her mouth.

"Look at him wave you on," quipped Ruby from the backseat. "Better hurry, Jim, he doesn't want that supper to get too cold."

Sure enough, Mr. German sat in his idling Jeep high on the opposite bank, motioning for us to come across. I inched the car to the bank-cut to look. Though he had spared spreading gravel on his field road, he had managed to firm up both sides of this ford with good stone, and the stream itself looked shallow enough, six inches deep, maybe. Before Sarah could protest any-more, I shifted into first and slowly inched into the water.

"Let's hope he has a good chain in case we get stuck," I muttered, as we all listened to the welling water, the rubber pushing against the foreign feel of liquid, the tires parting this blue sea. Halfway across, Ruby wished she had her fishing pole, and Sarah exclaimed again how she couldn't believe he expected people to pick in these kinds of conditions.

On the other side, the water dripped from the car as we pulled up beside him and got out. "How many pickers refuse to cross?" I questioned, amazed, like Sarah, that he could pull this off, that he actually asked pickers to ford this water. But he just muttered something and waved off my question. Then he pointed to several rows, said pick anywhere you like and come to the house when you're ready to check out. He didn't wait for any more ques-tions.

Such was the commencement of our berry quest, our exploration of other people's fields. We already had gleaned some unspoken advice from my grandfather's field, but what could we learn elsewhere? We took breaks from preparing our Eden-in-progress to travel the region, to understand how other berry farmers laid out their bushes, parked the cars, dealt with birds and weeds, or handled money. How did each farmer keep the customers happy enough to return? We were spying, in other words, checking out our competition and filling our freezer at the same time. What better way to learn how to operate a pick-your-own farm than by visiting one, or two, or five. And so we did.

The German's field, though full of fine fruit, obviously flunked for access. "Not sure you need to go back there," Ruby said as we forded the stream again and headed home. "That is, unless you need a car wash." She was a teacher's aide at Sarah's school, her husband the school janitor, the two of them resident grandparents for all of the kindergarten through seventh-graders. Sarah always came home with Ruby-stories, like the first-grader with a lisp who kept repeating, "Ms. Miiimic (drawing out the first syllable in its own long pleading request). Ms. Miiimic, I need a 'poon for my pudding." They both cackled at that. For weeks, Ruby would sneak behind Sarah and whisper in her high falsetto, "I need a 'poon for my pudding, Ms. Miiimic."

After we paid the German, Ruby decided she would wait till we had our own field before she picked anymore. In the meantime, Sarah and I visited the other two berry patches in the county, both small, half-acre plots at most, both not well tended. One closed shortly after we visited. The other still opened every June, despite its rubble road for access. These blueberries sat in the middle of one of the many hippie enclaves that dotted the county. So even though its road was as rough as the German's, that didn't matter. The owner already had an established group of pickers, all living nearby.

We parked the car beside a people-less patch, empty except for the birds. No one greeted us, no one else even stood in the field, and no houses were in sight. An abandoned peach orchard bordered the blueberry planting, another agricultural enterprise gone awry, it seemed. We headed to a check-out table shaded by a maple tree. A giant glass jar rested in the center along with a sign saying, HERE ARE THE BUSHES. FIVE DOLLARS A BUCKET. PLEASE PLACE MONEY HERE. An honor system—good for the owners in terms of freeing up time, but where was a "Welcome to our field?" And what if someone stole the money?

We grabbed two buckets and walked down the rows. Poison ivy climbed the bushes ("Watch where you put your hand," I warned Sarah) and we had to duck under the shiny strips of foil called bird-scare tape that draped the

whole patch like Christmas tinsel. It was torn and out of place, flying everywhere, but no matter, the birds kept coming anyway, starlings and robins
landing right beside us in the next bush, unusually unafraid, boisterous, and
bolstered by unhindered access to blues.

We didn't know much about pruning yet, but we could tell these bushes
hadn't been touched, their canes spindly and full of dead growth. As a result, the berries were puny, smaller than the German's, pinkie-nail-size versus thumbnail or bigger. It took a long time to fill a bucket, and we ended up
combining our pickings into one. So much for filling the freezer from this
patch.

As I placed our five-dollar bill in the jar ("What if you don't have the
right change?" Sarah wondered), I noticed under the table a bag of 10-10-10
fertilizer. "Jeez. Look at that," I said, pointing with my sneaker. "So these
aren't organic blueberries we just picked. Oh, well." So much for my stereo-
types of the "alternative" in alternative community.

The next few summers, from 1992 to 1995, we visited more patches, refin-
ing our judging skills, evaluating a whole spectrum of criteria from location
and customer parking to the health of the bushes and flavor of the berries.
At the farm with an ideal location, near a major town, people packed the
field, hustling to find the best spot before someone else. But like the hippie
patch, these bushes had poison ivy vining up into many of the branches.
Pick a berry and go home with a blistering hand.

At another patch behind an elderly lady's house, the bushes hadn't been
pruned in years. They formed a massive jungle that most pickers avoided,
preferring instead to pick along the periphery. Sarah and I ducked and
crawled under this canopy to pop up in the middle of the hillside of blue.
The picking was terrific here, the berries heavy and untouched, but crawling back out, we spilled half of our buckets.

The most impressive operation was also the largest, twelve acres of blueberries, all pick-your-own, all on top of a mountain on the West Virginia/
Virginia line. Our neighbor Joe had prodded us to go, so finally we drove the
two hours to have a look.

This place was incredible. An hour from any town of size, and at the end
of a mile of a rough, dirt road, these fields validated what Joe and his strawberries had also shown: location was nice, but often irrelevant. Pickers packed

each field, and already-full pails and boxes lined the shady sides of their cars. *"Twelve acres!"* we kept whispering to each other as we drove along the ridge to the check-out stand. We could see the blue glinting between green leaves and heard in the backseat the rattle of our empty containers.

We waited in line as Mrs. Miller, one of the owners, weighed out the pickings of an earlier bird than us. Their five mounded buckets confirmed what we suspected: the picking was good. Mrs. Miller then weighed and marked our empty containers (so she'd know later how much to subtract at checkout), told us where to pick, and sent us out.

Under the heat of summer's fruiting sun, we sat in the middle of an acre of Bluecrop and listened to the chatter of other pickers. These blueberries weren't organic and we sure couldn't imagine tending twelve acres, but our pails filled that day with round and ripe berries and with the thought that yes, we, too, could do this.

❧ BLUE INTERLUDE ❧
Blues in History

Who knows when we humans first picked and ate a blueberry? As an anthropologist friend told me, it was probably about the same time we figured out how to work our thumb and fingers, about the time we learned how to pinch a plump ripe berry off the bush.

And who was that brave person to take the first bite? Did she watch birds and bears eat this fruit, or did she just stumble onto a bush and say, "Lunchtime!"? What words, if any, did she know by then—"sweet" or even "blue"? In so many ways, that first bite changed our history.

Thoreau understood the significance of both berry and first bite, and in one of his last uncompleted works, *Wild Fruits*, he documents the many earliest written accounts of Indians eating berries.

The first known record of humans and blueberries comes from 1615 when the explorer Champlain "observed that the natives made a business of collecting and drying for winter use a small berry which he called blues . . ." Like so many other tribes, these Algonquins made a kind of bread from cornmeal and dried blueberries, what Thoreau calls a "huckleberry cake," and this proved to be a staple to carry them through the winter.

In 1639, a Jesuit named Le Jeune in Canada, observed of the Indians that "[s]ome figure to themselves a paradise full of bluets." This sentiment arose over 200 years later in the state of Washington when in 1843, a Methodist missionary described berry season among the natives as "one great holy-day." He continues that they "preferred to spend their summer Sundays in the meadows of 'Indian Heaven' instead of listening to sermons that promised a Christian paradise." So heaven for these native pickers from different times and regions must include or simply be a field of blueberries!

Then in 1672, John Josselyn in his *New England Rarities* calls blueberries "sky-colored," comparing them to the berries of his England home. He remarked how Indians dried and sold them by the bushel to the English newcomers who put them into "puddens, both boyled and baked."

In the Pennsylvania wilderness of 1743, Bartram described how "an Indian squaw" dried her huckleberries over a small fire. And in

1748–1749, Kalm wrote that when the Iroquois "designed to treat [him] well," they offered him "fresh maize bread, baked in an oblong shape, mixed with dried huckleberries."

Thoreau states how common this huckleberry cake was to all the tribes "in all parts of the country where corn and huckleberries grew." Lewis and Clark found this on their western expedition in 1805, and Thoreau believes that "if you had travelled here a thousand years ago, it would have been offered you alike on the Connecticut, the Potomac, the Niagara, the Ottawa, and the Mississippi."

How well we would have eaten by the banks of these many rivers if we had kindly taken this offered gift.

Chapter 11

❖❖

What We Fear

L oneliness, for starters.

And failure—failure of this blueberry dream of a farm: What if it doesn't work? What if we have to move and give up this idea? What if we never can call ourselves blueberry farmers?

And then a different failure—failure of this art of writing, my talents, to mature into beauty, something valued by others. What if I never publish a book, never reach that marker, that moment of validation? Will I still be a writer?

Then there are the usual fears of death and accidents, pain and hunger, poverty and homelessness.

Loss of any sort—of partners and pets especially, but also of arms and fingers and eyes and ears. And loss of kinfolk and friends, what friends we have.

Which brings us back to loneliness. Like a shadow it follows us even on cloudy days. We try to ignore it, forget it even, and then we turn suddenly to feel its fullness fall over us. Envelop us.

Why? We have each other, a beautiful homeplace, good and meaningful work.

But we also have this longing, a deep desire to belong.

We humans—all six-plus billion of us—seem like a connected bunch, with our phones and e-mails, but we all know this is far from true. Loneliness, "the absence of a place in a connected community," affects millions of people worldwide and with far-reaching effects, especially to people's well-being. Loneliness has been connected to hostility, substance abuse, eating disorders, depression, anxiety, and many health problems. One study found that divorced nonsmoking men had nearly the same amount of premature deaths as married smokers. As one writer notes, "For men, apparently, the breakup of a marriage can be nearly as lethal as a lifelong habit of smoking."

Thankfully, mercifully, Sarah and I have each other. "We'll just grow old together and be hermits," she often jokes in her better moments. In the darker times, though, we both struggle, sulk in our stew of frustration, in this unfulfilled desire to feel a part and not apart.

In many ways, our homesteading dream produces a certain amount of isolation. Look at the history, the accounts of Kansas settlers in their sod huts or Alaskan pioneers in their log cabins, and they, too, struggle with this paradox of wanting aloneness without loneliness.

Unlike the Alaskan wilderness, we do have people living nearby, but these folks have their family for neighbors, excluding us. Kin, after all, is the first and longest lasting form of connection. For us, our closest kinfolk, Sarah's family, live 150 miles away, and we visit them often. We try to see my family a couple times a year as well, but distance is an even greater barrier; my folks live 300 miles away in Pennsylvania, my sister 1,100 miles away in Kansas . . . all a way, way away.

For various reasons, we have no children, and this also creates more isolation for us. We might meet a neat couple at a health food store, and then around the corner comes their eight-year-old. It's not that we hate kids—far from it—but parents focus energy on raising their offspring. This translates into finding playmates for youngsters, not on making connections with childless adults.

In his book, *Healthy at 100*, John Robbins researches cultures that have the longest lived adults. From the Hunza of Pakistan who dance in their nineties to the centenarians of Okinawa, he discovers commonalities of exercise, diet, and community connection that allow these individuals to live happily and healthily well past the typical lifespan of people in more industrialized nations. When it comes to valuing each other, these elders far surpass us.

One "cure" for loneliness in our Western society is to go shopping, to buy something, a distraction, really, but something. In comparison, these people living in their traditional cultures visit each other rather than go shopping. "They have need of few belongings," Robbins articulates, "for they belong to each other." He concludes that an "abundance of positive, meaningful relationships is one of the secrets of the world's healthiest and most long-lived peoples."

Deep down we know this, know that our level of stress could lessen if we join a group. But we can't find this group, it seems, no matter how much we try. So in our worst moments, we swear off people ("They're a bad habit anyway") and hunker down with our dogs, Grover and Grace. And deep down, we know that these furry creatures also release stress, improve our health, connect us to a pack.

But no matter how much they try, these two mutts can't lick away that shadow of loneliness that still keeps creeping back.

Chapter 12

❀❀❀

The Not-Manual

We bought the best blueberry manuals we could find, including the one from Cornell, which was a huge binder affair that was also hugely expensive. These "authoritative" books expertly covered such topics as soils, diseases, and insects, but the more I read, the more holes I kept tripping into. None of them, for example, covered organic practices; none of them even mentioned this idea. And none really addressed some of my most basic questions, like how do you plant 1,000 bushes? How do commercial growers manage this onerous task of getting the roots out of sun-baking black pots and into the ground in a reasonable amount of time, a month, say, instead of a year?

At a fruit-growers workshop one winter, I listened to a horticultural expert from Virginia Tech, the nearby land-grant school. He specialized in small fruits, knew his bugs and berries, and as an aside, mentioned that they had just finished planting a test plot of blueberries on their research farm. *Ah,* I thought, *he'll answer this how-do-you-plant question.* Afterward, as he collected his materials, I introduced myself and then asked how they planted their new patch of blues. He veered off on a tangent about varieties, but didn't really answer the question, so I queried again. Finally, he confessed, "Well, we just dug a hole and socked it in the ground." That scientific. The simplicity embarrassed us, and we both understood that he couldn't answer the larger question of how to do this on a massive scale.

Eventually, like for other problems, if the manuals and experts offered no answers, I asked my neighbor Joe. If he had no advice (which he would never admit), I made up my own method. And really, the answers I searched for often could come only from the field itself and those of us trying to make it something blue, but I didn't know this at the time. The manuals and experts offered general tips, or told about how they approached a similar problem, but no book could ever be written to tell a farmer how to farm a specific field.

The field *is* the book, and despite the easy tendency to think otherwise, the field is not a blank page. It has a history to remember, a topography to read, and a soil to taste. Ideally, the farmer has gleaned enough knowledge from other fields and other generations to know how to ask the right questions and work toward the right answers. But for greenhorn farmers like us, where do these generations of experience come from? Often, nowhere.

At the time, I knew we were making do, just not how much. I had yet to learn this language of the field, and instead I kept trying to rely on the manuals, getting lost in their thick vocabulary about soils and nutrients. I wanted a translation, a how-to book specifically for new organic blueberry growers and specifically for this field. None existed, of course; none ever could.

Except maybe for this: a retrospective laundry list of what we did after we spread the fertilizer. *The Not-Manual* I wished for as I tried to learn a new language.

- Till in fertilizer. Wear a face mask for all the dust you'll kick up, and go easy on the steep turns at the bottom of the field. No tractor tipping allowed.
- While you're circling round and round on the tractor, forget about that test plot planted behind the house. Those six plants are too small to worry with now, and too slow to bear a fruitful sampling. After nights of debate, order six varieties that sound the best in the catalogs, and go with blind gumption that they'll be good. Like your grandpa, hope you won't bumble too much down this blueberry path.

- In the field, spread grass seed on the acre-and-a-half you're not planting in blueberries, not yet anyway. Hopefully your lovely partner will crisscross the field hand-flinging the seed on a windless day. Keep seed out of blueberry beds . . . don't need more weeds there, only blues.
- Bedspring seedbed. Find a discarded box spring, chain it to tractor, and drag smooth the soil. Easiest task on this list.
- Pray for gentle rains. Hardest task on this list.
- Admire new grass as it feathers across the bare ground. Be thankful for little erosion.
- Take a break from the tractor work and on a misty day, arrange for the local fire department to come burn the pile of trees stretched across the middle of the field. Help them spread out the cardboard tinder, soak it in gasoline, and step back as the brittle pines become torches. Watch from the fire trucks as you share lunch and stories. Admire how the flames reach as tall as the trees once did, and how the heat pushes a fog of steam across the whole field.
- A month later, hire your neighbor and his dozer to push the remains of the burn pile off the cleared field into the woods. Plant pines in front of this ugly heap to hide it from future pickers.
- In the now empty field, lay out beds. Takes two people, two tape measures, a zillion stakes, and at least one very large bucket of patience. Do it on graph paper first. Give each plant four square feet for the shallow mass of roots. Allow for plenty of tractor-turning room at the field edges. And don't get the beds too close because if you do, later you'll curse yourself every time you mow as loaded canes whack you across the legs.
- Plow up beds and stay within the contour and stakes you laid out. Admire the clods of rich earth crumbling in the sun, but don't let the tractor wander downhill. Look backward at the plow and forward at where you're going *at the same time.*
- Know while you plow that you'll also pull up massive quantities of sticks, roots, and rocks. (And you thought you had finished cleaning the field?) Become depressed for a minute or so, and then start back to the raking and grubbing and gathering of so many pickup truck loads of debris. If you're lucky, your parents might travel from another state to help.
- Fill plowed furrows with peat moss (blues love the acid). Get the huge bales on sale at the hardware store that's decided it needs to move a

half mile to a bigger box. Spend a day hefting the wet bales, ripping them open, and kicking them apart so they evenly cover each bed.

- Also fill plowed furrows with rotted sawdust—again, more acid and better "soil structure." (Read manuals to understand what that means.) Don't use fresh sawdust; it'll rob the nitrogen from your plants (again, refer to manual). Get the dark, old sawdust delivered in a small dump truck, something that can straddle the beds and spread the sawdust, saving you the labor. Be sure dump-truck driver has enough fuel. Swear under your breath when he runs out in the field. Watch as he sticks a hose into your truck to siphon out enough gas to get home. Try not to guffaw in horror as he spits out a mouthful. Don't imagine what he tastes.
- Spread more fertilizer, the bags you saved just for these beds, just for these blueberry bushes. Try not to think about Joe.
- Try not to think about the stack of essays you're supposed to be grading, either. Who needs a job? Just keep driving that tractor.
- Till again, this time just the beds. Watch your roto-tiller so sweetly mix the peat, sawdust, and fertilizer in with the soil. Again, with emphasis, *look both ways at once.* Stay in the contour lines of what you and your wife so carefully laid out.
- Get off tractor to admire the loose soil. Tilled in, all of these amendments make the earth crumbly, heaven to a blueberry plant.
- Shape beds by hand, especially where your tractor wandered out of the lines. Make terraces by raking smooth each foot of bed (a bed is eight feet wide and over 200 feet long, and you have ten beds to rake).
- Buy another pair of gloves . . . and another pair, and another.
- Take a break from raking to work on irrigation system. Find a friend who is a curious genius willing to build a special contraption called a ram pump, a two cylinder monster that uses the force of water to pump the water, no electricity, no gas-powered engine, just the steady *thump-thump* of a heart filled with water.
- While your friend builds the pump (reconfiguring it three times because he's surprised by the amount of force), lay out pipe—over 3,000 feet to deliver water to the field. Again, if you're lucky, your parents and a friend will help with this work, especially with snaking the long sections of one-inch pipe through rhododendron hells.
- Sing "Hallelujah" when the pump finally works, and you watch water rise 233 vertical feet to fill a bucket at 7 gallons a minute.

- Once pump is running and beds are shaped by hand, dare to straddle these meticulously formed, terraced beauties with a tractor, this time with a potato plow on back. Down each bed, make two furrows, four feet apart. Ask wife to walk in front of tractor with a notched eight-foot stick, your guide to help keep you straight (something she is already good at).
- Don't run over wife.
- When finished, plant blueberries. One thousand of them.

Part II

❧⚘❧

Grow

(1995-1996)

a clapper for the bell of this wide sky
the blossom a cup of bee-sipped wine
the bumble of a bee

Chapter 13

❦

"Grow, Little Plant"

Sarah is the best planter, her frame covered by denim overalls, her hazel eyes shaded by a wide-brimmed straw hat. Grover and Grace, our dogs, nap nearby or romp in the woods after squirrels. They come back to interrupt our work, nuzzle us for a rub, and then lay down again, watching over us as they drift back to foot-twitching bunny dreams. They are the grace notes to the steady rhythm of our planting song.

The tune goes something like this: First, Sarah slides the measuring stick along the trench, marking each four-foot center with a pint of cottonseed meal, fertilizer to help these newcomers overcome transplant shock. Next, she sets the potted bushes near each mound of stinky meal. And then she plants herself, sitting on the ground, a booted foot in the trench on each side of the blueberry bush. She squeezes the pot, taps the bottom, turns it over, and slides the plant into the open furrow—one smooth, practiced motion of release. The mass of roots has grown entangled in the dark, so she breaks some tendrils to promote good spreading. Sarah positions the plant in the trench at the right height (not too deep, not too shallow), and pulls dirt to cover the roots. She gets up, steps around the base to tamp tight the loose soil, and settles the new plant into its new home. After the first few, Sarah pops along at a three-minute pace. She blesses each by saying, "Grow, little plant," willing it to survive before planting herself at the next spot, repeating the refrain.

Through these long April weekends, I'm always thinking, plotting how to do each task most efficiently as I work around Sarah. I haul the potted babies from truck bed to the aisle ahead, guessing where she'll need them next and trying to keep each variety in its designated row. When she runs out of fertilizer, I fill the bucket from another fifty-pounder of cottonseed meal, then lug the weight down the hillside.

Mostly, though, I work behind her, moving the water hose, raking, always raking, and gathering the high stacks of empty pots she's accumulated (they look like leaning towers of top hats). Between plants each open trough gets filled with water at least once, sometimes twice. The tilled-in peat and saw-dust act like sponges, so we saturate the soil to prevent the peat from rob-bing moisture from the bushes. Once the water soaks in, I rake the trench shut and form small inch-high ribs of dirt around the bottom of each bush, pretty little dams to retain future rain.

Rain—a word we listen for every day on the radio forecast, a word we seldom hear, except in our prayers and passing questions, as in "Wonder when it'll rain?" or "Think that little white cloud up there, that loner, could throw some moisture our way?" Joe says farmers are never satisfied with the weather, and I begin to understand what he means. We have chosen a drought year to plant our field of 1,000 blues, a spring season so dry it stunts the hay crop and kills the corn seed as it sits in the soil unable to sprout.

Thankfully, we have our ram pump. When we're working in the field every day, we let it run overnight, its water flowing into the pond, its *thunk-thunk* entering our dreams. But when we are away from the planting for a few days, we shut down the pump. The next morning we head to the field and before we load the truck with bushes, I open the valves, release the air, and set the pump to its two-beat rhythm, *thunk-thunk, thunk-thunk*, a deep bass that fills the valley. By the time we reach the pond a half mile away, the overflow pipe gushes with clear water from Lost Bent Creek. I switch one more valve, and the water chugs up the last steep section of hill, filling the column of one-inch pipe and then slipping out onto the forest floor. We can hear the distant pump even up here, through thick woods, *thunk*ing along.

If we had more money, we would finish the irrigation system with a tank or reservoir here at the top, something to hold this flow and then feed it out by gravity one trickle at a time to the field below. But we have only a trickle of money now, so no reservoir and no irrigation system. Instead, the water seeps into the woods until we have the dozen hoses all connected and laid out to deliver it to the bushes. Over 800 feet of garden hose snakes across the field to carry water from pipe at hilltop to bed at field bottom. Once the ram pump starts pushing water to the top, it's difficult to turn off the system or divert the stream into our pond, so the water runs constantly. We try to use every drop.

We work long weekends singing this new song. Sarah uses her saved-up leave and takes off Fridays while I speed-grade all my papers so that we have three clear days to work together. Like the Sunday morning when we hauled these bushes home, we are back in our new house of worship, the church of *Vaccinium corymbosum*, the high order of the highbush. The long pews slowly fill with yellow and red twiggy growth. Until they leaf out and grow taller, their wind song is soft, subtle, as if they are trying out their new voices.

The double-row bed is my idea. Like with our trench-and-soak planting method, we're creating our own practices with scant help from manuals or experts. On paper I draw out the ten beds with fifty plants in a row, a hundred in each bed. No manuals offer photographs of anything similar, but I want to squeeze as many plants onto this parcel of land as possible, and besides, it looks neat and tidy on paper. The guidebooks recommend alternating varieties in order to increase pollination and fruit-set. So we make sure each bed grows at least two different kinds, Patriot and Spartan at the top, Bluecrop and Blueray in the middle, and Nelson and Berkeley at the bottom. The season will progress down the slope, early varieties at the top, late at the bottom.

During the week, every evening after school, we call the dogs and walk the half-mile road to admire the new pond and check on our plantings. Every time, we pass the pots of unplanted plants as they wait by the stream. I don't want to tally, don't want to know the weight of work hanging over us, but can't help keeping a rough count: 150 in, 850 left; 300 in, 700 to go. . . . Slow and steady, I think, but we've been hard at it already for too long.

On one of these visits to the field, Sarah notices the bushes look different, somehow smaller. Our choir of tiny twigs has suddenly become maimed, crippled, tinier than they already were. I look and see a stub of stalk where three branches once pushed into the air.

Sarah, with sore knees from planting, cries, "Something's eating our bushes!" And I, too, am shocked at this realization. I crouch to inspect. No deer prints, so that leaves groundhogs, squirrels, or rabbits. Then we find telltale pellets beside a few bushes—Bugs Bunny's cousins.

Sarah quizzes Grover and Grace, "What is it, puppies?" and I follow with "And why aren't you doing your job? Get these bunnies!" The dogs circle the field, noses down, acting like they want to keep their jobs. Grace, the collie-lab, black-streaks this way and that, busy on a hot trail, and Grover, the poodle-terrier, tags along, trying to keep up with her long legs. Sometimes he'll pause at a grass clump and snort into its roots, scenting some mole that's already scooted away. They might kick up a white-tailed bunny, but I have little faith.

The next day, I buy a live-trap, a solar electric fence charger, and enough wire to circle the whole acre. As a teen on our family farm, I helped build fence, but never an electric one, and I was never the boss, never had to make sure posts set plumb or the wire stretched taut. It takes me a week of evenings to read the directions, set the posts, hook up the charger, and run the long strand of skinny wire. Since it's rabbit I'm after, I set the wire at three inches above the ground. In places where the orchard grass has already grown thick, this means shoveling a trench beneath the wire to kill the green stuff so that it doesn't kill the electric current. In some sections, this trench stretches through the thick grass for over 200 feet. I take pain pills every night before bed.

In the live-trap we finally find the right variety of apple to bait the rabbit, and a few days after we purchased the metal contraption, the dogs circle and terrify an already frightened occupant. I hold high the trap and its startled rabbit to save her from the mutts, and Sarah insists that it is female because of so many babies causing so much damage. The creature looks innocent, her marble eyes brown and blue, her nose twitching and sniffing for any escape. I carry her home, the dogs jumping and circling the whole way, and then I drive the rabbit five miles away to release her into some other woods. When I open the trap door, I have to shake the creature free, break loose the cower that holds her body. She finally bolts and I yell, "You and your babies stay here and don't come back."

I think she listens. That, and the fence jolts a few wet noses into staying in the new grass and avoiding our blueberries. We wait another week to make sure the fence works. When no new nibbles appear, we settle back to the planting song, bush by bush, weekend by weekend, soaking each blueberry with a gallon of creek water as we go.

The rabbits injured 100 of the 300 bushes already planted. We prune out the damage and expect strong roots to force up new stems. But this chomping-induced interlude costs us two valuable weeks in April before the bushes break dormancy. How long can the 700 potted bushes wait?

We try to quicken the planting song but have fallen into a paradox because of the drought: the faster we plant, the less we get in the ground. To ensure they survive transplanting, we have to water these youngsters once a week. So instead of long evenings socking bushes into the earth, we spend long evenings soaking the ones already there. We take turns walking from blueberry to blueberry, water-spouting hose in hand, pausing at each one long enough to saturate the soil and fill the little dams. On good days, I give each bush a minute's worth of water; on short evenings, that diminishes to thirty seconds. At home, Sarah charts our watering progress on graph paper stuck to the refrigerator, each bed numbered, each date recorded for when last these thirsty plants had a small drink of water. We keep waiting for rain.

Finally, in early June, with Sarah still teaching and the remaining plants just sitting in their sun-soaking pots, I call my parents for help. They are recently retired, and anything but tired. In fact, their energy amazes us, and we often laugh at how we wear out before they do. Dad has two speeds: idle with a crossword in the armchair, or full-out with chain saw in the woods. Mom has a few more speeds, but is more the long-hauler, liking board games that go late into the night. I know how hard they will work, and they know how hard we have struggled, so with a call, they travel the 300 miles.

They have never planted blues, only picked, so in the field, I give them a quick lesson, and together we tackle the last four beds. Mom kneels to plant each bush, Dad rakes and waters behind her, and I do a little of everything. Shiny, fragile leaves cover the bushes now, so we handle them with even more care. The bull in Dad sometimes breaks a twig or two as he drops a plant in place, but no matter—better that than to watch each plant desiccate in a black pot. Sarah rushes to the field every afternoon after school, wanting to participate and witness the progress. Together, the four of us push through the remaining 400 bushes, and in three days we get them all in the ground.

The final morning when we've emptied the truck the last time, Mom and Dad gather tools, and I hike to the far end of Bed 6 with a shovel and the last blueberry bush. New leaves, green with bright yellow veins, jostle against my face as I hug the pot and weave between all the other bushes. The red label hanging from a stem says Spartan, a variety name that implies strength, even courage and simplicity, though I'm not sure that's what the breeder had in mind. This plant has traveled far, from the flatlands of Michigan to these mountains of Virginia; it's been crowded and pushed too many times, dunked in cold stream water, and waited in its pot a long six weeks. Now, I hope it'll spread its many roots in this rich soil.

I spade open a hole and then kneel, tap the container, and slip out the circling, pot-bound mass. Like we've done with all the 1,000 others, I grab the bottom tendrils and rip them apart; the tearing sound—like muscle cleaving from bone—no longer bothers me. This needed violence allows the roots to escape the now imaginary confines of their past. If left unbroken, the fibrous mass will never spread out, never truly become established, never survive.

With a prayer of "Grow, little plant," I place this measure of our song in the last hole and cover its roots.

🌸 BLUE INTERLUDE 🌸
Working off of the Farm

While we struggle with getting so many tender plants in the ground, we also struggle more than ever with our off-farm jobs, especially Sarah. She has taught six years, the last three with kindergarteners, and she is completely drained. We both know that two months of summer rest will not heal her and that she cannot face another class of crying pupils. The constant shoe-tying, babysitting-instead-of-teaching, and parent-lack-of-caring has split her head open with a migraine every day. When the administration tells her that next year's class will have at least thirty five-year-olds, and they have no money for a teacher's aide, she breaks. "Jim, I just can't do it anymore, I just can't." I hug her sobbing body and search for solutions.

That same year, 1995, we pay off the mortgage. We scrimp and pinch and horde so that three and a half years after we buy the farm, we finally own it outright—no bank, no debt, no mounting interest. Though we have spent much of our remaining savings on the bushes and irrigation, we still have my teaching job, an untenured, annual-contract one, but fairly secure nonetheless. We punch the numbers and realize that we could live on my salary while Sarah takes a leave. She can tend the field, or find part-time work elsewhere, anything but having to face a roomful of youngsters again.

Our struggle with off-farm jobs is far from unique in agriculture, especially with small farmers. The USDA's 2007 census reveals that "[o]ff-farm income . . . received by U.S. farm operators and their spouses has risen steadily over recent decades and now constitutes the largest component of farm household income." Thus, to stay on the farm, most farming families often have to work off of the farm. One report summarizes that "[t]he off-farm income share of total household income . . . rose from about 50 percent in 1960 to more than 80 percent over the past ten years." What was once seen as a "'temporary response to the Great Depression,'" now is "regarded as a 'regular feature of almost all farming societies.'"

As our nation has transformed itself over the last century moving away from an agriculturally based economy, the message for those still wanting to farm has become, "Get big or get a job." Be a not-farmer in order to also be a farmer. I know growers who drive school buses, work in machine shops or banks, and many with a spouse who teaches. The off-farm job provides health insurance for the whole family and guarantees a steady income when a drought or hailstorm ruins that year's crop. Though we don't know it at the time, our off-farm labor fits a very large, national trend, and this leads to several ironies.

One paradox comes from the Internal Revenue Service. They demand that a farm shows a profit at least one in five years. This is their way of weeding out tax write-off scams, but for start-up operations like ours, the five-year rule makes little sense. But tell that to the IRS.

The Department of Agriculture's 2007 census underscores another irony: small family farmers, most of whom also have some off-farm income, own 91 percent of all the farms in the country and "70 percent of the land owned by farms." They control what happens to the lovely rolling hills that so many admire, but those lovely rolling pastures are often worth more sprouting houses than corn.

Yet, in this census these small family farms only accounted for a small percent of agricultural production. More and more, the large farms produce what we eat (63 percent in 2007) while the small farms produce what we value but don't buy—clean water and open land. As one researcher notes, "Small family farms manage and operate the bulk of farm assets, including the soil, water, energy, and natural habitat resources associated with farmland use." If we want to keep these resources, we should also keep the small farmers who manage them. Seldom if ever do we factor in the economic benefits of these services, and seldom do we pay the farmer to farm well.

Chapter 14

❧❦

College of Mulch and Sciences

If you look at him just right, Brian has the build of a blueberry plant, a Berkeley, maybe. A skinny body for a stem rises to a black mass of curly hair that appears as if it never gets pruned. And this bush of a head bears some amazing fruit. He holds a doctorate degree but years ago gave up on academe to live in a commune, an "intentional community," he calls it. And he is a person full of many fine intentions.

Take his mulch experiment that he tells us about at a local sustainable farming conference. Brian wants to help farmers find the best mulches so they can reduce weeding and eliminate herbicides. When we tell him about our newly planted field bare and waiting for a healthy cover of mulch, he eagerly agrees to help. And we soon learn that when Brian talks about mulch or compost or carrots, or when he takes his long, fast strides across a field, you feel his excitement. Sarah guesses that as a youngster, he was the hyperactive genius who befuddled every teacher. You run to keep up and are glad to siphon off a little of so much energy.

· · ·

In June, the bushes a month in the ground, Brian comes to help set up the experiment. Other than our parents, Brian is our first guest, the first person to witness our new project. We wonder how he'll react.

To get to the field, you turn at the white cinderblock church onto the gravel "lowway" (opposite of highway) named Berry Hill Road. This parallels Lost Bent Creek, past huge hemlocks and poplars, through woods for a half mile, all of it down slope. Then you turn left onto our farm lane, cross the creek, and begin to wind another half mile upward. Again, trees line this single-lane, shaley road, and several turns bend around the hills, so you never can see more than one hundred yards ahead. At the pond, bear left across the dam, and then put the car in low gear to make the final steep climb through big pines. A last hard turn and you finally see the woods open to an expanse of sky.

In the field, Brian's first words: "Wow!" followed by a long pause, and then, "You did all of this?"

We nod and watch him forget to close his car door as he hikes to the bushes. He keeps looking around at the field's expanse, and then down at the plants, his shaggy hair shaking.

"They look great! So green and healthy," he says as he bends to rub a leaf. Then standing to wave his arms, he asks again, "You cleared all of this and planted all of these by yourselves?"

We tell him we had help—hired dozers, called in family to get the last bushes in the ground—but he knows we've done the great mass of work. And having done his share of farm labor, he appreciates, and keeps repeating, "This is great."

Then we begin. Brian takes out a clipboard and asks what we want the best mulch to do. With his help, we set criteria: a good mulch will last a long time, handle easily, stop the weeds, and hold water and soil in place. It'll also keep the soil temperature in check and our wallets from emptying.

Brian writes this all down and draws out a map of the two long beds we'll cover. For his experiment, he plots and numbers twenty sections, and then randomly assigns each a type of mulch, saving a few patches as bare ground controls. We stand alongside and watch. He's thorough, I think, and takes his work seriously.

Sarah and I have already amassed piles of three of our four mulches: bales of old hay and dump truck loads of sawdust and chipped bark. We still have to gather the pine needles. When we set to moving material, Brian proves he also knows how to handle a pitchfork.

We start with the hay, lugging heavy bales to their assigned plots. The smell of dry grass reminds me of the fields and barns of my youth, except here I unbale the mown clover instead of baling it. We keep the hay a uniform four inches thick, per Brian's orders, and surmise that this, the easiest to spread, will also be the easiest for the worms to digest and the fastest to disappear. We shake out the bats, blanketing the bed, loose stems sticking to our sweaty arms. A few strands even tangle in Brian's black hair.

Next we shovel sawdust, one scoop at a time from the enormous pile into our old pickup, and then one scoop at a time from truck to blueberry bed. Thankfully, the drought has broken with two huge thunderstorms. But that rain also soaks the sawdust, so we heave water as well as spongy specks of wood.

Then after a packed lunch in the pines, we back the truck to the other pile, the mountain of chipped bark. The coffee brown, humusy material fills truck bed pitchfork by pitchfork, and then it covers the designated plots fork by fork. Though I cringe at its expense, I appreciate how this mulch covers the ground in a thick carpet, not billowy like the hay, but dense enough to last a while.

We keep an eye on the clouds, aware that another storm could fester up. And Brian gives us a new term, "sucker hole," a circle of blue in a sky of gray, a belief that the threatening storm might disappear.

We work on through the heavy air, tackling the last mulch, pine needles, which don't already sit in a nicely gathered pile. We should've started the day with this, the hardest task, but we save it for last, and as a result, trudge into the woods with rakes and burlap sacks. Instead of buying expensive bales from out of state, we decide to steal the straw from our forest floor. Under the pines, we rake the dry, orange needles into long heaps, pack these into burlap sacks, and then drag the bulging sacks to the designated berry plots. Once spread, the rust-colored needles create a gorgeous cushion to cover the bed. Brian even comments on how he could take a nap right there between the bushes on this soft mat of needles. I agree, but also can't imagine gathering enough needles to cover a whole acre. Brian only nods in tired agreement and heads home for a shower and a real bed.

A month later on a blistering July afternoon, Sarah and I try to keep up with Brian's long strides as we march across the field. He's returned to evaluate, test the plots, see what's working and what's not. We start with the control plots of bare dirt. Beside a blueberry bush, he probes the earth with a soil thermometer. When Brian pulls it out, he shouts, "Good Lord, I knew it would be hot, but not *this* hot!" Six inches into the ground, on the hottest day in July, the gauge reads 95 degrees. I think I can hear the shallow roots of our just-planted bushes sizzle and fry.

We move up a row to probe beside blueberries that have four inches of pine needles. This time the temperature gauge shows 75 degrees, and instantly I become a believer. The other mulches, the hay, sawdust, and woodchips, also have soil temps in the mid-70s. "So it doesn't matter which mulch," Brian notes, "just cover the earth with something."

He gathers samples of soil for other tests, mainly water retention. And he can tell even as he digs, that the soil beneath the mulch is moister than the control plot's bare ground. On his clipboard he scribbles notes about these temperatures, moisture levels, and also makes observations about erosion from two recent gully-washers.

We joke, offer him a pitchfork, and point to our new pile of chipped bark made by five dump trucks. He politely mentions another farmer he needs to visit, another field test to monitor. But he does say to let him know when the berries are ready—he wants to taste these fruits of his labor.

As summer progresses, we make our own notes, tally our own results. We predict correctly on the hay—too quick to rot, plus too many introduced weed seeds. The tawny pine needles earn A-pluses on appearance and performance, but fail the economic test. When we figure how long it will take to gather enough for an acre, we turn off the calculator. We want to grow blueberries, not gather pine needles.

The mulch of sawdust fools us. What I think is well rotted is not, despite its coffee-brown color. Two months after we set up the experiment, the one hundred bushes under sawdust appear stunted, while the rest of the field flourishes. Too late I realize the sawdust has robbed each plant of needed nitrogen. We rake back the mulch and apply more fertilizer, but I fear these bushes might never recover.

The chipped bark from a local sawmill becomes our choice of the four mulches. It decomposes the slowest, handles easily, and definitely holds moisture. Likewise, most weeds whither under it. It doesn't come free, yet for our scale, it saves the most money and body aches.

We spend the rest of the summer pitchforking the chipped bark from the mountain of mulch. As the calluses thicken, I realize Brian has given us a new field of study with texts like multicolored stretches of mulch, soil limits and capacities, and a simple thermometer. Sarah and I have enrolled in the College of Mulch and Sciences. The field and this curly-headed genius are good teachers, but the course work so heavy and complex, I doubt we ever graduate.

✿ BLUE INTERLUDE ✿
Roots and Fungi

Given the right soil, a blueberry bush's roots become both massive and shallow. One of our grower manuals has a photograph of a man holding a just-dug, mature plant upside-down above his head. The roots form a huge mat, a dense, fibrous "umbrella" for this smiling farmer.

The massiveness of these roots only goes so deep, though. Most of the tendrils stay in the top two feet of soil. Add to this odd arrangement the bush's fondness for very acidic soil, and you have what for most plants would be an uncomfortable situation, a soil too "poor" to grow much. That is unless they have allies like fungi.

To get a better understanding of the science beneath these plants, I queried my friend and biologist, Gary Coté, and as always, he provided ample information.

"Nearly all plants have some kind of an association with fungi at the root level. Most trees, for example, have fungi that coat their roots, called *ectomycorrhizae* ('outside fungus root'). We know most of these as common mushrooms, so when the time is right they send up their fruiting bodies around the tree to disperse spores and we see a crop of mushrooms (or don't see a crop of buried truffles).

"The trees provide the fungus sugar along with other nutrients. These fungi, in turn, send out their hyphae throughout the soil, taking in minerals for the tree. I've stood under pine trees and thought how the carbon in the mushrooms was fixed out of the air by photosynthesis in the pines, using chlorophyll containing magnesium taken up by the mushrooms. Even more beautiful is how the fungi can send their hyphae through the soil, engaging with more than one tree, even shrubs and herbs, thus uniting the forest into a sort of superorganism. Seedlings or stressed trees may take sugar from the fungus, the reverse of normal. Therefore, these young or stressed trees draw on sugars from the stronger trees, through the connecting fungi.

"Unlike trees, though, most plants join up with fungi that actually invade the roots of the plant, so-called *endomycorrhizae* ('inside fungus root'). These fungi do not produce the characteristic forest mushrooms, but instead rely on wind and burrowing animals to spread their spores.

"Some plants have specialized *endomycorrhizae*. The Ericaceae Family is one such group. Blueberries and other members specialize in acidic, nutrient-poor soils. The fungi help them by pulling minerals out of the soil, like with the trees. Even more important for the blueberries, probably, is the role of the fungi in getting nitrogen. In highly acidic soils, much of the nitrogen is tied up in rotting organic matter, a form that plants cannot use. Fungi, however, specialize in digesting that kind of organic muck. I heard someone once describe a fungus as an inside-out animal. Their digestive tract is the whole world, and they secrete enzymes outward to digest anything they find to useable compounds. Thus, they can turn the decaying animals and plants into nitrogen useable by other plants.

"So for blueberries in their favorite acidic soils, minerals are hard to absorb (and often rare). Fungi are good at absorbing stuff; plants are good at making sugars. It's a perfect collaboration."

Chapter 15

❧❧

Homestead Hint Number 2:
Throw Out the Electric Clippers

I sit outside in a chair from the kitchen, my wet hair too thick and too shaggy. I haven't visited a barbershop in several months but now it's time. Sarah stands facing me, ready, for the first time, to cut my hair. Though she has never wielded scissors like this, I stay calm. I have all summer, time enough for any mistakes to grow out. Or if we have absolutely horrible results, I can go for a buzz cut at a local barber. That, too, can be hidden under a hat in the berry field; that, too, will grow out in time to look presentable for school.

So *snip, snip* go the scissors, the cool blades resting against my scalp, my shoulders and lap filling with the remains of a too-long mop. Sarah circles, pauses to rest her hand or to reevaluate. She is unusually quiet as she touches her thigh to mine, leans in for the right angle of cut. I hope the silence means she concentrates extra hard, and not that my earlobe might get nipped. *Snip, snip, snip,* we plug on.

We get the idea for this kitchen-chair barbershop from the Watermans, homesteaders we visited once in Vermont. They had no phone or electricity, made their own presents, and cut each other's hair. Why not, we think, at least with my head. Ten or fifteen dollars a month to the barber adds up.

When I look in the mirror after brushing off those first Sarah-trimmed hairs, I am impressed. No blood, no arguments, and my hair looks decent. Not great, but good enough for summer and the first cut.

Later that year we travel to Pennsylvania to visit an old friend who happens to also be my parents' haircutter. We ask Tiffany for a lesson, which she kindly gives. ("A strip down the middle first, to get the right length, and then measure everything against that.") Sarah watches as Tiffany quickly works around my head. As usual, I'm the guinea pig, but I can tell from Sarah's dimpled brow and intent eyes, that she understands these instructions. After leaving a big tip, we head home with new confidence.

For the most part, Sarah has cut my hair ever since, and we haven't divorced because of any false snips, though we have had snips of a different kind. Like the one time, the only time, Sarah braves sitting in the kitchen chair to allow the scissors to fit onto my thumb and finger. "Just trim the ends, maybe a half inch at most. Nothing more." Slowly I clip and keep stepping back; I want to make sure my line across her shoulder blades stays straight. So, a little more on the left to even it up. Then, a little more on this side. . . . The requested half inch becomes an unrequested inch and a half, the piles of soft blond hair littering the ground. "That's *not* what I wanted," Sarah grumbles as she takes back the scissors. The only hair I ever clip again is Grover's, our shaggy dog.

Sarah's beauty-shop endeavors are not all perfect, either. The worst really isn't her fault, no matter how much I try to blame. We have to travel back home for my parents' anniversary, a big to-do celebrating their fortieth, complete with them marching to the altar to restate their vows. I am to dress in my best suit and read an essay to honor them. The piece is written and ready, but my scruffy head is not. We buy clippers, the electric kind that buzz with a juicy hum that vibrates every molar in the back of your head. We haven't tried out this new toy yet, but I've watched barbers use them for years—just plug and go, right?

Sarah puts on a blade, hits the switch, and takes one swipe down the middle of my head, stopping with a stare. "Jim, I don't know about this," says my drama-queen wife, hands at her sides.

"It'll be all right."

"But it looks funny."

I have a reverse Mohawk at the moment and doubt it could look any sillier.

"Just go ahead."

"Okay," she musters and swipes away. Three more strokes and she turns it off, still not even a quarter done. "You go look," she commands.

Into the house to the bathroom mirror and then a yell, "*Sarah!* What have you done to my head?"

"You said to keep going, so I did," says my wife, telling it straight for once.

I try to control my anger.

Somehow the blade on the clippers is a special *angled* blade, with teeth at different heights. So instead of a smooth peach fuzz, I'm left with streaks, some clear white to my scalp, some three-quarters of an inch of blond. My head has become a miniature NASCAR racetrack, complete with curves and a growing, oily slick spot from my sweat.

After more curses and blame-throwing, we throw out the electric clippers and revert to the antique scissors. Sarah does the best she can to cut my hair evenly, but Mom's first comment, "What have you done to your hair?" proves what we fear—these lines are deep. Mom soon forgets my hair when I confess that I've forgotten my suit. So off to the local clothing bank we traipse where they outfit me in a worn but serviceable suit and tie. Even from a distance, in the many anniversary photographs, my new streaked and contoured hairstyle still shows.

Recently, after my last haircut, Sarah pauses longer than usual when she finishes checking the ears and bangs. "What's the matter?" I ask.

"You have a bare spot here and here," she points, her finger touching above my temples. I head to the mirror to check, and sure enough, the first sighting of a hairline heading north. And here I thought I was safe because my maternal grandfather died with a full shock of hair.

In another twenty years, will there be any hair left for Sarah to cut? I guess baldness could be the ultimate cheap haircut.

Chapter 16

❧❧

Homesteading Alone?

Homesteading implies a certain amount of independence. A common synonym is, after all, *self*-sufficiency. But like our pitchforks, this belief only holds so much. And like our blueberry plants, we also need good soil, plenty of sun and rain, and healthy doses of community. When we moved away from our native lands, we already ripped up our roots. Could our own tendriling masses spread out, find enough nutrients to sink deep, to survive in this place we now call home?

Though we talk of the blueberries as our children, they can only provide so much. We need other people to swap pet-sitting and recipes, to supply us with nails and fertilizer, chocolate and coffee. More important, we want to find friends, like-minded folks who will share meals and laughter.

Floyd County has one high school, one tavern, and one stoplight. Roughly 13,000 people live here, and many of these folks proudly call up their eight generations of ties to this land. To get to know these native neighbors, church seems to have the most potential, so we leave our sanctuary of wooden stems and visit one with wooden pews.

One Sunday we don our best clothes and drive thirty minutes to a

United Methodist Church (UMC), a massive brick building on Main Street in a nearby town. We both grew up Methodists, and Sarah's grandfather was a minister. We shake the greeter's hand, an older man in a finely tailored suit, and slip down the left side, the huge tinted windows filling the sanctuary with gentle light, the vaulted ceiling making everyone speak in hushed tones. We slide into a pew and read the bulletin, opening the hymn book to the right pages, scanning the announcements, trying to get a sense of the people in this congregation.

The sanctuary feels empty, and many of the long pews are vacant. Two older women in front of us whisper about a friend's operation while glancing at us, the white-haired one saying, "Oh, my," over and over.

Then I feel a tap on my shoulder. Turning, I look into a wrinkled face covered thick with makeup and a fancy hat. "This pew is where I always sit. Would you move?"

"Of course." We oblige, shuffling over to the other end of the long bench. She sits in our warmed spots and leans over to join the other two whispering about their friend.

The church feels even emptier, the opposite of community. We never return.

A month or so later, we try again, this time following a neighbor to his church only a few miles away. The Presbyterian chapel constructed of river rock sits tucked back against a woods with a hayfield across the road. It doesn't have the vaulted ceiling, huge windows or grand pretensions of the big UMC in town. A few of the men wear ties, but none have coats, and the women enter in simple dresses. Many greet us, welcome this young couple, and we see we are some of the youngest people present. Only a handful of the small congregation doesn't have graying hair.

We should not have gone on this particular day, Memorial Day. The minister wears a flag clipped to his lapel, and the sermon mixes God's wrath for evil with the United States of America's grand conquest of that dark force. I want to leave five minutes into his speech, but Sarah and my own manners prevent this. I am a guest, one who appreciates sacrifices made by many, including my relatives, but I do not believe in war. Peace depends on a God of love, not wrath. I want a community that believes the same.

I'll have to look elsewhere.

.   .   .

That logical elsewhere seems to be the "alternative community" that peoples a significant portion of Floyd County, a community we already have met through Brian. The fertile soil, clear water and air, cheap land, all the qualities that attracted settlers seven generations back, also pulls in many "back-to-the-landers" in the 1970s. Though we don't wear tie-dye or dreadlocks, we think we might have more in common with these folks.

We subscribe to their "moonthly" newsletter, *The Museletter*, a stapled to-gether collection of gardening info and poetry by the likes of Redmoon, Starchild, and Fern. It also includes announcements for "womyn's" drumming and the fire-circle dance at summer solstice on top of Buffalo Mountain. *The Muse*, as folks call the newsletter, tells us of one of the commune's free pan-cake breakfasts every Sunday morning, an open house, of sorts, and a quiet way to meet others.

In jeans, not our Sunday best, we travel the long hour of curving roads to this commune on the other side of the county. We are impressed by the neat-ness of their place, the orderliness of a huge garden and a well-stocked root cellar. Twenty-five years ago, they laid out the commune so that the kitchen/eating house sits centrally, with individual sleeping cabins spoking outward in a circle. None of the buildings has indoor plumbing and few have elec-tricity, all of it supplied by solar panels. They heat and cook with wood.

On our first visit, after consuming sweet, home-canned blueberry top-ping on a stack of wood-griddled hotcakes, we spend hours with Harry, the unassuming leader of the commune, a tall, skinny man with a full beard and ponytail, and his wife, Liza, also slender, also with intense blue eyes. He tells us of the history of the place, their concentrated, ongoing "dream-work" where they share and analyze their nightly dreams. From her we learn of their new healing endeavor, the use of magnets to increase the blood's circulation. We share our lives as well, our histories and blueberry dreams. The conversation is long, wide ranging, and exhaustingly enjoy-able. Though we don't like the long drive, we see potential here, so we plan to go back.

Like most of the alternative hangouts in the county, it is, as Sarah calls it, "a huggy kind of place." Handshakes show a lack of hipness, coldness in-stead of coolness. Even in his e-mails, Harry always signs, HUGS, HARRY a new name Sarah and I playfully call him, but only between ourselves. On our first visit, instead of the Methodist church's suit-and-tie handing out bulletins, here at the commune, we are greeted by a few handshakes, but mostly awkward-for-us hugs. On the second visit, the hug is the only greeting used, and we think we are in.

Three months after our first visit, we return on a summer Sunday, the humidity already curling Harry's hair. Sarah gets to the meetinghouse ahead of me, and as she climbs the steps, Harry comes out the door to greet her. Sarah, shy and usually reserved in new places, opens her arms to hug a greeting; she wants to be cool and accepted by these new friends. At the same time, "Hugs Harry" holds out his right hand, his arm a straight shot from his body—a greeting, he thinks, to a new guest.

He has forgotten Sarah, has not remembered the previous two visits, the hours of talk, her pretty blond hair, our purchase of magnets. He is meeting her again for the first time.

Sarah drops her arms and shakes his hand limply, then quickly hurries around him into the dark heat of the kitchen.

After that day, we return a year later, to see if anything has changed. It hasn't. The distance has grown longer, the people seem to all have known each other forever, and Harry and Liza still want to sell us more expensive magnets. The attractive forces from our first meetings have long dissolved.

Still, every day I wear their expensive magnets under my feet.

But Sarah long ago threw hers away.

Chapter 17

Relief

We need an outhouse, a privy, a john. We can't expect people to pick blueberries all day and not relieve themselves somewhere, and I don't want to stumble onto some City Jane squatting in the woods, or worse, seeing her slip into thicket to return with poison-ivied privates. So we need some sort of "relief station," as one manual calls it, some place for folks to do their business.

While Sarah and I tend the plants and fork mulch, we ponder our privy problem. It's not so much a problem of where to put it or how to build it, but more specifically, how to move it. We have an outhouse already, just not by the field where we need it.

Behind our house, beside our test-plot blues but a half mile from the field, sits an unused privy already built. When the previous owners remodeled the farmhouse ten years earlier, they added plumbing and the first bathroom, making any outhouse obsolete. For some reason, though, they also hammered together this new outhouse, but they never dug a hole. So the massive john just rests on top of the ground, a huge, two-seater lawn ornament.

This seems like a good time to call Ben, my father-in-law, a reticent, retired engineer who has taught me how to replace spark plugs or change belts

on washing machines. When the in-laws visit, I always have a ready list of
"Ben-and-Jim-jobs" where he supplies the know-how and I try to do the
grunt work, or at least hold the flashlight.

"So what do you think? Can we get it up to the field?" I ask when we
climb the steep hill behind our house.

Ben, as always, chews a toothpick and doesn't say much as he scopes and
considers, kicks a corner and pushes a wall. But this time, unlike all the
others, he has a smirk.

"Are you sure you want to do this?" He can't wipe the smile off of his
face, a grin of wonder and amusement, and mostly disbelief that anyone in
1996 would still be interested in outhouses. He creaks open the door, the
heavy spring rusty and loud. Peering into a hole he shouts, "Doesn't look
like they used it much."

"No, seems like they just built it to look at," I agree.

Then gently Ben closes the door, only saying, "I don't know, Jim." This
from a navy man who survived World War II. He walks around the structure once more, pushing, testing, assessing.

Finally, Ben turns and can't hold back anymore. "Why a two-seater?" he
asks. "I thought it was a privy."

With one more push on the side to test the structure's soundness, he throws
his toothpick away and says, "If you can get your tractor up here, we can get
this to the field."

"No problem," I answer his challenge. The tractor is new, small, and four-
wheel-drive. I haven't driven it up such a steep grade, but despite Sarah's
concerns ("It won't tip, will it?") I think it possible.

First, though, the demolition. Up the hill we drag hammers and crowbars, ladder and wasp spray, dust masks and earplugs. The nails release reluctantly, a low squawk turning higher pitched as the pry bar pulls each one.
The hemlock lumber has weathered to a silver gray, but each released nail
reveals the original colors of these rough planks, small circles of yellow and
orange, rows of stars on dusky boards of night.

When I fetch more tools, Ben, in his seventies, climbs the ladder and begins prying apart the tin roof. By the time I return, he already has loosened
two corners and the third teeters. He climbs back to the ground and then

together we lever the last corner with our crowbars. The roof pops like a giant jack-in-the-box, and we carry it down the hill to the pickup truck.

Next we tackle the doors and walls, slowly undoing the privacy of this privy. Sarah joins us, both hands swinging hammer. The nails screech, hammers clang on crowbars, walls wobble. "Stand back," Ben shouts as he releases the first heavy wall and it falls with an air-lifting *whump*. Each wall we heft down the hill to slide on top of the roof, filling the truck bed with a prefab outhouse. And through it all, Ben keeps his grin, keeps wondering how he got suckered into this.

The head toilet-demolition engineer stops us after the third wall falls. We rest and examine what remains: a floor, a back wall, and the two side-by-side holes. "Time for the tractor," Ben says, pointing to me with his hammer and I hike down the hill for the blue machine. I put the noisy diesel in low gear and weave up through the yard of flower beds to back against the remains of the john. Ben, with gloved hands and face mask, slings a chain through one hole and out under the floor to hook it to the tractor. And then I begin the slow drive back down through the yard, again in the lowest gear. I have to turn sharply to avoid a bed of lilies, and this makes Sarah instantly yell, "*Stop!*" The tractor's back wheel has started to lift off of the ground, and she points and points until I finally see. I give an "oops" half smile, and then straighten the front wheels to drive through the lilies and avoid tipping.

Once tractor and outhouse reach the gravel road, I notch up the gears and begin to slide the whole works down the road. The wood timbers roar as they roll against the gravel. Sarah drives ahead, the truck loaded down with roof and walls that stick over the bed rails. And right before I push the throttle, Ben jumps onto the outhouse platform. He grabs the wall, pulls down his cap, and rides along.

In the field, we return the privy's privacy. With the tractor, we slide the floor over a hole I already dug and level it on blocks. Next the sides, each one Sarah and I heave while Ben quickly nails a brace, plumbing it level. The tin roof is the heaviest, the hardest to place, so again the tractor lifts the bulk. I operate the machine, while Ben and Sarah prop each side of the roof, hoping that the sucker won't slip and land on top of them. It slides in place smoothly, and I climb on top to nail it solid.

Before we finish, Sarah gets us to pose. We prop the door and Ben and I each go to sit on our separate holes. "See, this is why it's a two-seater," I joke. Ben just shakes his head, chuckles, and waves his hammer to the camera.

After the shot, Ben points his thumb to the door, motioning me to leave our just built "closet." "Excuse me, Jim, but I need to christen this," he says, smiling.

Later, as he tucks in his shirttail, he offers, "It works just fine." Then looking away, "And I didn't even get a splinter."

Chapter 18

❧❀❧

Certified

Janey, the organic inspector, is obviously a cat person. Her small frame, pale skin, and dark hair don't hide her distaste for Grover, our little mutt who's escaped his pen to pogo-stick his greeting to her. She just holds out her hand, waist-high, pretending to pet, to be nice as we grab the pooch and thrust him in the bathroom where he whines his lack of understanding at just being a dog. We ignore the racket and offer Janey springwater and a chair at our kitchen table as she pulls out her file on our farm, and we sit to watch her peruse our records.

She is an acquaintance, someone we know from farming conferences. And Janey's a substitute for the state's main organic inspector, who also grows blueberries and doesn't want any conflicts of interest. Janey sips her water, turns pages, examines our receipts and records, notes what she wants to see when she walks in the field. She clicks her tongue to fill the silence, repeats, "Let's see, let's see," and we sit on our hands, hide our anxiousness. She knows the paperwork of how to certify us, checks each task off her list, but her background is in agricultural economics. When she asks a third question ("So, why so much cottonseed meal?"), we realize we know far more about growing blueberries than she does.

Outside, we unlock our sheds and barns for Janey, show her the pallets of fertilizer we'll spread in the spring, and she reads all the labels, looking for suspect bags or bottles of "illegal" spray. She inspects our fertilizer spreader, the sprayer, the tractor, and I wonder if she's ever driven even a small one like this. She hugs her clipboard, clicks her tongue again, and I avoid making eye contact with Sarah. I can only imagine how much of a smirk both of us are trying to hide. Janey's doing her job in a thorough, honest manner, but she knows so little, we realize we could be lying and hiding tons of chemicals in another barn, have a separate file of "real" receipts, and she'd never know. Still, through all the tongue-clicking, I feel like my pants are down. We want the official label, so we hide our feelings and go on.

In the field Janey peers into the outhouse, again looking for suspect bags of fertilizer. "Nope, nothing there," she clicks. Then we all walk the field, the aisles we've newly mown just for her visit, the bushes green and happy. She asks me to bring a shovel because she wants to dig in the beds, wants to see earthworms, as if a worm will tell her, "Yes, these guys are honest." I scratch back the mulch and turn over a scoop, but find nothing. We walk down to the next bed, scratch and scoop again, and again, nothing. "Um," Janey clicks. "Wonder where they are?"

I say something about the summer heat pushing them all deep, and all the while I wonder, *If we don't find a worm, will she not certify us?* I move to another bed, and still no worms. Finally on the fifth hole, one red crawler wiggles free of the clod. Janey rests back on her haunches and says, "There. That's what I need to see." Sarah and I both breathe sighs of disbelief and relief.

As we hike out of the field, the inspector admires the bushes and says she wants to pick for her own freezer next season. We tell her we'll put her on our contact list, and then we hold Grover as she finally drives away.

Not until the next year, 1997, do we receive our official papers stating our farm is certified. We have become one of the first certified-organic blueberry farms in the state of Virginia, and probably one of only a few in the Mid-Atlantic region.

All thanks to one wiggly, sun-stunned worm.

❧ BLUE INTERLUDE ❧
Meditation on Organic

In 1990, right before we bought our farm, organic foods and beverages represented $1 billion in sales in the U.S. market. In 2007, that figure rose to roughly $20 billion, representing just under 3 percent of all food and beverage sales. This growing niche market has increased roughly 20 percent every year. That's a huge amount of carrots and tomatoes, blueberries and apples all grown in theoretically better ways.

And there's the rub. In theory, organic certification protects all parties involved in our food system, including consumers, farmers, farm workers, the soil, water, air, and all the flora and fauna of each farm. The USDA's final passing of the National Organic Standard in 2002 made organic practices legitimate while also standardizing the rules for the whole nation.

In contrast to our one-acre patch, all across the country and planet, the scale of this "new" way of farming has become a problem, one that the writer Joan Gussow takes apart. "*Organic* does not necessarily mean that the food was grown in an ecologically, energetically, or socially sustainable way," she argues. A hundred-acre field of organic carrots is still a monoculture open to the problems of erosion, pests, and lack of diversity, it still depends on a vast quantity of fossil fuel both to till and to ship it across country or globe, and the final orange spear is still usually only affordable to the wealthy.

So maybe farming organically is getting at the heart of a healthy food system. But we still have a ways to go.

❧❧

Chapter 19

❦

Meeting the Mennonites

Over the course of our first years in Floyd County, we attend two Methodist churches, a Presbyterian, a Lutheran, a Unitarian, and a commune's Sunday-morning pancake social. We even sit for a year in silence with a new group of Quakers, and this for a long while feels fully right, a place to contemplate the larger world with a group of like-minded folk, a community, literally, of Friends. But then the leaders decide they want to build a new house of worship, one with plumbing. Several of us find nothing wrong with the beautiful old church where we gather to sit in the round every week, the high ceilings and wooden floors warm in the morning light. Plus, the outhouse works fine, especially for so little use. The larger group, however, votes to form a Building Committee, and we end up in an unfriendly setting.

After the Quakers, we realize we will never find a "church home," to use my worrying mother's phrase, and eventually, thankfully, she stops asking. We live too far away from larger towns to find diversity, and really, we just don't believe many of the dogma required to join. Still, we have that longing to belong, that lonely shadow to throw off.

A half mile from our house sits a small, white-painted, cinderblock church.

About the same time we plant the blueberries, a group of Mennonites erects a new sign beside this 1950s building. At the bottom they paint, EVERYONE WELCOME. They have just moved to the county, newcomers like us, strangers in a strange land. I've read and admired bits of their long history, their continued opposition to war. Though we have never attended a Mennonite gathering, we figure it worth a try.

We like especially that we can make the Sunday-morning journey as a walk up Berry Hill Road, a tree-lined dirt lane that parallels Lost Bent Creek. What better way to consider creation than to amble with water music and wood thrush warbles.

We are nervous the first morning and the creek's song does little to soothe our jitters. I scratch at my tight necktie, which I loathe to wear but I do at Sarah's insistence. We don't know what to expect so we dress our best.

We needn't. Ezra Zook warmly greets us at the door, an older, trim man with thin white hair and wire-rimmed spectacles, a carpenter, we later learn, a fitting trade for this man who follows Christ. In a plain black suit and white shirt, no tie, he tells us his name and that he's the minister and then he introduces Rebecca, his wife standing beside him. She, too, has gray hair, but hers is thick and wrapped in a bun. "We're glad you came today," she echoes his sentiment, and we proceed to sit near the back.

Others introduce themselves, all warmly but shy, the handshake firm but the eyes quick to look away. I keep hearing the last name of Zook from several, and eventually they explain that they're Ezra and Rebecca's son or daughter-in-law or grandchild. When we sit down to begin the service, I see roughly five or six families, and guess that about half of them are kin to each other.

The service runs the typical course of most churches—a few hymns and prayers, scripture readings and an offering, and a long sermon based on a few Bible passages with a scattering of wise words to remember. No silence like the Quakers, and no organ or piano like the Methodists and Presbyterians. Though I don't know the hymns, they become my favorite part, that communal force of voices pulling forth harmonies to create something larger than any one person.

On the walk back home, we compare reactions. During the service, Sarah and I both noticed the silence of the Mennonite women, how little voice they have in anything but the songs. We're uncomfortable with this, but also realize that this group of strangers has been the most welcoming we've encountered in a very long time. Even though we know we'll probably never officially become Mennonites, we decide to return, not every week, but regularly enough to learn names, to share stories, and to join in their high-reaching hymns.

Chapter 20

Bees, Blooms, and the First Berry

The first year after we've planted the blueberries, we follow our "parent-ing" manuals. They tell us to prune lightly, and this we do. They tell us to provide so many pounds of nitrogen per plant, and this we do, though not easily. And they tell us to pick all the blooms and kill all the weeds. This we try to do.

The blooms, those beautiful hanging cups of white. Oh, just for an hour to be a bumblebee and buzz through this fragrance-filled air! To land with a delicate dip of plant, to crawl inside this white-walled chalice, to swim in the honeysuckle-sweet scent of blue, to know the shimmer of soft light and sip from this wine that only a bee can sip.

But no, no bee-loud dreams for us. Only, as I remember John Keats's "Ode on Melancholy," an "aching Pleasure . . . / Turning to poison while the bee-mouth sips." Sarah and I stoop, plant by small plant, to strip off all flow-ers. The books instruct and this we do, forcing the bushes to put all energy into growing strong roots. So grab a stem and "wipe" it clean of any white. Then drop the blossoms and bend to the next, the trail of spent blooms fall-ing like snowflakes on April-greening grass.

The bumblebees keep working ahead of us, refusing to give up gathering pollen. We wear gloves and wiggle each branch before stripping it, shooshing away the black-and-yellow creatures.

At the end of a bed, Sarah and I rest in the grass and agree—we have plenty of bees here. Despite our honeybee failures, it looks like we needn't worry about pollination. Our blues will have an abundance of wild bees visiting these flowers, all ensuring a crop of berries, just no honey. Oh, well. There is other sweetness here, like watching a giant bumblebee plunge so deeply into a tiny cup that only the tips of his back, black legs stick out. I want to touch this creature, to nudge it even deeper, but instead just sit beside a bush and watch the bees arc away and back, circling each bush, alighting at last on the ready flower.

Despite the manuals' advice, we want to taste, to sip a little of this bee-made wine. Sarah decides to save blooms from a few bushes of each variety, so we can at least sample and savor these hoped-for fruits. For two months as the cool of spring turns into summer's warmth, we walk to the field most every evening. We monitor these blooms, witness the white cups fall away after the bee's last visit, and then watch the small globes grow and swell. Slowly they fade from green to pink and then starting at the blossom end, the minute pink saucers turn to blue, light and tentative at first, but darker with each moment of sun. Every few days, we touch the berries, twist them slightly to check the color near the stem. We handle them so much that we rub off their thin white "veils" and leave our fingerprints on each one. They're not ripe until fully blue to the stem, the books tell us, and for too long, we have to wait as this last bit of pink disappears. Like a sunset, the shades of red darken around each globe to that final color of night.

Then at last at the very end of June, we see a berry blue all the way to the stem, and another, and another. We give a slight tug, and they roll off easily, the tiny clasp of stem releasing into our hands. We sit on the mulch beside the bushes, our hands cupping only six berries. I hesitate, want to watch Sarah eat first, to savor the first bite after years of dreaming and sweating and watching. She says, no, we eat at the same time. I close my eyes and place one on my tongue. Then gently, I press it against the roof of my mouth. The skin breaks and all the hoped-for sweetness spreads across tongue and cheeks and body. Again, I remember Keats and his "Veiled Melancholy" in

"her sovran shrine." She can only be seen by "him whose strenuous tongue /
Can burst Joy's grape against his palate fine."

What joy and what melancholy will we find here in this, our Eden, these,
our berries that taste as good as we could have ever hoped? We kneel to
search for more, knowing we will always hunger.

Part III

❀❀

Fruit

(1997-1999)

flicker of sun
this blue flame
of ripe berry

Chapter 21

❧❧

Filling the Field

To fill our field with people takes a bucket of patience and about three buckets of energy. By mid-June, our conversation goes something like this:

"I think they're ready, Sarah. We should open soon."

"I don't know. . . . There are a lot of green berries out there."

All the while, we pick and pick just for us, filling our freezer before the mad rush.

Two days later:

"Oh, crud, I think they're ready, Jim. We should open now!"

"I don't know. . . . There are a lot of unripe blueberries out here."

We worry ourselves like this until we settle on June 25 as the official opening date. And then we spend every hour getting ready, mowing grass aisles, weed-eating around each of the 1,000 bushes, scrubbing down the berry hut. We want pickers to enjoy their time here, to return and pick often, so we sweat through the dusty, machine-driven days.

And then all evening, every evening, we make the calls. "Hello, this is Jim Minick at Minick Berry Farm. I'm just calling to say our berries are ripe and ready for you to come pick." Often with the list so long, I hope for just the answering machine, for a quick one-minute message and onto the next.

Usually though, in the country way, each call takes a half hour to catch up on a year's worth of weather and news, enjoyable, but also exhausting.

Or, there are the cold calls, the folks we kind of know, but not well. Like Isaiah Cox, the excavator who built our road, dug the pond, and cleared the field four years ago. I call to tell him the berries are ready and the next week, his wife, Dorothy, arrives with her sister, thankful for the call.

But many cold calls turn colder after the first hello. Like with our neighbors. I call everyone who lives within a mile or two of us, a ridgeline of houses we pass every day on the way to work. Most I know, some I don't. And most, except for Donna and a few others, never come. They'll pick Joe's strawberries, but they have never touched a blueberry, and have no interest in trying. I have no idea why and attempt to "whatever" this out of my mind and move on, but I can't stop gnawing that bone.

Then there is the problem of how many people to call. We don't want everyone to arrive at once and completely pick the field clean by the end of the first day. Ideally, a set number of folks would come each day, but how do you determine that number, and then, impossibly, how do you control the flow of pickers?

I want to draw on my neighbor Joe's decades of pick-your-own experience so I ask for the advice he loves to give.

"You're working too hard, Jim." He sits back in his recliner, grins, and wags his finger. He's relaxed now that his strawberry season is over. "No way can you control any of it. Just put the ad in the paper, call your list of people, and then get out of the way."

He's right, of course. And eventually, that's just what we do—make all the calls, place ads in local papers, and open the gate, 8:00 to 8:00 every day but Sundays and Wednesdays from late June through late July, sometimes even early August, four to six weeks of PYO madness. Joe advises against these hours, recommends his dawn-to-dusk, seven-days-a-week policy, saying folks will come earlier anyway. Then he adds, "The season's so short, you gotta get the people here to move the berries there," pointing his finger this way and that for emphasis.

"And why Wednesdays, Jim?"

"To give the field, and us, a rest," I reply. "We have to get out for groceries at some point," I joke.

He just shakes his head.

❧ BLUE INTERLUDE ❧
Picking with HD

Despite his curmudgeonly stuffiness, his convolutedly beautiful sentences, and his sometimes contradictory habits, Henry David Thoreau has shaped me and helped define how I live in this world. In college, when I read him for the first time with any close attention, I cut class to tramp through the woods, searching for my own small cabin with its two windows and writer's desk. I tried to suck the marrow out of all the life I unearthed. And I even labored over an analytical paper applying the psychology of Abraham Maslow to my new hero. Of course, in my sophomoric wisdom, I found both HD and me to be fully self-actualized.

So years later, imagine my blue-tinted surprise when I stumble onto Thoreau's last two unfinished manuscripts, *Faith in a Seed* and *Wild Fruits*. I know he goes huckleberry picking after his famous one-nighter in the county jail, but I have no idea that he so thoroughly loves blue- and huckleberries, so intensely studies their habits. Always he relishes their flavor, these "little blue sacks full of swampy nectar and ambrosia commingled," a sweet enough reason to excuse a person from any book lessons.

For Thoreau, too, believes in skipping school to wander in the woods and pick berries, because one can learn more while picking than while in a classroom. He even declares that the school of huckleberries teaches him more than Harvard, claiming that doing his "journeywork in the huckleberry field . . . was some of the best schooling that [he] got, and paid for itself." When he heads out with his pail, he feels "an expansion of . . . being," a sense of "[l]iberation and enlargement," and suddenly, he says, "I knew more about my books than if I had never ceased studying them. I found myself in a schoolroom where I could not fail to see and hear things worth seeing and hearing."

A sampling of these worthy things HD sees and hears: blueberry bushes encircling a pond and becoming its "eyelashes"; fox dung that contains the remains of a groundhog and huckleberry seeds, making Thoreau note that the fox, like us, wants at least two courses with his meal; and on "Sassafras Island in Flint's Pond" his favorite wild bush, the size of a tree, that "must be about sixty years old." HD climbs this tree and finds "a comfortable seat with [his] feet four feet from the ground."

He exclaims that "there was room for three or four persons more there, but unfortunately it was not the season for berries." Oh, to have the chance to pick with Henry, to sit in that ancient berry-tree, to converse on blue varieties and bluer dreams.

For HD shows me that berry picking is a holy act. He finds equal value in both the gathering and the eating. In *Wild Fruits* he notes the "value of these wild fruits is not in the mere possession or eating of them, but in the sight and enjoyment of them" and also in the journey, the exploration. Everywhere he picks, from field to burnt-over forest, from swamp to mountaintop, he finds Nature "inviting us to picnic." And this fruit is her holy body that we "pluck and eat in remembrance of her." "It is a sort of sacrament," he states, "a communion—the *not* forbidden fruits, which no serpent tempts us to eat."

Two other times, Thoreau connects holiness with huckleberries. When he finds himself in a huge patch of black huckleberries, he calls the place "some up-country Eden," "a land flowing with milk and huckleberries."

Later, when he climbs one hill to find berry bushes "bent to the ground with fruit, [he thinks] of them as fruits fit to grow on the most Olympian or heaven-pointing hills." He continues, "It does not occur to you at first that where such thoughts are suggested is Mount Olympus, and that you who taste these berries are a god."

For Thoreau, and for all pickers, the holy acts of gathering and eating transform us, help us to know that we, too, sometimes can become gods.

Chapter 22

❦

First Official Picker

Five-year-old Callie plops the five-dollar bill in my hand. "Thank you, Jim and Sarah," her small voice warbles as she scrunches her shoulders and tilts her head.

"Oh, no, Callie," I reply. "Thank you for being our first official picker."

This brings a giggle and an even wider grin. Then she runs back to Ashley for a hide-and-hug behind her mother's leg.

Sid, Callie's father, works in the library at school, handling the whole university's interlibrary loan program. When he sees all of my requests for books on homesteading, Wendell Berry, and such, he decides to introduce himself. On his office walls I see posters of Zappa and the Grateful Dead, and a banjo leans in one of the corners. He takes off his round glasses, and I realize he could easily pass for the traditional picture of a long-haired, bearded Jesus Christ, if by chance, the Savior liked Frank Zappa and Jerry Garcia.

Sid, Ashley, and Callie live in town an hour from our farm, he tells me, but they also own thirty acres in Floyd County. Soon we figure out that our two chunks of land are less than two miles apart. "We're neighbors," I say, and he smiles and agrees.

Eventually the five of us spend afternoons together hiking these two "neighboring" farms, swapping meals and garden stories. On their land, Callie shows us her small plot of radishes and carrots, and Ashley points to motherwort, comfrey, and other herbs she plans to sell at market as tinctures. They give us advice on the farmers' market and we answer all of their questions about their six young blueberry bushes.

Then in the early spring of 1997, we all hike up our farm road to skip stones on the pond and walk through the long rows of the blueberry field. The stems have turned a bright red and yellow, and Sarah kneels beside one to show Callie the swelling buds. Sid sees our huge pile of mulch next to the trees. "Looks like you have a little work left," he says, nodding to the mass of chipped bark. After we tell him we still hope to cover two more beds before bud-break, he offers to help, swapping labor for berries. We readily agree.

The next weekend, Sid, Sarah, and I back our ailing pickup to the pile and start pitchforking. Steam rises from the dark brown mulch, the whole mound looking like the arched back of a giant, sleeping dragon. The previous month, five huge dump trucks wound up our narrow lane to empty their loads here, to form this steam-breathing, slumbering dragon. So pickup by pickup, we take it apart.

Soon, we throw off our jackets, then our long-sleeved shirts, the three of us working in our T-shirts in the cool March morning, as if summer has already arrived. We sweat like the hot season's already here, too. A pitchfork of wet mulch weighs roughly twenty pounds, so our quick pace at the start soon slows. Sid and I heave the peaty stuff into the truck while Sarah forks it forward, into corners. Then she does a little trotlike dance step back and forth across each layer, packing it in. Even though we might only haul this load 300 feet, we want to make as few trips as possible.

Sarah shouts enough when my forkfuls of mulch keep sliding to the ground. And because the tailgate has fallen off, and one side of the pickup's bed has a severe rust problem, the weight of the mulch makes the back of the truck swell like a puppy's belly.

I drive around the bottom of the field, thankful for the four-wheel-drive, and then I slowly pull into the day's aisle. When I open the truck door, I squeeze out between berry canes, grab my fork, and climb onto the very top, ten feet in the air. From there I try to pitch the mulch in between the bushes where Sid and Sarah rake it into place, smothering the weeds and tucking in these babies with this quilt of warm chipped bark. Sarah darts from this spot to that, choking up on the long handled pitchfork and pointing to holes where I need to throw the next batch. Sid flings his ponytail back and forth, obviously used to both the hard labor and the added weight of his hair. And I just keep thinking how terrific this all is that before the buds break open, we will finish this huge task with a little help from a new friend.

By the end of the day, we've moved six truck loads, covering the last two beds. And despite wearing leather gloves, we also cover our school-soft hands with blisters.

So on June 24, the day before we officially open, we invite Sid, Ashley, and Callie to pick, to join us as we try to fill our freezer before the onslaught of customers. Sarah and I have fallen in love with the flavor of Spartan, so we pick this early variety exclusively, the two of us working on each side of a bush, our hands walking us down the long row.

But we encourage Sid and Ashley to try all of the varieties, knowing they might find another they like better. The family wanders the field, sometimes saying to each other, "Um, this is a good one," calling Callie to sample. From the middle of the field, Sid shouts out, saying he's on Bed 5 and asking us to name the varieties. Ashley, like us, favors Spartan, but Sid can't decide if he likes Blueray or Patriot better. And Callie says she just likes them all. She's brought her own special picking pail, hot pink with special flower decals on the sides. She picks a few, then bends to find a bug in the new mulch and add it to her berries.

After an hour of picking, our buckets full, we climb the hill to the berry hut. I weigh their berries, and Sid and I agree that he has a few more buckets yet to pick to work off his day of labor. So Sarah and I are surprised when Callie comes running from the car with her tiny fist holding a green bill.

"What's this?" I ask her and Sid who stands behind her.

"Some money for your berries," Callie smiles.

"But *we* owe you more berries, you don't owe us," Sarah says.

"Daddy said to bring it to you and make sure you take it, so here," she thrusts it into my palm.

Sid watches, says, "We figure she's eaten and squished that many today." Then after a pause, "Plus, we want to be your first official customers."

With that, we thank them all and begin the season, our first blueberry income, child-touched and generously given, stuffed deep in my pocket.

Chapter 23

❧❧

Stricken

One of the first strangers to call after reading our classified is a deep-voiced man named Bear. He shows up that evening with his neighbors, Pam and Jesse. Out the kitchen window we watch their Chevy truck drive up our lane. We have just cut into a warm pie, so I scarf down the last bit of dessert, and hurry out the door. The pie is blueberry, of course, and I know my teeth and tongue must glow purplish blue when I smile.

In the field I shake hands, give the threesome buckets, and point them to Bed 5. Bear, a burly, red-headed giant, leads the way into the field while I head to the berry hut.

I clean up after a busy day and then am drawn to their laughter down in the field. They're teasing Bear about his dog named Hooch, and when I show up, Bear takes a break from picking and sits beside a bush. His voice sounds like gravel in a wheelbarrow as he tells me about his bulldog-terrier mutt.

"Hooch always eats and drinks whatever I do," he looks at me, pauses, then adds, "including beer. If I'm having a hot dog, he has to have a hot dog. If I'm eating some Doritos, he has to have some, too. He just whines and hops around aggravating me until I have to give in."

"So one day I was sitting on my porch sipping some whiskey. Now, have you ever had Merry Berry?" he asks me.

"You mean moonshine with canned fruit in it?"

He nods.

"I've heard of it but never tried. Sounds potent."

"Well, this was liquor poured into a jar full of peaches. Let them peaches steep for a month and nothing better. One peach probably equals three shots of whiskey."

Bear takes a berry out of his bucket and eats it, slow and easy.

"So ol' Hooch sees me eating a peach from this jar, and he starts his whining and begging, jumping from side to side, tugging on my pants. I tell him, 'You don't really want this. I know you don't.' But he don't listen. So I give him a peach and just like that, he gulps it down.

"That don't slow him down. He wants another and starts pulling my pants again, so I give him another." Pause as he pretends to sling a peach to his dog. "And then another, and another, and another." Each time, he says, "another," Bear flicks his wrist, the imaginary fork throwing the imaginary peach. "I give that mutt five of them peaches. Pretty soon, ol' Hooch, he starts wobbling across the porch. He's looking a little green, you know, a little frothy at the mouth. I says to him, 'I told you, Hooch, but you wouldn't listen.' Then he leans out over the porch and vomits all five of those peaches into the yard.

"Now if I ever offer a peach to the old dog, he absolutely refuses."

And then Bear gets on his hands and knees and becomes his dog Hooch. He snarls and shakes his head, red hair flying, loose jowls trembling as he imitates the mutt's emphatic, growling "*No*" to any peach, liquored or plain.

Eventually, Bear picks up his bucket and begins picking again. And soon we talk berries and pies, and Pam finally asks, "I don't want to be nosy or anything, but did you just eat blueberry pie?"

"Yeah, why, does it show?" I grin wide and point to my teeth.

They all nod and confess to holding in their laughter when I first greeted them. They didn't know what to think of my stained smile, my purple tongue. "I even poked Jesse," Pam admits. "I wanted to say something, but then I thought you might have some awful disease."

We walk out of the field making up names for this new disease and settle on *blueberrium dentata*.

They go home to also become stricken.

Chapter 24

How To

Always, always take a bucket. Even if you plan to harvest just a few as an evening dessert, you'll end up picking more than you can ever eat at one time. So take a bucket, maybe two.

Perfect your own method of carrying the pail. I like to slide the handle under my belt and buckle it in, so I have both hands free. Some pickers hang the bucket on a rope around their necks. Sarah hates both methods and instead slides the handle into the crook of her elbow, like the way her grandmother carried a purse. She still picks with two hands, and is usually faster than everyone else.

My grandma started me on raspberries, not blueberries. Out by our pond, the purple vines tangled so thickly that the first trip often required more path-making than berry picking. There in those thickets, I developed my techniques, the vine-tip-pull, the under-the-leaf-check-for-the-big-ones, and the tiptoe, stretched-arm, fingertip reach. I came home to Grandma with stained tongue and hands, and we soon ate steaming raspberry pie.

Of all berries, blueberries by far pick the easiest. Our dog Grover, blind now, can even pick these by sniffing and bumping around the bushes until he finds a clump. Then he slobbers over the bunch until he eats them all, whatever the color—green, pink, and blue. We scold and shush him away, laughing but also hoping he doesn't get sick again on the green ones. Though I don't have Grover's problem of eating green berries, I still have his tendency of eating too much—and also getting that bellyache.

Early in the quiet of a new day offers the best time to pick, the droplets of dew sparkling on each blue jewel. Eat and your hunger is nourished, your thirst quenched. Or, to also satisfy the hunger of your eyes, pick in the evening, when the heat has dissipated and the sunset colors the field auburn and gold, the berries fading to specks of purple as dusk settles.

Along with a bucket, a hat helps as well as sunscreen and maybe a stool. My grandpa often picked in his blueberry patch while sitting on his lawn mower or an old milking stool, and some of our customers do the same, toting a stool to each bush. A good picking partner helps, too, for lively banter and a little competition.

The actual act of picking blueberries requires a bit of practice, mainly to distinguish ripe from unripe. Cup hand under a cluster and as Sarah says, "Tickle the berries." The ripe ones will giggle off easily. They'll also be blue all the way to the stem. Unripe berries require tugging and have some pink at the stem. Though these will "blue up" off the bush, they won't have the same sweetness as the fully ripe, so try to pick just the ripest. But I confess I never can. I like to "clean" a bush *and* try to keep up with speedy Sarah.

Though sometimes in the sweat-drenched heat of July, I forget this pleasure, the next day or season, I still look forward to the gathering, the quiet filling of bucket and belly, and the heady taste of these sky-colored berries.

⁂ BLUE INTERLUDE ⁂
Frederick Coville

In 1910, the USDA printed Bulletin No. 193, titled *Experiments in Blueberry Culture*. Frederick Coville wrote this slim book, and in doing so, he radically changed our understanding of blueberries.

Before Coville, scientists and gardeners of all sorts tried to domesticate wild blueberries. They took fine specimens from the wild and planted them in their best soil, treating these bushes like other garden plants by amending the earth with lime and rotted manure. Almost always, the blueberry bushes died. But Coville, through years of failures, persisted to finally figure out this mysterious plant.

Probably his greatest discovery was that blueberries, along with rhododendrons, laurels, and other similar plants, love and require an acidic soil. His *Experiments in Blueberry Culture* documented his many trials and observations. He noticed that in the wild, berry bushes avoid what we normally call "rich" loam, the alkaline dirt that grows so much of our food. Instead, these plants thrive in peat bogs and acidic soils all across the country. He replicated this "poor" soil in his lab, and eventually succeeded in pinpointing the needs of blueberries.

In addition, Coville discovered that blueberries love a peaty soil; they need cross-pollination with another blueberry to bear well; they have chilling requirements to flower and fruit; and they benefit from fungi that penetrate their roots and help them take up nitrogen. This "father of the blueberry" also perfected the methods of propagating blueberries still used one hundred years later.

Frederick Coville's obituaries written after his death in 1937 illustrate how widely respected he was. One appeared in that year's USDA's *Yearbook of Agriculture*; another was published in *The National Geographic Magazine*, the outlet for the society for which he served as a board member for over forty years. Both obituaries comment on his distinguished career in the USDA as a botanist and blueberry breeder. But they also reveal Coville's wide interests: he explored Death Valley in 1891 and wrote a definitive book on the botany of that desert; he did similar work in Alaska and also researched plants used by Native Americans; and among other accomplishments, he was the first director of the National Arboretum.

Coville's writing reveals a brilliant mind coupled with a hard-working, yet modest personality. His breeding efforts to develop and select outstanding varieties of blueberries show a tireless persistence and devotion to both the blueberry and good science. His records must have been meticulous, for in all of his searching for the ideal berry, he propagated close to 100,000 bushes. As James F. Hancock articulates, "A testimony to the greatness of his efforts is in the fact that 75 percent of the blueberry acreage in the 1990s was composed of his hybrids," and seven of the top ten cultivars were Coville progeny. In our field, three of our favorite varieties, Bluecrop, Blueray, and Berkeley, came directly from this one man's work.

Chapter 25

❧❧❧

Wired

Among our neighbors and friends, I count at least five with the first name of Joe. The one who lives farthest away happens also to be a homesteader and a fine friend. Joe and Rita left their city jobs in the 1970s to get "back to the land" on a farm even farther back in than our blueberry field. Now, in 1998, these teachers live in a house with plumbing and electricity, but they love to tell stories of their early days, when they raised two kids in a cabin at the end of a long, rutted road, a house uninsulated, unplumbed, and unwired.

Joe is far from unwired these days in both personality and technophilia. If he can grow a little more broccoli in an already huge vegetable patch, he'll squeeze it in. If Apple produces a new computer, he owns it. He loves his garden and his gadgets.

So on their first visit to our field, Joe hikes all through the bushes, praising the vigor of the plants, the size of the crop. I try to keep up, while Rita and Sarah just stand and watch.

"Look at these berries! This is great, Jim," he keeps repeating. "But you need a Web page! You need to let people know you're here, share some recipes and your writing, you know, give them directions, pull them in. You need a Web page, man."

I'm doubtful, not so wired up for the Internet. "We're a small farm in the middle of the nowhere of nowhere," I reply. "I just can't see a Web page helping us . . . what? Sell blueberries to Hong Kong?"

But Joe persists, even after they leave, and eventually, he gets me wired in to his idea as well. "But we can't spend too much money on this," I insist.

I know Joe knows his technology and that they're both frugal. Rita finds treasures at every junk shop she visits, and Joe has a shed full of old school doors, heavy oak. He has no plans for them, but that'll come eventually. So when I finally give the okay, he finds a way to host our Web site on one of his servers. And even more amazing, Joe agrees to create and maintain this site for us, all for free berries. Later, when I research what Web masters normally charge, I realize the generosity of Joe's offer.

I send him several essays about the farm, and Joe begins to assemble our Web page. He designs a green and welcoming mountain as the backdrop, and then a hanging bunch of blueberries for our masthead. He pulls in photographs of pickers picking, pickers eating, pickers picnicking, pickers loaded down with buckets of blue. He suggests several pages—an introduction to us and our farm, a "day in the life," and a page on our organic certification and another on the ram pump. We also include health benefits and, of course, recipes and directions, the two most frequently used pages.

What Joe brags about most, though, is the icon he spent days fiddling with to get just right. To visit any of these pages, to move forward or backward, you click on a blueberry—quarter-size, plump, real enough to eat.

The Web page fulfills even Joe's high expectations, let alone my low ones. If a customer asks about our farm history, I give a brief version, and then point them to the Web page. If they want to know Sarah's best blueberry pie recipe, I find myself repeating, "Visit our Web page." If they get lost on their way to the field, I know they didn't print off the directions. I repeat the address so often that I have to laugh at my initial skepticism.

We invite Joe and Rita to come on one of our "closed" days, so we can relax, not tend to customers, and instead enjoy our friends' company in an empty field. We've already picked several buckets for them, and when they arrive, we pick alongside. We want to make sure they leave with plenty, a year's worth of blue eating, as we bartered, but we also just want to visit, catch up, hear about their kids, their work, their own homestead.

As always, Joe brings a new electronic toy, this time a digital camera that can take a "streaming video." The field empty of pickers seems kind of boring to me, but not to Joe. He wants a panoramic view of the whole shebang for his video, so he stands in the bed of our pickup truck, but that isn't high enough. So he climbs on top of the cab. Rita warns him to be careful, and he dutifully moves slowly as he turns in a circle, camera a foot or so away from his squinting eyes. When he climbs down, he shows us what we can see around us: pines swaying, sky full of sun, and wind blowing through bushes.

The next day, if you click on a blueberry icon, you can view this panorama on our Web page, and in the background you can just barely hear Joe saying, "This is great."

Chapter 26

❧⁂❧

My Folks and Manny

M y folks drive the 300 miles twice during the monthlong season. They have helped to plant and weed these bushes (their "grandbabies," we tease Mom), and now, they help pick for market. Dad wears his sun visor with a sweatband and V-necked T-shirt, and Mom wears her "special" picking Capris, pants she expects to get dirty. They remember their old belts this time, and use the leather to strap buckets to hips. Dad, as usual, is in a hurry, eager to claim a bed and get picking before too many customers arrive. We send them to bed number six, the most loaded for the day where the six-foot canes now bend to a three-foot height. My parents work here all morning without taking a break.

I check on them often, help pick for a little while, and try to ease their hard tempo. I know Dad's back can only handle so much of this bending, but they're both set on making sure we have our quota of at least fifty pounds for Saturday's market. That's roughly eight buckets, and by lunchtime, they have the white pails all lined up along the back wall of the shed, ready for us to take to the house and refrigerate.

At lunch, Mom lays out her regular tablecloth (a new feeling, I imagine, to the picnic table) and then pulls from her cooler ham and Swiss cheese, pickles and Pringles, all Dad's favorites. I've learned to monitor his moods, can tell when he's overdoing it, but haven't yet learned how to tell my seventy-year-old father when to slow down . . . and in their fifty-plus years of marriage, neither has Mom. But as he chomps on a carrot and Mom lays out more food—desserts, of course—I see they are in a good mood.

Sure enough, after a short lunch and no real break, they head back to where they stopped picking earlier. This time, they pick for themselves, or more precisely, for all of their friends back home. They save the biggest and sweetest berries to travel on ice all the way to Pennsylvania where they'll share with the neighbors. It is a generosity touched with pride at the size of this fruit they've helped to raise in so many ways.

On my parents' second visit, we have a painting-party. We need signs, markers to help people know where to turn off the state road, where to pick, where to go to the john. We scavenge old boards and flat rocks, lay them out on benches, tailgates, and sawhorses, and dip brushes to become, for a morning, artists.

On the rough lumber, Dad and I slap on a background of white, two coats, and set them aside to dry. We try to keep ahead of Sarah and Mom, who, in their best elementary-schoolteacher-writing, neatly paint the many letters and numbers, all in blue, of course. First, an outline, making sure of the spacing, and then the filling in, the dabbing at corners. Mom leans over her artwork, careful to stay in the lines. Sarah crouches to the task, her brush-strokes quick and efficient, each letter giant and straight.

Every blueberry bed needs a number at each end, so they paint 1 to 10 on flat pieces of shale, and Dad and I haul them down the field, neat markers to save us all from getting lost.

For the check-out hut, the women letter MINICK BERRY FARM, CERTIFIED ORGANIC BLUEBERRIES $1.25/POUND, and PLEASE SUPERVISE CHILDREN. Once dry, these get nailed by the door, and we hope the last one will prevent our bushes from getting destroyed by rowdy kids.

Sarah wants a USE LOW GEAR at the bottom of our steep hill, so she dips her brush to this. We've already had too many people ripping up our gravel, and one lady even panicked and stopped halfway up. She put her Cadillac in reverse and then backed it into the ditch. The sign, we hope, will forewarn and slow any hurried, harried picker.

Like a schoolgirl, Mom giggles all the way through painting a board to say RESTROOM! Our outhouse is tucked in the woods, not at first obvious, so the sign will hopefully prevent the question. But Mom knows when people see RESTROOM! they think water and sinks and handles to flush all the stink away. She puts an exclamation mark at the end to highlight her joke.

We add THANK YOU to the pile, to put near the end of the road as a farewell to exiting pickers. And then the biggest board receives BLUEBERRIES with an arrow to point the way to the field. Dad and I add stakes and drive them all into the ground.

At the end of this painting soiree, we find two extra white boards. "Can't let these go to waste," I comment, and ask for ideas. Sarah decides to letter WATCH FOR TURTLES on one, and Mom, tired of the jostling, head-jerking water bars across our lane, wants SLOW, MANY BUMPS on the other. These last two placards become the most commented on. "I looked for turtles but didn't see any," one picker might say after closing her car door. Or another, a child, asks how many turtles we have.

And then later Zeke, a wide-faced newcomer, gets out of his car with a handshake and a huge grin. "Where's Manny?" he asks.

"Manny? Manny who?" I'm thrown off, sensing some joke I don't get.

"You know, *Manny.* I read he's here."

"Sorry, but I don't know any Manny."

"Oh, but I thought *you* were Manny. Aren't you Mr. Bumps? You know, *MANNY* Bumps?"

And then I finally get it. "Oh, no, not me," I say. "He lives out in the woods and waits to jolt your car when you're not looking."

❧ BLUE INTERLUDE ❧
Elizabeth White

Sarah and I are not the only ones to have a certain time in our lives colored blue by this fruit, years we remember well for how they shape us, years we still call "the blueberry years." Elizabeth White, like us, also knew this blue shade of light, the long association of hand to berry to mouth. She, too, called them "the blueberry years," and she, too, remembered them as "a joyous memory."

Born in 1871, White grew up in the Pine Barrens of New Jersey where she helped her father manage one of the largest cranberry farms in the country. Often the two of them noticed the wild blueberry bushes near their bogs and commented on the need for a well-developed variety. They wanted a blueberry to extend their cranberry season and give extra employment to their pickers.

In 1911, Elizabeth White read Frederick Coville's *Experiments in Blueberry Culture* and immediately contacted this scientist who had started to understand this remarkable plant. Within three months, Coville journeyed from Washington, D.C., to visit Whitesbog, New Jersey, and so began over twenty years of collaborative work that gave us the domesticated blueberry.

With her father's financial backing, White offered Coville assistance and land on which to test the many potential plants. But she also gave the scientist much more—a link to the local people, called Pineys, and their vast knowledge of the wild blueberries that thrived in this swampy terrain. She knew the natives spent days each season in the woods picking these berries for market. So White offered them money and the potential for immortality by having any worthy bush named after the finder. In the next five years, the Pineys brought her berry samples from many potential plants and in the off-season, she would then travel in horse and buggy to find and move these to the test field.

Of the one hundred wildlings transplanted, only a few proved worthy of propagating. The best, found by Rube Leek, caused White and Coville to struggle with naming this particular plant. "Rube" as White commented, seemed "a poor name for so fine a variety." "Leek" obviously was no better and "savored of onions." Finally Coville thought of adding the last initial to Rube, and thus Rubel, a gemlike moneymaker, was named. Though its berries appear small by modern standards, farmers still grow this variety today especially after scientists discovered in its fruit high concentrations of antioxidants.

Elizabeth White's writing shows an extremely gracious personality. The Pineys had been denigrated in the local press as a backward, ignorant people, but White knew better, even declaring that she was a Piney herself. Once in 1916, she paid tribute to her friends by writing, "When we get in the woods and swamps, I am the one who reads haltingly and with imperfect understanding and must rely implicitly on my piney guide." This from a woman featured in *The Saturday Evening Post* as "The Blueberry Queen."

White also had great business acumen. According to Mark Ehlenfeldt, the USDA's blueberry breeder, White's greatest accomplishments were "gathering germplasm and developing a commercial market." Not only did she expand markets for her domesticated blueberries, but she also created demand for the bushes themselves, sending them all across the country. And when enough other farmers established blueberry fields, she helped organize the first blueberry growers cooperative.

Another example of White's business savvy came by chance. She once saw cellophane used to wrap candy, so she contacted the supplier and soon became one of the first in the United States to use this material to sell her beautiful, now-visible berries. And later in life, Elizabeth White started her own business cultivating hollies and other Pine Barrens flora. Eventually she became nationally recognized for her horticultural work with these plants.

Elizabeth White called herself "a practical dreamer." She knew the hard realities of months of labor that might bear only hard lessons, but she also knew the successes often borne by such work. And these successes bore more dreams. Once in the late 1930s, she even wrote that she "dream[ed] of cultivated blueberries, shipped by the train load— blueberry specials—to every part of the country." Yet she knew it was "hard to measure a dream accurately."

White also understood that the blueberry, for all of its commercial success, still lived as a beautiful plant, one that "few plants can compare with." She ended a 1920 promotional pamphlet by describing this beloved bush in all the seasons.

In the spring, the young shoots and leaves . . . are a rich bronzy red . . . [showing] the greatest variety of . . . delicate tintings. One plant has dark bronzy leaves and white flowers, the next displays its clusters of pink buds against the daintiest green. . . . [Then] [f]or a few days longer the air is filled with an elusive spicy fragrance and the fine high orchestra of the bees. [In summer, the] blueberry fields are never more lovely than just before the berries are ready to pick. [Come fall,] [w]ith the first frost, the reds flame again. Most of the plants are brilliant in autumn coloring, some astonishingly so. . . . In winter the color charm of the blueberry fields does not fail. . . . The blueberry twigs above the snow make a red tracery, which in the distance softens to a rosy haze.

Elizabeth White, tireless promoter of all things blueberry, valued this plant for its beautiful company in all the seasons of her blueberry years.

Chapter 27

⁙

A Handful of Jewels:
A Day in the Life

L ate June.
Early morn and the field silent but for wren and towhee songs. This bowl in the forest holds the morning shadows, and the sky floats in it clear as a ripe berry. Sarah sweeps the berry hut while I set out buckets, and then together we perform our daily ritual of "walking the field." Before anyone arrives, we savor the sun tipping the pines at field edge, the hooded warbler singing down by the pond, the dew soaking our sandaled feet. We cruise up and down grass aisles, look sideways into so many bushes filled with blue. These plants have started to reach maturity, meaning that some have reached six feet in height, and also meaning most are loaded.

We talk quietly and pause to sample a few berries for breakfast. Sarah jots a scrap-paper of notes of where to send pickers and where to pick ourselves. Yesterday's crowd harvested mostly from the early varieties, so those beds need a day or two to recover, but Blueray and Bluecrop, our midseason and heaviest bearers crowd the aisles with their arched and weighted stems. Here first, we agree, and then if we have an overflow of customers, we'll send them to the bottom of the field where the later varieties are just turning ripe.

Back up the hill on the path we hike so many times each day, to the shed and our buckets. Market is two days and seventy-five pounds away. We pick our way down the bed, Sarah on one side, me on the other, cleaning each bush of ripe blueberries. We wonder who will show up today, but talk little, focusing instead on the movement of fingers, the cupping and rolling of handfuls of berries, the thump and thud of buckets slowly filling. The sun breaks over the pines, and the dew-covered berries become jewels in our hands, sparkling, bright, even, maybe, illuminated, lit from within. This beauty, this quiet, quick work, this stillness before the rush of the rest of the day, we hold and relish.

The spell breaks shortly after 8:00 A.M. when we hear the first customers downshifting to climb our steep lane. Sarah continues to pick while I carry full buckets into the check-out shed. Soon, car doors slam and a voice rings out, "Morning, Jim." I step out to greet Donna and her two children, Sophia and Caleb. Donna with her curly hair and love of gossip comes every week with her kids, her three-legged stool, and usually another friend. I grab pails and escort them to a good row, and soon Donna's buckets fill with the quiet staccato of berries.

The gravel on the lane rattles with more cars emerging from the woods to fill our grassy parking area between the berry hut and field. I try to guide the parking, greet new and old friends, hand out buckets, and point folks to the best picking. As we guessed, the morning bustles with the chatter of pickers and the movement of blue from bush to finger to bucket, from scales to pan to car, with a few samples along the way.

By mid-morning, more than thirty people have spread across our field, so Sarah stops picking to help with the customers. We direct more cars, parking to pack them in. We give handshakes or hugs, we weigh and make change, and we tote buckets—empties down field, full ones up.

Through all the work, we visit. I hand new buckets to the Hoovers, one of the Mennonite families. Samuel, their youngest, waves to me and points to his waist where a bucket dangles from his belt, just like mine. A row down, I overhear Sarah and Ruby comparing our field with the German's we visited together years earlier. When she sees me, Ruby jokes, "I feel like I'm missing out, Jim. I expected to ford a stream to get here."

I smile at her joke and then hear someone waiting to check out, so I hurry away. After the customer pays and leaves, I stand at the top of the field. Below, I watch so many people surrounded by bushes of blueberries and busy with the ancient task of gathering food.

Through all of the hiking and hauling and "howdys," we repeatedly answer questions: "Why blueberries?" "How old are they?" "Which is your favorite?" "Why organic?" "And by the way, how's that pump work?" We often retell stories several times a day. Occasionally, I'll even hear Donna fielding these questions in her high, smart voice: "They planted them three years ago in '95." "No, the deer don't seem to bother them much." "I like Patriot best, but Sarah and Jim say they like them all." She, too, has come to know this acre, to love the fruit of these bushes.

By early afternoon, all of this day's pickers have headed home to freeze their morning's work, the full pans of blue nestled snuggly in backseats and trunks. Sarah and I sneak to the house to squeeze in lunch, return phone calls, and, maybe, if we're lucky, take a nap. Always, though, we listen for cars, watch the road for any pickers turning up our lane.

By 4:00 or so, the evening shift begins. I hurry out the door to follow the first batch of cars, while Sarah fixes a picnic supper. By the time I get to the field, some pickers, regulars, have already grabbed buckets and headed into the field. Two retirees wait by the check-out stand, interested in the ram pump *thump-thump*ing below us. I answer their questions about pipe lengths, pressure and flow, and then start them on a bed. While they pick, I sit at our shaded picnic table, tally our totals for the day, and make notes for tomorrow. Periodically, I check on the two men and other pickers, and after about an hour, they all hike out of the field with two buckets each. They praise the size of the berries, "big as nickels and quarters," as their own coins jingle in our money tin.

Sarah arrives with supper, my stomach grumbling with relief. At the same time, our neighbors, Frank, Amy, and their teenaged daughter, Georgia, pull in, ready to fill their freezer with their yearly quota. Frank, a tall, balding accountant I sometimes carpool to work with, asks, "Where to?" As we walk down the field, he cajoles his wife and daughter, the younger dark-haired and dark-eyed like her mother. "I expect three buckets each from both of you," Frank says, trying to sound serious, but we all know the women will pick as much as they want. Such is life for Frank who has grown used to living in a house full of women. I start them on a bed at the bottom of the field while Sarah lays out a fine spread of pasta salad and homemade bread by the hut. I hurry back to dine.

With bellies full, Sarah and I walk down to check on our friends. We are too tired to do more than sit on the grass and visit. We tell them about Sarah's new job, teaching part-time at a homeless shelter, a job that still gives her summers off, but also half days in the winter to prune and make baskets. Frank pauses between bushes to tell us the neighborhood gossip. As he does, Georgia slips behind him to steal from his bucket. She grabs a handful, quick jab of fingers from his bucket to hers, turning her back each time, pretending to pick her own bush. Then on her third berry heist, Frank catches on. Without pause, this loving father grabs a handful of just-picked berries and smashes them on top of his daughter's head. Not one to miss her chance, Georgia wheels around and jumps to squish a handful of blueberries on his bald head. They both try to wipe the juice from their eyes.

Later, as we all walk up the field toting full buckets, Frank asks if we expect any more pickers. "No, probably not," I reply, wondering why he asks.

"Great," he says, hinting at a surprise. After Frank pays for their berries, he opens their car trunk and pulls out wineglasses and a bottle of Burgundy. We sit around the picnic table while Frank pours everyone a full glass, except Georgia who doesn't like the stuff. In this quiet at the end of day, we sip and relax in the goodness of the moment, and watch the sun settle below the far ridge, its rays brushing the field one last time.

Chapter 28

❧❧❧

Shaking Free

Eileen comes often, sometimes shaking free an hour from her work as a probation officer, loosening her day like she shakes out her hair whenever she readies to pick.

These side trips during her lunch hour require creativity with her dresses. If she plans ahead, she brings jeans and T-shirt, walks into the woods behind our berry hut, and changes. Once, with no one in the field but Sarah, Eileen changes back into her dress right in the middle of the field, the red-tailed hawk circling and watching. Another time, she forgets her jeans, but this doesn't slow or baffle her. She sets her bucket on the car hood, grabs the sides of her gray dress, and tucks the hem into the top of her underpants. The ballooning folds billow around her bare legs as she marches into the field. Like the other pickers, I try not to stare.

One Saturday, Eileen brings her two children, Timmy and Sarah. With big, brown eyes, the five-year-old girl wiggles her loose tooth and keeps calling Sarah's name—"Sarah, look at this." "Sarah, I brought you the biggest berry ever." "Sarah, watch my tooth." She has never met another Sarah and marvels at the sweet-sounding word shared with this adult who runs a blueberry farm.

Over lunch at our picnic table, Timmy and Sarah eat their carrots and

Eileen tells us this story. A couple of weeks ago, she and the two kids were in the garden when Sarah said she had to pee. "Well, do it right here in the garden," Eileen exclaimed. "The house is too far away and you're all muddy."

Little Sarah looked around and found what looked like a mole hole. "I'll do it in this hole," she shouted to her mother. She squatted and watched as the ground suddenly buzzed. A few urine-covered yellow jackets waded out of their nest, angry and trying to fly. "I yelled at her, 'Run, it's a yellow jacket's nest!'" And then while her daughter giggled, Eileen added, "I've never seen a bare butt move so fast."

On a different day, Eileen brings her kids again, and this time, she thinks they're old enough to pick a bucket each. They labor and whine, sweat and pout, but they also keep at it, competing with one another and learning to balance the patience of standing at one bush with the quickness of hands. When they flag, their mother reminds them of the reward—a visit to their favorite swimming hole. "And remember, no eating until they're paid for," Eileen shouts as the two go searching for what they think is the best picking spot.

An hour later, their faces red from the sun, Timmy and Sarah proudly carry their full pails to the scales. They're careful, too, watching their buckets to make sure they don't spill any. Earlier, Sarah tipped her precious berry pickings onto the ground. After a moment of crying, the two then crouched together, the older brother helping his sister repick her berries out of the grass.

In the check-out hut, they insist that we keep their buckets separate from their mother's and each other's. "Mine are cleaner," Timmy claims, and I try to ignore the grass and bits of mulch in Sarah's. We weigh their fruit, write down their totals, and then once their mother says okay, the children grab handfuls of blue nuggets. They scoop up their berries, stuff as many as they can into their mouths, gorge on this reward of picking your own.

"It's not like they just ate," Eileen comments. Then, "Come on. Let's find that swimming hole."

They run to their car, and Sarah almost spills her bucket again, but thankfully catches herself. Then they wave on their way down the lane, their smiles wide and stained blue.

❧ BLUE INTERLUDE ❧
Other Colors

Sure it's blue, blue-jean blue, bluebird blue, deep blue of these blue mountains. And if untouched, it should also have a veil of white, a cloud cover over this ocean globe.

But it's also a blue tinged with purple—purple of royalty, purple of the shadows hiding inside its blossom's cup. This hint of dark comes out if the berry hangs too long on the bush, becomes overripe, and also when the "bloom" of whiteness rubs off between fingers as it travels its purpling road from bush to finger to mouth.

The purple pops when a blueberry is cooked. Then the heat of oven performs an alchemist's trick, turning blue to purple of pastries, purple of slumps, purple of cobblers and jellies and pies. Purple bubbling under batter of grunt. Purple to stain your teeth.

Before a blueberry turns blue, it really is pink, the blush of a child's cheek, the soft red of a sunset as it slowly burns down the shoulder of a green mountain. Pink turning to red turning to blue. And like a sunset, all of this slow coloring happens at such a pace that you fail to notice until night falls, and the stars speckle the blueberry sky.

Before pink, a blueberry is really a green berry—the size of a pea, but harder and not as dark, and not hidden in a pod, but out and tinged with red at the very lips of what used to be blossom tip. On a bush, in a field full of bushes, these tiny green orbs dangle like thousands of clappers inside thousands of invisible bells.

Before all of this, before the purple and blue and green, a blueberry really is white. And this white really is a bell, the bell of a blossom that rings and rings the invisible din of scent, all of it pealing the blue sky with waves of sweetness, all of it music to a bumblebee's ears.

❧❀❧

Jim and Sarah with their morning's harvest. (*Unknown*)

Berries ready for market. (*Sarah Minick*)

Preparing the field for planting. (*Jim Minick*)

Each bush was carefully planted . . .
(*Jim Minick*)

. . . and mulched. (*Jim Minick*)

Jim and Sarah's father "tested" the
two-seater outhouse in the field.
(*Sarah Minick*)

Neighbor Joe enjoyed some of the first young blueberries. (*Sarah Minick*)

When mature, the bushes bore thousands of pounds of fruit. (*Ricky Cox*)

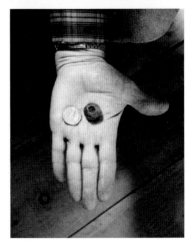

Many blueberries grew as big as quarters. (*Sarah Minick*)

Large berries made happy pickers. *(Sarah Minick)*

Proud pickers. *(Sarah Minick)*

These pickers helped create the farm's Web page. *(Sarah Minick)*

Pickers dressed in blue for a day in the country. *(Jim Minick)*

Child tasting brigade.
(Sarah Minick)

Child tasting brigade on
the move. *(Sarah Minick)*

A service dog
pitched in to help.
(Sarah Minick)

Jim and his uncle in front of the berry hut. (*Sarah Minick*)

Jim's parents helped paint signs. (*Sarah Minick*)

Sarah's parents enjoyed a picnic. (*Sarah Minick*)

The farmhouse in spring. (*Kathryn Minick*)

Always, Jim and Sarah's lives centered on the blueberry field . . . (*Sarah Minick*)

. . . and friends who came to pick.
(*Jim Minick*)

They picked and picked all summer . . .
(*Jim Minick*)

. . . and hiked to check on the bushes in winter. (*Sarah Minick*)

Sarah and a much-loved picker.
(*Jim Minick*)

Jim and Sarah prepare to end the season . . . (*Linda Jones*)

. . . and eat a lot of blueberries. (*Ricky Cox*)

Chapter 29

Hungry

Greta drives likes she picks berries—swiftly and with intent. In her small blue car, she always rips up our steep lane as fast as she can, and out on curvy country highways, we've seen her leaning into turns, zipping by too quickly. She likes speed, it seems, or she's always late, or both.

In the field, when Greta opens her door and stands to stretch, I'm always amazed that she can fit into such a little car. With her broad shoulders and towering height, she reminds me of those Olympic athletes from East Germany who won so many swimming events years ago. She has that wide grin and big bones typical of that country, her native Germany. When she greets us with a hug, her "hello" wells up deep and thick from the bottom reaches of her body, like it, too, has traveled far to get here. And always while we talk about school and kids and berries, Greta looks toward the field, hungry and ready to pick.

We know Greta and her husband, Nat, because Sarah taught one of their daughters. They live at the end of another long dirt road, where the couple owns a retreat center, one of the many hippie outposts in the county. There they offer weed walks, women's weeks, yoga classes, and drumming retreats. Nat, a musician, plays nightclubs in the lean winter months. At Christmas, his huge white beard under a balding head often gets him suckered into playing Santa at the local schools.

In the blueberry field, Greta comes regularly, early in the morning, and she doesn't hide her primary purpose—she comes to eat her breakfast. At first we don't mind; we encourage customers to sample each variety, find ones they like. But Greta doesn't sample—she forages, she hunts these berries, she dines and devours so much blue. She knows her favorite bushes, too, so there she heads, where for the first half hour of picking, her hands work quickly but her bucket stays full of air.

One year Sarah and I hear of another berry farm two counties away that starts charging a one-dollar picking fee just to enter the field. At first we scoff at this, at the idea of it, the miserliness. And then we remember Greta. We won't charge a fee, we decide, not yet anyway. And we probably won't say anything to Greta, either. How would you without sounding rude? "Please don't eat your breakfast here?" No, she's a friend and customer, just keep quiet for now.

We watch their daughters grow, sprouting another few inches every year they return to the field. While they go pick or play with friends, Greta praises the one's love of painting, the other's love of dance. They have their mother's blond hair, the wide forehead, and blue eyes. And despite some struggles, they're learning German, learning their mother's tongue.

But that all ends too soon. On one of her errands in her tiny blue car, out to pick up the girls or buy groceries, Greta rounds a blind curve to find the front end of a pickup truck facing her—a drunk driver across the middle line. Greta has no time to brake, no time to react, no time at all. The truck crumples her car into the bank, crushes Greta's strong body, and leaves a hole in so many lives.

If only I could offer Greta a thousand more blueberry breakfasts.

If only Nat could once again hug his wife.

If only their two daughters could wake to find their mother washing berries at the kitchen sink.

Chapter 30

❦

Berry Hut

A high porch roof covers the front of the check-out hut offering shady chairs for tired pickers. The porch also shades the door, an entry special-made by Sarah's brother, Matt. He carpentered for us one that splits in the middle, a Dutch door like the kind Mr. Ed always leaned out over.

Three steps lead up to the door. If someone sits on the steps, which make a good rest, they might admire this wood's tight, light grain. The lumber for steps and door we milled out of two beech trees. They once shaded the hollow where the pond now puddles. The rest of the lumber for this structure came from the pines saved when we cleared the field. The yellow boards each hold orange and purple suns, knots where branches once grew.

Inside the shed to the left, we stack buckets, red and white, all waiting. Behind the door, we keep broom, hoes, and a golf club to whack away any of our dogs' poo.

Across from the door, first thing in sight, stands a bookcase, salvaged and painted blue, of course. On it we sell blueberry cookbooks, Sarah's herbal vinegars, specially stenciled pint boxes for gift berries, and then all of Sarah's baskets, which also fill a hat tree. My sister gives us a blueberry cookie jar, which holds free recipes, until a child almost knocks over the glass container, so it goes back to the house.

Along the back wall, a long, wide VIRGINIA GROWN banner covers parts of the open studs. Above the bookcase we tack up health articles on the benefits of blueberries along with our official letter from the state saying we are certified organic. Also on the walls: pruners, old belts to hold picking buckets, hats, rolls of bird-scare tape, beetle traps, an old car horn, and a dog leash. On the south and west walls, two salvaged windows bring in pine-shaded light.

Two corners of the berry hut hold more shelves and more boxes of boxes—pints and quarts, wooden and plastic, squares nested inside other squares—all to hold round berries. The small loft above holds still more boxes, this time soda flats, the shallow pasteboards once holding Cokes now ideal for ten pounds of blue. We spend all year collecting them for all those customers who forget to bring their own take-home containers.

In the center of the berry hut sits a dining-room table bought at a yard sale, and on top of it rests the whole purpose of this shed: the scales. I bought them at auction when a country grocery went out of business. Across its back, a white panel faces the customer, the words HOBART above the circular portal. This window the size of a half-dollar fascinates every kid who has to be held up by his waist to watch the numbers roll and roll and roll. On the other side, I place a bucket on the shiny metal plate and I, too, watch the numbers roll to settle on five or eight pounds. If the child is young, I might ask her to say the number. If a little older, I might ask her to do the math of subtracting a half pound from the total to compensate for the bucket's weight.

When we weigh the berries, Sarah and I stand on a braided rug made of heavy wool by my grandmother. Years ago it somehow got stained beyond household use, so here its worn reds and browns have found a second life and a daily dose of crushed berries to give it a darker shade.

But the rug's real purpose is to cover what's underneath. Hidden there, between two floor joists, is a secret box, a hold for our stash of money. It's Sarah's idea, a place to keep most of the cash in case some picker decides to become a thief. When we built this hut, I crawled underneath to nail up the bottom of this safe, and then inside, I drilled a thumbhole to pick up the now loose piece of floorboard.

On busy days, when the twenty-dollar bills are rolling in, we wait for that lull that always comes. Then Sarah tells me to watch, play lookout, while she turns back the rug, lifts the small trapdoor, and trades out twenties for more ones. She gets nervous when doing this, so I might whisper, "Hurry," just to goad her, or I might pretend someone has run up to surprise us both, yelling out a "Hello there" in mock seriousness. This always gets a pinch in my behind.

We never make love in the blueberry field, never feel the crush of grass under our bodies, never enjoy that kind of fruit.

The one time we try, we decide to sleep on the wood floor of our just-made berry hut, "to break it in." But there, eye-level to our two dogs, we keep getting interrupted by their slobber and wet noses. Who can blame them for becoming thrilled to have us so close, to be wound up by our unwinding? They keep licking our faces, and we shush and shove them away only to find a wet dog tongue in eye or ear or mouth.

And then our mutts hear a coyote far off, a lone high whining yowl. The dogs scramble past us where we lay by the door, but they stop on the threshold, fear keeping them close. They lean their hot fur against our bare feet and legs, and when the coyote howls again, the collie and terrier both lift their jowls, open wide, and howl a return, the terrier's so high pitched as to sound like a pup's.

"I don't think this is going to work," Sarah says, stating the obvious.

"I don't know what you could mean." I sigh and roll to my side and start laughing. Then I join the dogs and howl with the coyote, the bare-butted moon hanging above us.

Chapter 31

❦

Worms

Sometimes Sarah is a little dramatic, maybe, even, overdramatic. When she tells a story about one of our dog's antics, she'll raise her eyebrows, throw wide her arms, and get the emphasis in her voice just right. She can tell a story far better than I, but she never ever exaggerates. If, for example, our thermometer reads zero degrees one chilly winter day, Sarah calls her mother in sunny Charlotte to tell her that it was "negative fifty zillion degrees this morning." But like I said, exaggeration doesn't exist here on Berry Hill Road.

So one Saturday early in the blueberry season, I hurry home from market. I've been up since 5:30, loading and unloading the truck with table, signs, and coolers of berries. By mid-afternoon, I am exhausted but I'm also anxious about Sarah. Saturdays are one of our busiest days in the field, and she's been soloing it all morning, in charge of who knows how many pickers. I drive up our lane to find only a few cars parked in the field, but Sarah's numbers in our notebook confirm a very full morning. When I find her down among the bushes, Sarah leaves the picker she was checking on and we walk to the check-out hut for privacy. I can tell something's troubling her, but she waits till we are inside the building.

"Jim, we have a problem. A very *big* problem," she says in a low voice. She looks behind me, out the door and window to make sure no one else is around.

"What?" I ask, worried and curious.

"We have worms! Lots of them. I mean tons of them. Millions of them climbing out of every berry. When Eileen checked out this morning, I tried to ignore them crawling on her berries, but she saw them, too, and said, 'Oh, well, guess they add a little protein.' But then Danica came and they were squirming around the rim of one of her buckets. She was kind, too, and said this just proved we were organic. But Jim, this isn't good. I'm scared."

I know these creatures, tiny pale-green fruitworms, skinnier than a fishing line. Our manuals say the mother moth laid her eggs on our blooms and green berries a month or so ago. As the fruit ripens, the egg grows to hatch a worm that burrows into its host berry to eat and grow and finally emerge right when the paying customer is ready to hand over her money for a hard-earned bucket of berries.

"We've had them before here and there," I say, trying to downplay her worry.

"Yes, but never like this. This is an infestation, Jim! A major infiltration of our field." She pauses, looks at a flat of berries sitting on the table, and then points to three minuscule worms. "See? One, two, three, three; worms right there in only a second of looking. This is *bad!* What are we going to do about it?"

I don't know how to answer, what to say. And I know the "we" in the last sentence is usually me when it comes to bugs and sprays and such.

A picker slowly hikes up the hill, a full bucket in each hand. We both see him, and Sarah whispers, "You look now and tell me if I'm wrong."

We greet the man, help him with his load. When I place a bucket on the scales, I read the numbers and glance onto the surface of blues. And sure enough, I see several small worms inching around berries and bucket. I pour the contents into the man's container, a white dishpan, hoping to bury the creatures. But others show up, minute but even more visible against the white plastic. The man doesn't seem to notice, or if he does, he's quiet about it. I don't look anymore, try not to draw attention to them, then I make change and thank him as he heads out the door. "Come on back," I holler. He says he will, but Sarah and I both have our doubts and hope he's not wearing bifocals.

. . .

The next week I call Phil, a bearded, blue-eyed professor at a nearby land-grant university. I met Phil and his wife, Susan, at a local bird-club outing the previous year. When I heard he was an entomologist, I asked if he knew much about blueberries and their pests. He said he knew a little and liked blueberries well enough. I invited him to come pick.

When I call him this time though, I try to hide the urgency in my voice. "Why don't you and Susan come pick? We have several bluebirds and tanagers visiting our field right in front of people as they pick. And, by the way, I have some bugs I need your advice on." I know Phil's a busy man, so to sweeten the request, I offer free berries.

Phil's schedule delays a visit for two weeks. When they finally come to the field, Susan's smooth face is smiling as soon as she gets out of the car. "We heard your tanager already, and a hooded warbler down by the pond, and maybe a water thrush down by the creek." I grin, recognize this as birder-speak for "This is a great day, isn't it?" But Phil is quiet, a little reserved, and I worry that I've asked too much of his generosity. We grab buckets and head to the bushes.

We only have a few other pickers in the field, so Sarah and I pick alongside Phil and Susan. We want to make sure they leave with enough fruit, and we want to learn our bugs. Soon, the picking is interrupted by Phil's, "There's a lacewing," or "Look at that scale." His excitement has overcome any reservations, it seems, and we move from bush to bush, picking a little, but talking more and more.

He points out some of the fruitworms, their telltale frass connecting clumps of berries, but after walking around for a bit, Phil observes, "There's really not that much fruitworm sign here, so I'm not sure you need to deal with it." Sarah and I both agree and mention that we hadn't seen as many in the last week or so. "Sounds like they peak early in the season," Phil offers, "and then their numbers fade. I'd either try spraying Bt (an organic fungus that kills worms) or you could just ignore them." I am relieved, the worry-gene inherited from my mother, for a moment, turned off.

But then Phil points to more and more scale, soft-bodied pests that hug the twigs in unobtrusive clusters, blending in with the bark. They are like aphids, he tells us, and they'll suck the juice right out of the plant. My worm-worry-gene suddenly mutates to a scale-worry-gene. "A coat of dormant oil in the fall will take care of them," Phil recommends, and I make a note to read up on sprayers and oils.

We pick less and less, as Phil walks from bush to bush, forgetting his bucket and pulling out his small handheld magnifier. "You might want to get one of these," he advises, holding up his tool, and I remember my neighbor Joe saying the same. Joe loves to walk his strawberries, pick a leaf, and hold it under his lens, this hidden world suddenly revealing itself.

Now I watch Phil doing the same, bush by bush, leaf and berry and twig shown in a different way, as a world full of tiny life. And amazingly what Phil examines most often is a world full of beneficial bugs. He makes sure we know the ladybeetle and its voracious larva sometimes called aphid lions. "These larva can eat a thousand aphids each," Phil praises. Both larva and adult are abundant in our sorrel-covered beds. But I don't know the hover fly, or the harmless parasitic wasp, or the lacewing, its light-green body dwarfed by delicate, transparent, and well-named wings. All of these "new" insects, Phil tells us, eat or parasitize a swarm of different insects, especially aphids, caterpillars, and scale.

"These insects love your place," Phil compliments. He says our organic practices have helped make them happy here. Then he asks if we know how to identify lacewing's eggs. When we say no, he goes searching again and quickly uncovers several on leaves and even on a few berries, pinhead ovals suspended at the end of filaments of thread. Some are the same pale green as the adult, and some are white; the latter, Phil informs, are empty because the insect just hatched. I hold a leaf with a tiny egg. Even when I blow softly, the stiff thread barely bends, the egg stays balanced, and in so doing, the lacewing prevents any hungry ant from having an egg breakfast.

Between the four of us, with all of the bug-traipsing and bird-watching, we only pick two buckets of berries. But smart Sarah had picked earlier, and so when Phil and Susan get ready to leave, we're able to fill the backseat of their car with some extra flats full of blueberries. As Phil wedges one container in place, he pulls out a plump berry. "Here, you hold on to this one," as he places a single berry back in my hand. "It still has a lacewing egg not yet hatched. Keep it here in the field."

I thank him and place this small world and its embryonic inhabitant on the berry-hut windowsill. A day later when I check, the egg is hatched, the lacewing flown to sup. And suddenly our acre of blueberries has become a parasitic wasp parlor, a lacewing lodge, a ladybug lounge, a hoverfly home— the field far more than just a field.

❧ BLUE INTERLUDE ☙
Blues Evolution

So how did a blueberry become a blueberry? How did it evolve to bear such sweetness?

"It's all because of birds," says my friend, biologist Gary Coté, a fellow teacher at Radford University who also enjoyed our blueberries. I asked him for help in understanding this plant's evolution, and he graciously and eloquently replied:

"You probably know that blueberries are in the plant Family Ericaceae, the heath or heather family. One characteristic of many members is the urn-shaped flowers. The genus *Vaccinium* includes blueberries, cranberries, bilberries, and the Mount Ida grape popular in teas.

"The blueberry's section of this genus is basically a mess. Apparently the two versions of blueberry, the highbush and the lowbush, can freely cross within their group as well as with each other. And I've read they are doing so promiscuously in areas north of the glacial limits. This sounds to me like blueberries were isolated into small pocket populations during the Ice Age and started to separate into distinct species. But when the glaciers receded, the plants were not sufficiently far along to maintain their distinctiveness and are now busy collapsing back into one or a few species. The species (*V. corymbosum*) that produced the domesticated highbush blueberry has no less than six species in its ancestry.

"As to how it came to have a tasty berry, I can only guess, of course. Many members of that family have juicy, if not always tasty, berries. On the other hand, some have dry woody capsules for fruits (think rhododendrons). I don't know which is ancestral, but I suspect the woody ones, which means at some point in evolution, the ancestral *Vaccinium* started producing berries. How this happened, as I said, I can only guess.

"Why it happened is pretty clear, though—the blueberry became bite-size for a bird. From the plant's point of view, birds eat the berries and defecate the seeds somewhere else, along with a good dose of fertilizer. Other animals also contribute to this propagation game, including bears, chipmunks, squirrels, even turtles. Birds are best, however, since they can fly and spread the seeds far and wide. And they make small deposits, only a few seeds at a time, which means a better chance to live with less competition. Imagine how many seeds would be dumped in one location if a bear gorged itself and then left a deposit!

"From the bird's point of view, carrying the blueberry's seeds must come with some prize. Thus we have enticing sugar, the plant's reward, a small dose of energy. Same with size and color, both evolved to attract winged creatures. Birds have trouble eating anything bigger, and it's not to the plant's advantage to give the bird more than it needs. And the color blue is easy to see.

"So basically, we are the home wreckers in the evolutionary marriage of birds and blueberries, insinuating ourselves and stealing berries meant for birds. (So are bears, for that matter.) When we eat wild blueberries, we really are stealing. When we domesticate the plants, we basically try to woo the plant away from the birds. We offer the plant this deal: if they make blueberries fat and juicy to our liking, we'll take over propagation. We do a better job than the birds, I'm sure. Still, based on hundreds of thousands of years of evolution, the blueberries are really for the birds."

Chapter 32

❧❧

Affinity

We expect winged visitors to our field, and the manuals warn to be ready, to take action since blueberries are "bite-size for a bird." The thick books even illustrate how to set up a huge, eight-foot-high net over the whole acre-field, with massive, anchored posts and even more massive costs.

And I remember my grandfather who spent evenings waiting in his berry patch, rifle across his lap. Confined by emphysema to his garden tractor, he rode out after supper and picked off robins and starlings before dusk. He handed me his other rifle and together we tried to kill any settling, berry-hungry bird. But they kept returning, always honing in on the most loaded bush at the opposite end of the patch.

To be honest, the feathered creatures never really raid our Virginia field, never come in great numbers like the books warn or like they did on that Pennsylvania patch. I even hang two bluebird houses and have a resident family. When I take a break at the picnic table, I watch these "sky-colored" birds dart among the bushes, and yes, round berries fill their mouths, but also I witness them hunting the green plants for bugs, and it seems they eat more insects than blueberries.

One family of pickers tells us of another patch where they picked blueberries last year. There the farmer uses a cannon to scare away birds. "It would *boom* and *boom* and *boom!*" the ten-year-old son shouts and waves his arms with each *boom*. The father explains how it exploded at random times, so you never knew when to expect it. "I felt on edge the whole time," he remembers. And then the mother adds, "We really appreciate the peace and quiet of your field." No plans for cannons here, I think to myself, and then realize this family won't ever return to the boom-deafening patch.

Since we know of this affinity of berry and bird, and since I was a good Boy Scout, always doing my best to be prepared, we decide to take some preventative action. We buy bird-eye scare balloons, round yellow affairs that once blown up, their red and black circles supposedly look like a hawk's eye swooping in for the kill. One morning in the berry hut, we sit in our wooden folding chairs bought at a church yard sale and begin to blow up these new-plastic, awful-smelling balloons. Sarah, ever the competitor, says, "I bet you a back rub I can blow this up faster than you."

Of course, I can't back down. "You're on." Before I even finish the words, her cheeks puff and her balloon begins to inflate. I take a deep breath, put lips to foul-tasting balloon, and blow hard. But little happens. And Sarah's is already half filled, the bird eye already looking scary. I blow more and more and only get a slight swell, a little expansion. Soon I start to feel light-headed, my lips numb, and I let go of the balloon's pinched neck, the precious air whizzing out. "Shoot, Sarah. I can't do this without hyperventilating." I throw my sagging balloon at her as she ties off her fully inflated one.

"Guess I get a back rub," she gloats and grabs another.

"Yeah, yeah," I poke her in the ribs as she starts blowing her second balloon. She pinches the air and pokes me back as I head out the door. I figure I can at least work on our other bird-scare device—flashy reflective-tape, inch-wide strips of heavy foil that catch the sun and stir up a whirring racket in the wind. These I unroll, cut to length, and string above the berry plants. I like how both balloons and tape are simple tools, no electricity, no batteries, just a little current of air and shine of sun to hopefully scare off feathered marauders.

But the manuals warn that birds, like deer and humans, quickly adapt, readily learn that the bug-eyed balloon is harmless. The trick is unpredictability, to move the tape and balloons often, to set the cannon, if used, to fire at random intervals.

These random acts of unkindness we accomplish with bamboo and leftover pipe. We harvest the bamboo from Sarah's folks' home in Charlotte where a skinny jungle of thirty-foot-tall sticks has taken over their backyard. We tape and tie our ten-foot-long haul to the side of the car, forcing the passenger (Sarah) to ride with her window down so she can hold on to these wind-wiggling rods for 150 miles. Luckily the load doesn't get smashed on the highway.

In the field, I pound leftover chunks of irrigation pipe into the berry beds at twenty-foot intervals. The bamboo poles go into the pipes, and we stretch the reflective tape above the blueberries and tie it off on the poles. Each big-eyed, Sarah-blown balloon also gets its own bamboo rod where it dangles and bounces with the breeze. Once a week Sarah and I march across the field, moving the bamboo to different pipes, and hopefully creating a random effect. But who really knows if it fools the birds.

It does fool one picker. He picks all through the windy morning under the whistling foil. The racket impresses him, and he pauses often to try to figure out how the bright strip works. When he's filled his buckets and readies to check out, he asks, "So I guess you have to unplug that shiny tape every night?"

Chapter 33

❦

Forgetfulness

Sometimes I forget these bushes are individuals. I'll look at the whole field and mark out the tending tasks of the day, the traps to check, calls to make, and buckets to clean.

If I'm lucky a friend will wake me from this dull sleep. Katie, our friend and hired help, for instance, often greets each bush with, "And how are you today?" before she kneels to pick. Or Sarah, in the winter as we prune, reminds me, "Each one calls for its own shape. The blade never cuts the same."

One July afternoon, tired from the morning's twenty cars of pickers, I sit at the picnic table and watch a male scarlet tanager, redder than the gum tree's leaves of autumn. He flicks his black wings from bush to bush, searching for the ripest berry. He plucks it in his beak, flies to the pine bough above me, and eats this, the sweetest berry from the most beautiful bush.

This I cannot forget.

Chapter 34

❧❧❧

Don't You Know

Louise, sweet Louise with her round glasses and quick smile. She works as the secretary at the local elementary, which means she runs the school. Sarah worked with her for six years and even taught her son, her only child, in fourth grade. With short, wavy hair and a handy sense of humor, Louise laughs often, knows everyone's business, and works as hard as anyone I know.

Once she gives us a tour of her garden. We "ooh" and "aah" at the straight rows of cabbage and corn, but then she says, "Now over here . . ." and we trail her to a different patch, and then "over here" to another, and another. She really has four gardens, any one of them the same size as our own patch.

"What do you do with all of this?" I ask, "especially now that Mark's in college."

"Can it," she responds in her usual quick way. "Can it and give it away. Here, you need some cucumbers, don't you?"

Later she shows us her cellar, newly rebuilt after a house fire destroyed the old one. "Of all the things I lost, I hated seeing that burned-out cellar the most. All that food and work . . ." her voice trails off.

These new shelves are lined with hundreds of jars of tomatoes and greens, pickles and peaches, cherries and beans. "My goodness," Sarah whispers. "You sure have restocked this."

"Just last weekend," she tells us, hand resting on a shelf, "Mark brought home his whole fraternity, and you can imagine how much food twenty-five young men can eat. 'Bout wore me out." She smiles. "And they want to come back soon, don't you know."

Louise only has three blueberry bushes in her garden-filled yard, and they don't grow well for her, so she comes to our field often to stock up. On one visit, as she fills the bucket tied to her waist, she shares her deer troubles. "The deer have eat up most of my rhododendrons," she complains, "and now they're so bad they're bedding down right in the bushes, right beside the house!"

Fred, her husband, read in the local paper that soap shavings ward them off. "So I pulled out my cheese grater and I grated thirty bars of soap."

"All by hand?" I ask.

"Yep, all by hand. Then I spread those soap shavings all around the bushes, just like fertilizer. Covered that ground with white. The next night, those deer just came right back and bedded down again, right there in those bushes."

Louise pauses to wipe the back of her hand across her forehead, the sweat dripping behind her glasses.

"Last week when it rained, those shavings all started to lather up, bubbles of Ivory all over the place. Soon a river of suds floated down the driveway and out onto the state road. Fred just stood at the window watching it all foam up and float away. He asked if I had seen it, and then said, 'That's one way to clean the driveway.'"

Every time she arrives, Louise asks her usual question, "Seen any snakes?" She has taken a shotgun to her garden to blast a poor black snake, so I know she is serious in her fear. I always say no, none in the field, which is true for the most part. I might have seen a garter snake along the edge of the patch, but never *in* the field, not yet anyway. But, of course, I don't tell this to Louise.

Once I've satisfied her question, off she'll march into her favorite variety, always carrying at least two buckets, always greeting whoever is near. Even if she pulls up by herself, she never picks alone.

And she never lets us dally in the shed. If she's filled her buckets, she'll call out from the bottom of the field, "Jim, I need another bucket." Off I'll go with five, knowing she'll keep whatever I can offer. I don't mind huffing buckets for her. With a friend one time, she filled nine buckets in three hours, over seventy pounds.

One day while Louise's out in the field picking, Sarah hears something sliding in the rafters of the shed. She looks up to see a black snake dangling, a third of its long body pointed straight down from rafter to our scales. Sarah grabs the broom and waves it above her head, back and forth in front of the black, slithering head, and the snake quickly withdraws into the attic crawl space. There it hides only a few feet above anyone who enters.

Soon Louise walks in with her five buckets ready to check out. Sarah never says a word, and the snake doesn't move.

And Louise never knows.

Chapter 35

Religious Moments

Patty and Clara step out of their JESUS SAVES bumper-stickered car. I know Clara as gentle-souled—she comes often, speaks quietly, always smiles. But she brings a friend this time, and soon I avoid ponytailed Patty. Like her hair pulled so tightly, she has none of that gentleness. In the field I overhear her railing against the local school board for not allowing prayer in school, and I'm amazed by the sheer hatred in her voice. *How can someone like this love thy neighbor?* I wonder to myself.

At check-out time, just the three of us stand in the shed. They place their full buckets of berries on the table between us and say, "The Lord has blessed you with a bountiful crop."

"Yes, indeed," I agree, and then think, *And you don't know all the work the Lord required to get this bounty.*

Patty, sensing an opening, proceeds to ask, "Are you a Christian?"

"Of sorts," I reply.

"What sort?" She does not hesitate.

I move buckets, wonder what Jesus would've said with such an attack, wonder why I can't just walk out that door. But instead, I measure my words: "More open and liberal than you."

That doesn't slow her as the well-oiled lines spill out. "Are you saved? Do you know Jesus as your personal friend? Have you gone to the altar to ask for his forgiveness?"

I say nothing for a long time and we all wait out the oxygen-depleting silence. I weigh their berries, calculate their totals, and I do not look up, do not make eye contact. I am both amazed at this lady's gall and angry by her prying sanctimony. Clara says nothing, just watches me pour berries, while I can feel Patty staring hard into me, waiting.

Finally she asks again, "Do you know Jesus?"

I put the last bucket down, look at them both, and say, "I know him well enough." Clara bends to the table to write the check, while Patty invites me to their church, into Jesus' open arms, into this warm world of definite answers. I ignore her and watch Clara's steady hand, the pen writing our name and her slow curving signature.

"Thanks for coming." I watch them leave and hold in my disbelief.

In college, I studied New Testament Greek, which meant I committed myself to four semesters of 8 A.M. classes meeting four times a week. When I enrolled, I thought I might follow my previous mentor and become a minister, so the Greek would help me better understand God, Jesus, and their mysterious teachings.

But the closed bud of my life burst open in those first years away from home, away from a confined and confining existence I helped create. I had feared life then, or at least the wild aspects of it, like alcohol and women. College quickly cured this, helped me overcome this straitjacketing fear.

Through those semesters of too-early classes, I struggled often with waking up and with understanding the New Testament's original tongue. Christ's words didn't always translate as the King James Bible claimed. We bumped against words like *erchomai*, which means *coming* or *going*, or *pneuma*, which means *breath* or *Spirit of God*. One word in this slippery language changed the meaning of a whole sacred passage.

As I parsed verb tenses, I also wrestled with creating a fresher identity, a more open idea of who I wanted to be. And retranslating the Bible actually helped. I found what became my favorite passage, Matthew 10:7: *"Aggiken a basileia ton ouranon."* I worked through to the translation of "The Kingdom of Heaven has come," and King James translated the Greek to "The Kingdom of Heaven is at hand." Either way, my professor loved to challenge us by saying, "The Kingdom of God is here, now, among us all, not above, not in the heavens." We spent a whole class exploring the ramifications of that one line.

And though I had read Matthew often, this was the first time I saw heaven in the palm of my hand.

"Aggiken a basileia ton ouranon." The Kingdom of Heaven is among us. I still love this, love the sound of it on the tongue, how it makes me realize that this tongue is part of the very kingdom, that I *am in heaven* even now, here on this farm that demands so much sweat. That I am in and of the Kingdom with every breath, *every pneuma*. I joke about creating the Garden of Eden with our blueberry field, but God, too, is a jester, and maybe the joke is on me and Eden everywhere.

I sweep out the berry hut and work over my conversation with Patty, my answers to her jabs. "I know him well enough," I repeat, but not really. No one does, not even those in the fold. I want to be open to this heaven, to the myriad possibilities of his teachings, of what God might be. To do so means for me to live outside of the strictures of organized religion. I almost smothered in those strictures as a child and cannot imagine going back. But I realize I'm as entrenched in trying to be open-minded as Patty is in being open only to Jesus.

I shake out the braided rug. "Are you saved?" I repeat. From fear of life and death, I hope so.

Restack the buckets inside the door. "Do you know Jesus as your personal friend?" Probably not, unless he exists in the lives around me, in Sarah and our pups, this field of living plants and all of these pickers.

And then I take a break and sit on the steps, back against the doorjamb while I look over the field. "Have you gone to the altar to ask for his forgiveness?" Not sure. I want to believe that there is more than a life of the Fallen, that maybe we have the whole story wrong. That maybe every time I kneel to pick a simple blueberry, I am praying for gratitude, for grace, and this is enough.

"The Kingdom of Heaven is among us," I say again, aloud. And each time I say it, it takes on new meaning, and new mystery.

·   ·   ·

Two hours after Clara and Patty depart, Martha drives up, her straight
black hair framing her smiling face. Her bumper sticker reads CO-EXIST and
displays all the symbols of various religions. I know her as an outspoken art-
ist and agitator, hard-sticking to her liberal beliefs. She is the one school
board member the Christians criticize most.

Not only is Martha against prayer in school, she just won reelection even
after a controversial battle. She could no longer tolerate the local high
school's use of an old mascot, the "Indians." "We don't have the Cleveland
Jews or the New York Spics, but we love those Braves and Indians," she
carped to me once. And when she came to have a little power, Martha organized her supporters, put the motion before her fellow board members, and
had enough citizens there complaining. Now the cheerleaders all scream,
"Go Wildcats!" thanks to Martha.

I've never discussed religion with Martha, whose name makes me think
she had a religious upbringing. I don't even know if she attends a church. I
would guess she follows the "religion" of her art, the spiritual path of creativity, but this is just a guess. When she steps out of her Jeep, I hug her and
can't stop laughing. I tell her about Patty and her crassness, and Martha
says, "You're kidding, right? I know her all too well and she drives me nuts."
When I assure her that it was indeed one of her loudest opponents, Martha,
too, joins in my laughter.

If only Patty had stuck around, she, too, would've witnessed the cause of
our laughter—Martha's amazing T-shirt. She found it at Goodwill, she tells
me, and just couldn't resist touching it up a bit. In bright red, she painted on
the letters st. Now instead of the slogan saying BORN AGAIN," her T-shirt reads,
BORN AGAINST.

God, the Jester, I think. Eden everywhere.

Chapter 36

❧

New Religion

It takes us a while to realize we've become prophets of a new religion. We built a church, it seems, without intending, and now the rows fill up each day with worshipers, a congregation coming to take the sacrament, to eat the holy goodness of real food. The religion is "organic," and whether we like it or not, we've created this house of worship.

Our most devout members are cancer survivors. They've realized the error of their past diets and have converted to a strict organic menu. I listen to their stories, admire their courage, and am thankful they're here to enjoy a sunny day in our field. And that is life's essence, isn't it, one day to the next, taking care of finding your food in the most healthful way?

Elaine and Connie show up one morning in a shiny SUV with Ohio plates. They're strangers who like many folks stumble onto our Web page or hear about us from a friend. All of them drive the extra miles just because we're certified organic.

"All the way from Ohio?" I ask, after first greeting them.

"Just for your organic berries," round Elaine says, smiling. Then she explains that they own land nearby and hope to build and move here soon once they sell their restaurant business back north.

She is a large woman, and I can quickly tell, also large in heart. She loves the field, the quiet, and is not afraid to tell her own story. While Connie wanders into the bushes to pick, Elaine stays back, says, "We're glad you're here. We've converted to an all organic diet since I had breast cancer, and it's not easy finding fresh fruit like this. We're really glad to be here."

And of course, I'm glad they're here, strangers and friends, survivors all. We hear similar stories at least once a week, usually from women, sometimes from adult children or siblings who tell of losing their father or sister and then reading the often hidden truths of our food system. Usually, underneath there swims an anger, a disbelief that our beef could be called safe, or that so many pesticides wouldn't also affect our drinking water. They've had to educate themselves, read and search out information not usually covered in the media.

"And they call our food safe," Beverly, another cancer survivor laments in the shade of the pine trees, taking a break from picking. She, too, has lost a breast, and her mother, to cancer.

"When will people wake up?" she asks. I only can say I hope soon. And slowly, as more and more people find us, traveling to our small field from Blacksburg and Roanoke, over an hour away, I keep this hope, this faith.

But to be honest, I'm not a very religious person, spiritual, maybe, but religious, not really. Too many dogmas barking and biting at each other. So this organic religion makes me uncomfortable, makes me, even, skeptical. This skepticism is bolstered when I learn how the official organic rule defines "free-range" for chickens (an open door that the birds are too afraid to use). Or when I consider all the fuel that goes into even organic food to grow and cool and haul it everywhere. As Michael Pollan writes in *The Omnivore's Dilemma*, "Today it takes between seven and ten calories of fossil fuel energy to deliver one calorie of food energy to an American plate."

And again to be honest, when I truly analyze our own farm, I realize we're not really "organic," either. Oh, sure, we abide by the law and use only approved fertilizers and pesticides. Instead of my neighbor Joe's potent, petroleum-based standard of 10-10-10 that keeps him in red fields of strawberries, our organic fertilizers are mostly mined rocks and dried, pulverized blood and cottonseed. And even as we shell out the extra money for what Joe calls our "magic powders," even as we vow to never use synthetic or petroleum-based fertilizers or herbicides, I realize early on that we will never truly be "organic."

The word *organic* implies a circle, "a systemic connexion or coordination of parts in one whole," so says my old *OED*, an antique dictionary that doesn't even mention the word's new "connexion" to agriculture. Ideally I think of *organic* as a closed system where the farm supplies its own fertilizer (through animal manure and cover crops) and for us, our own mulch. But we don't have the land, desire, or knowledge to farm animals, and cover crops don't work well with perennial plants. To supply our own mulch, we'd have to invest in a huge chipper, a gas-gulping machine far from any ideal of *organic*.

The root of *organic* is organ, the vital parts of an organism. "Organic vein" is an old name for the jugular. So maybe farming organically is getting at the heart, getting closer to health. Maybe this organic religion will help us all survive this messed-up food system, transform it into something that doesn't value cheapness over all else, doesn't look at food as a commodity, or even, as a weapon, but instead understands the holiness of this world we all ingest with each bite, the holiness of our own bodies that is no different than the holiness of this one earth. Maybe.

❧ BLUE INTERLUDE ❧
The Benefits of Organic

The benefits of eating organically grown food have been known for several years now. A 1993 study, for example, published in the *Journal of Applied Nutrition* by Bob L. Smith compared mineral content of organic produce with conventionally grown. Over a two-year period in Chicago, Smith bought apples, pears, potatoes, wheat, and corn of both categories and analyzed them in his lab. He discovered a significant nutrient difference in favor of organic produce. The organic corn, for example, had 1,600 percent more manganese, 1,800 percent more calcium, and 2,200 percent more iodine than regular corn. On average, organic produce had two-and-one-half times more nutrients than conventionally grown, primarily due to the health of the soil and type of fertilizer. Smith noted that many studies, including a Surgeon General's, "have found that low levels of elements correlate with many health conditions," from "alcoholism, allergy, [and] cancer," to "chronic fatigue . . . , diabetes . . . , and rheumatoid arthritis." Smith concluded, "The elements found to reduce symptoms are the same elements found in this study at greater concentration in organic food."

On the Organic Trade Association's Web site, a more recent study confirms this older one. In 2001, Virginia Worthington, of Johns Hopkins University, reviewed "forty-one published studies comparing the nutritional value of organically grown and conventionally grown" foods. She found significant differences of several major nutrients. Overall, Worthington showed that organic crops have "27% more vitamin C, 21.1% more iron, [and] 29.3% of magnesium." The organic produce also had "15.1% less nitrates," the residues left from fertilizers and pesticides. Depending on how it's grown, the proverbial apple-a-day could help you a lot, or not at all.

Curious to find more research on the benefits of organic produce, I discovered several other studies. One, from *New Scientist*, 2002, documents a British study of salicylic acid in organic soups. This acid, a plant-produced defense mechanism, acts in our bodies as an anti-inflammatory that also combats bowel cancer and artery hardening. The British scientists reveal that organic vegetable soup has on average almost nine times more salicylic acid than regular, nonorganic soups.

As a result, the *New Scientist* concludes, "Eating organic food may help reduce your risk of heart attacks, strokes, and cancer."

The population most affected by this debate over how crops are grown are those with no voice—our children. In 2002, a research team headed by Cynthia Curl at the University of Washington proved that children who eat an organic diet are exposed to far fewer pesticides. Their study, published in *Environmental Health Perspectives*, focused on two groups of preschoolers, assessing diets and urine samples. The twenty-one children who ate conventionally grown food had a concentration of a certain pesticide nine times higher than the eighteen children who ate primarily organic food. This high level of toxin exceeded the Environmental Protection Agency's recommendations. As the authors conclude, "Consumption of organic produce appears to provide a relatively simple way for parents to reduce their exposure to . . . pesticides."

Eating is a political and environmental act. Each bite affects our health as well as that of all creatures, from the soil microorganism to the farmer. Granted, organic food usually costs more than conventionally grown, but what is the true cost of health? As Barbara Kingsolver writes, "Before anyone rules out eating . . . organically because it seems expensive, I'd ask [them] to figure in the costs paid outside the store: the health costs, the land costs, the big environmental Visa bill that sooner or later comes due."

And these costs include hunger and feeding the poor. They, too, are part of this organic web; they, too, like the children, like all of us, deserve health and good food.

We can improve the health of our planet and our own bodies by eating, growing, and sharing organic food, or we can improve the wallets of doctors and agribusiness CEOs while sending tons of soil and pesticides downriver every day.

Whatever the choice, we always create the same world that we eat.

Chapter 37

❧❦❧

To Market

The journey to the Saturday farmer's market—all twenty miles of it—starts every Wednesday. We don't walk or ride a horse up and over Alum Ridge and down along the Little River all the way to Radford; it just takes that long to pick that many blueberries. Each large pebble of a fruit travels by finger from bush to bucket, bucket to pint, field to the second-hand fridge in the garage; then from fridge back to truck, home to town, truck to table, and finally, again, from my fingers to the customer's. Along the way a single blueberry moves at least six times, like it has little blue wheels to motor it along, transport it to another place. But we know better. The weight of all this lifting burrows into our backs.

Sarah can outpick anybody I know. When the picking is prime, she fills a bucket in twenty minutes and can haul out of the field twenty pounds an hour, maybe twenty-five. She slips into the middle of a bed where most pickers don't venture. There she's surrounded by bushes bent from bearing so much, the tangle of green leaves hiding her, the plants taller than her blond head. She can settle in and disappear like a magic forest fairy. Other pickers walk by and never know she works just a few feet away. She has heard many secrets this way.

When she picks, her two hands work freely, fingers tickling the berries into palms. As the bucket fills, the wire handle leaves a white groove in the skin of her tanned arm, a dent that takes a long while to disappear. She makes sure I see it, this badge of hard work. But I know already, don't need any more proof than the row of full buckets lining the check-out hut's back wall.

At market on a good day, I can sell over 100 pounds, my record 140 pints. So prime picking means an easy four or five hours of work. But that kind of pace, that kind of magically overwhelmingly fruit-laden Eden, only happens once, early in the season. All the other weeks, we pick alongside everyone else who comes to the field, which means our picking pace for market drastically changes. Instead of three buckets an hour, we feel good some days if we can pick one an hour. That triples or quadruples our market-picking time. Then, we shoot for 50 pounds to take to market in order to break even.

So much goes to market, besides berries. I have to type up a checklist so I don't forget: table, recipes, signs, money, hat, gourds, and the special berry-imprinted tablecloth, fabric from my mom, hemmed by Sarah. The night before I pack the truck with everything but the berries—the table on the bottom, the garbage can of free birdhouse gourds for kids on top. Then at 5:30 A.M., I wake to fill coolers with pints of blue and head out. I wear my market shirt, a heavy-knit given to us one Christmas by kinfolk, Matt and Melanie. It has MINICK BERRY FARM embroidered above the pocket, yellow letters on a field of blue.

Like the town, the Radford Farmer's Market is small, a parking lot with new landscaping sandwiched between Main Street and the railroad yard. I like to set up facing the building next door, a three-story from the early 1900s that now houses a flower shop. On its tall brick side, some early 1900s businessman painted CUBANOLA CIGARS 5 CENTS, the bright yellow letters framed by blue background.

Other vendors offer new potatoes and bright-colored beets, fresh bread and homemade soap, sourwood honey and goat cheese. After setting up, I buy my dozen eggs from Tom, a fellow Floyd County farmer, because I know they disappear in an hour. I usually buy some of his early lettuce, too. One farmer from two counties away brings a freezer full of poultry and lamb, and Roger, another writer/part-time farmer, sets up crates of apples from his family's orchard, the russets and goldens bright in the sun. By 7:30, half an hour before market officially opens, the first customers wander in.

Like the pickers who visit our field, the shoppers come with their own tastes and stories. Some sample blueberries for the first time and go home with a quart. Others pass by, not interested in fruit, just out for a morning stroll. The market advertises local produce only, but at least once every Saturday, some bloke pulls up and asks for tomatoes and corn. He can't understand why these bestsellers aren't here, a month ahead of any reasonable ripening time for our region. He never gets out of his car.

Occasionally someone snips about our blueberry prices being too high. Sometimes I offer free samples, or preach the virtues of organic, but usually I don't bother if the nose is already too high in the air. I know most customers value our berries, value our labor in picking them, and appreciate their unadulterated health. And in fact, many people come just for our blueberries, like Walt, a retired doctor and fellow birder. He always has a quip and a bird story to whisper to me as we stand behind the table, like the flycatcher that daily tries to build a nest in his mailbox, a mass of grass and sticks that Walt daily destroys in order to get his paper.

Or Carl, a big fellow in white shirt and tie, who finds me the first Saturday and walks away with a small pint dwarfed in his meaty hands. The next week he returns and tells me he's a car salesman on the way to work, our blues his favorite breakfast. He returns every week, blueberries his only purchase.

Fellow teachers come as well, and they're always surprised by my presence in a parking lot pushing berries instead of in a classroom pushing words. Usually they want to know how long I've been doing this secret occupation, or how I manage to grade student essays and grow a farm. Only a few students ever find me, the Saturday morning too early for them. But Vesta, the housekeeper who cleans my office, always shows up. Her loud hello and bubble of a laugh make me smile every time.

Some market hours feel like minutes, the crowd steady, even thick, the berries flowing. I make change and small talk, bag purchases, and give away recipes and gourds. On these days I might sell out an hour early, turn away the latecomers, and close up shop to head home for lunch.

Some market hours feel like days, the crowd peaking at one or two people, and Jenny, the market manager, apologetic. She's a petite, blue-eyed woman with a big New York accent and a bigger hug. "I even put a photo of blueberries in our ad this week," she explains to me. I say it's not your fault, you did what you could, as I shift the containers, try to make my display more appealing. Next door, Tom, bearded, long-haired and quiet, whispers, "Maybe folks just aren't hungry anymore."

On these slow days, Jenny buys extra produce from everyone because she feels so guilty. And if I'm lucky, the health food store will buy my extra berries. But usually they don't, even though our price is right in line with what they purchase from the other side of the country. I never understand, so these leftover berries fill our freezer.

Sometimes on these slow days, Morgan, a golden retriever, visits. He likes my discards, berries too bruised to sell, and he pulls on his leash to get to my stall. His long blond coat shines in the morning sun, and he keeps ignoring my petting, pushing his head toward the box that he knows holds his treasure. Brian, his owner, lets me know Morgan should work for his treat, so we go through his routines of sit, beg, shake, and speak. After each trick, the warm tongue licks from my hand its blue reward.

To market often means to educate: we hand out recipes and flyers with directions to our farm along with the Web address. And always, we answer questions—why fresh and local and organic are best. Or how blueberries are so full of so many health benefits.

Once a new customer, a cheerful lady with curly gray hair, listens to my spiel about a study showing blueberries increase short-term memory. "Oh, I need all the memory help I can get," she exclaims as she opens her purse to buy a pint. I make change, thank her, and then help another customer, as the older woman walks off. When I look down, I see a bagged pint, forgotten. I carry the blueberries to her at another farmer's stand where she laughs and says, "Maybe I should buy more!"

Ten minutes later, she waves and drives away. Two stands down, the other farmer holds up the bagged pint and yells to me, "What do I do with these?" The customer has forgotten her pint again, and she never returns to retrieve it.

Our goal at market is to move berries, and ultimately to move people to come pick, so we don't have to. This happens occasionally with a few people, but most we soon learn would rather let us do the picking. They miss out on what Thoreau calls the sweetest labor, the holy act of gathering.

Some folks, though, do enjoy this sweetness as well. One Saturday evening early in the season and long after that day's trip to market, Sarah and I work in the finally empty blueberry field moving bird-scare balloons and cleaning up before heading to bed. But at 7:50, ten minutes before we close, we hear a car hauling up our steep farm road, and then there it is, our first Cadillac in the field. We are both beyond punchy tired, exhausted to a smelly weariness that only wants a shower and a bed.

"Who could that be?" Sarah asks. "And why do they come so late?"

"I have no idea." And I don't know whether to laugh in disbelief or get angry at the rudeness.

The Cadillac shines with a new washing, white with a blue top. I slog my way to the top of the field as an older couple jumps out. She wears a summer skirt, he loafers and a bolo tie, and they both smell freshly showered and perfumed. The older man has the warm creased eyes of someone who smiles a lot, and the grandmotherly lady carries herself with a dignity of someone used to money, but someone who also knows few strangers. I shake hands as he introduces himself and his wife as Sterling and Ellen Foglesong. I stumble on the name, have to ask him to repeat it, to make sure I pronounce it right. As we talk, I gather up two empty buckets and hand them to these so-well-dressed-I-can't-believe-you're-going-to-actually-pick pickers.

"Oh, no, we're not going to pick," Ellen chides, her face glowing in the setting sun.

"We bought berries from you this morning," Sterling adds, "and picked up directions."

I say yes, I remember you now, and I do, especially Ellen with her wide-brimmed summer hat, her ruby-bright lipstick.

"We love your berries," Ellen praises. "And we've eaten them all already!"

They both apologize for coming so late, and they both have a deep well of energy that makes me even more tired.

Sterling explains, "We're on our way to the Parkway winery for our anniversary dinner. And I thought since we were heading this way, we'd follow your directions to see if we could find you. Looks like we did!" he adds with a chuckle.

They admire the field, walk down to the first row, and see the berries still coming on, the bushes still loaded. And they promise to return the next week. I'm skeptical, of course, not sure I believe this country-club set would stoop to pick their own food.

But I'm wrong, thankfully, woefully wrong. Sterling and Ellen drive up the next Tuesday, the Cadillac still shiny. And they bring the whole family, two carloads of three generations.

And they return every year.

❧ BLUE INTERLUDE ❧
Eating Local

One hundred years ago, just about everyone ate local food. Our country hadn't yet become addicted to oil, so by necessity, our provisions came from close by, often from the garden just outside or the farm on the outskirts of town. That all radically changed when petroleum-powered vehicles replaced horse and steam, so that today we eat apples and iceberg lettuce refrigerated and shipped from the other side of the earth. The distance to a Connecticut kitchen is truly immense for a blueberry from Chile.

Thanks to consumer demand, though, eating local once again is becoming easier and more commonplace. And as more people become "locavores," they realize a wide range of benefits: the food is fresher and usually healthier; the hometown farmer earns more money; communities become economically stronger, circulating their money rather than sending it elsewhere; towns also save valued open farmland while enhancing food security; and we avoid the plethora of negative environmental problems wrought by world-traveling food. As Barbara Kingsolver likes to say, who wants to eat food more traveled than we are?

And though finding and cooking local food might take more time, might require you to eat "slow food" instead of fast, you'll also discover pleasure and neighborliness. This act of faith in one's home region promotes knowing your neighbors, those who eat all the extra zucchini from your garden, and those who buy eggs, produce, and meat from your farm. That knowledge, that neighborliness, along with the simply superior taste of fresh berries or just snapped asparagus, all brings pleasure to tongue and mind and body.

This desire for fresh, local food and the communities it nurtures has helped create a sudden bloom of new farmers markets across the United States. In 1994, according to the USDA, only 1,755 farmers markets existed. In 2008, that number grew to 4,685, almost 3,000 more. And in every one, consumers can directly connect the potato with the Powell family who grew it, the corn with the Claxton brothers who picked it that morning.

Community Supported Agriculture, or CSAs, offer another way to eat local. In this unique form of farming, members of a community become shareholders in a farm. By paying money at the beginning of the season, CSA members "pledge in advance to cover the anticipated costs of the farm operation and farmer's salary," according to the USDA. In return, they receive the bounty of the farm in the form of a regular delivery of lettuce, broccoli, corn, and all the produce the rich soil renders. Members might also purchase "shares" of eggs, meat, honey, milk, baked goods, and fruit.

Like farmers markets, CSAs also have grown in number. In 2001, one poll found 761. In 2005, that number rose to 1,144. Altogether, one source estimates that "CSAs supply more than 270,000 U.S. households during the growing season." That's a healthy dose of community sustenance.

CSAs differ widely in how they operate. Some require little of the member other than money upfront. Others offer or require more, like helping with the harvest or delivery of shares. A few, like Food Bank Farm CSA, a nonprofit in Massachusetts, distributes millions of pounds of produce every year to shelters, food banks, and soup kitchens in a four county area. Here, the community supports the agriculture, which in turn supports the community in so many ways.

The ultimate in local eating is, of course, to grow one's own, whether it's just a few potted tomatoes on an apartment balcony, or an ambitious half-acre homestead. Either way, the local eater-turned-grower anticipates that first squirt of ripe blueberry or that first bite into a juicy Brandywine. This plant that has demanded our body's energy to water and tend it, now completes the circle, gives us pleasure, nourishes us with its backyard health.

Maybe that's why one of the Obama family's first acts upon moving into the White House was to dig up the lawn and put in a garden.

They even planted a few blueberry bushes as well.

Chapter 38

❧

Homestead Hint Number 3:
Spray or Pray

When you invite people over for dinner, you clean the house, make it at least presentable. When you invite people to come to your farm and pick berries, you do the same—make the place at least presentable. And for us, this applies not only to the blueberry field, which we mow and weed, but also to our garden.

This garden has some of the best soil I've ever worked, a rich loam that crumbles easily between thumb and finger, a darkness empty of rocks and full of life. It lays by the creek in a bottomland below the house. The state road that carries all of our customers to the field cuts through our farm, divides house from garden and berry field. So when the carloads of berry-eyed pickers drive by, they actually look down into the garden. And they're not too berry-eyed to notice the plump cabbages, hilled potatoes, and shriveling, dead-on-the-vine tomatoes. This soil, rich in so much, also happens to be rich in tomato blight.

These are prize heirloom tomatoes that Sarah so carefully starts from seed on a special shelving unit that I built. These are the seedlings we so carefully water and talk to daily, and then when they are hardy and ready, we so carefully plant and stake in the garden. We nurture these babies for several months, waiting for that first juicy bite of an organic tomato.

Then about the peak of blueberry season, a moist air mass comes along bringing rain, but also heat and humidity. And like the settling of pillows, this humid air smothers our tomatoes with blight. The fungus loves the hot moisture and within two days, all our beloved tomatoes turn from a vibrant, dark green to a gray-spotted dull yellow, and then finally, to a brittle brown. The leaves flake in my hands like dried tobacco. Our dream of canned quarts of our own red fruits goes up in this blighty smoke.

Then enters Joe—Joe our neighbor who always loves to give advice, Joe who scoffs at our organic practices, Joe who grows splendid tomatoes.

After four decades of tending his fields of strawberries, Joe has decided to retire, to give up on his Red Chiefs, All-Stars, and Earliglows. "My back about give out," he tells me when I visit. "That and the deer eat me up." He still has his quick wit, but not quite the quickness of body. He pulls himself out of his recliner and leads me out to an old field. He wants me to see for myself, and sure enough, I witness huge patches of bare earth where this past winter the deer scraped away the snow and ate his berry plants, even pulling up the roots, leaving only dirt. "Can't grow nothing with this many deer," he leans on a fence post, his overalls baggy, worn shoes untied.

"But they won't touch my garden." He grins and we turn to inspect. "Watch yourself now. Don't touch that wire." He has rigged up an electric fence around his large plot of beans, greens, and tomatoes. And this isn't a typical electric fence with a safe charger—Joe can't afford such. Instead, he's strung a line from his house, wired it directly into his breaker box, and so this thin strand of metal is charged with more voltage than most, enough juice to jolt a man to the ground.

"Don't you ever get shocked?" I ask and watch as he gingerly opens the flimsy gate.

"Oh, just once or twice," he says, grinning again. He likes the danger, likes to know the deer that ran him out of business, the deer with their moist noses will touch this wire and jump twenty feet backward, snorting with fear and pain, but safely and permanently scared away from his garden.

I am impressed by the productivity of this patch. In one corner, Joe's transplanted enough strawberries for his own eating. When I point in surprise, he shrugs and says, "Couldn't give the deer the last word, you know." He's already eating beans from his first planting, the second and third short rows emerging and coming on. The turnip greens cover a wide swatch, their yellow flowers filled with bugs. "You come back in a few weeks and I'll give you some seed." He points to the greens. "Best eating in the world, and plant them once, and then you never have to plant them again . . . just step back and let some go to seed."

I admire the frilly green leaves. "How do you cook them?" I ask.

"Oh, throw a hunk of fatback in the skillet, and let that get good and hot. Then throw in as many greens as the pan will hold. Cook it down and eat it up."

He knows already that we eat little meat and no fatback, so he grins, can't help himself. "A little pork fat every now and then won't hurt you, Jim. Look at me," he pats his round belly. "Coming up on eighty and still plugging."

I just shake my head.

Joe only gets off the farm once or twice a month for groceries. And last week, I watched his red car zip by the house. He always honks and waves his hand out the window, but he never looks to the house and never stops. He fears he'll stay too long and "talk both of your ears off." But he does slow enough to peer down into the garden. And I know on his last trip he probably saw our blighted and pathetic tomatoes.

We circle his garden, inspect all the vegetables and berries, and I admire the weedlessness of it all. He just points to the worn hoe by the gate. "Out here every morning with the hoe. Have to keep up or they get ahead."

Finally we turn to the garden's center with its long row of staked tomatoes, bushy with heavy growth. At least a dozen plants, more than plenty for one person, each is tied to a stake with white strips of old cloth. When we stop by the first, I sense Joe has orchestrated this tour, has saved his prize robust plants for last. "Look at that tomato!" He leans over and roughly parts the healthy leaves. Under the mass of greenery, sure enough, a ripe and huge love apple sits.

He parts another bush and another as we walk down the row, each time admiring, each time naming the variety. At the end of the row, he spits out his tobacco. "I saw your tomatoes the other day." He looks away. "Got the blight, didn't they?"

I only nod when he looks back at me, his blue eyes twinkling.

And here it comes. "You know, Jim, you can't grow tomatoes without spraying. That blight'll just kill them all. I spray these once a week, *and* after every rain. Got to if you want to eat." He spits again, pauses.

"You just want to farm like my grandmother! But that won't work today, oh, no. There ain't no way you can grow a garden without a sprayer. Looks to me you either spray or pray! Spray or pray, Jim, spray or pray."

I know too well this argument, know Joe will harangue into the night if I engage, so I only laugh at his wordplay, shake my head, and say little.

After a while, when he's winded, he pulls out two grocery bags. "Now get you some of these." He points to the tomatoes.

"Oh, I can't, Joe. You've already given us a mess of beans."

But he insists, "There's more here than I'll ever eat, so you better take some and help make sure they don't go to waste."

So I do. I part the leaves, even though they have a film of white from the spray of poison, and I pick and pick this red fruit. Joe leans on his hoe, waits, and is quiet. He could gloat, could say like he has in the past, "I thought you were strictly organic?" But he's quiet, just watching and pointing out any that I miss.

When we walk back to the house, he hobbles side to side, and I stay beside him, even though my arms burn with the weight of his gift.

As I get ready to leave, Joe says to come back in a week or two to pick more, and, "Next year, you come up here and borrow my sprayer."

But we both know I probably won't.

Chapter 39

❧❧

Sweetness

I meet Liesel at the university's post office where she works. She is a compact, quick woman always with a slight lean forward, always moving with a certain controlled urgency. Small glasses magnify her dark eyes, and her voice still carries the deep accent of her German home. She married an American soldier, has lived in the United States for several decades, but still speaks a halting English that I love to hear, the accents and consonants still sometimes difficult. "I go back every summer," she tells me across the counter. "My sisters still live in da village and my cousin runs our family's winery."

She reads my monthly column in the local paper and asks about the berries. "You should come pick," I invite. And the next Saturday she brings her husband and visits our field. I'm at market and miss them, so later Sarah tells me about Liesel, how much she loves our field, and how much the blueberries remind her of her native land.

A few weeks later, Liesel returns on a cool, wet day, and this time I'm there to greet her, to meet her husband and sister, who is visiting from the homeland. As we walk down to a prime picking spot, the sisters reminisce about picking grapes in Germany. "We got up early to go sit in line at da river, waiting our turn for da ferry ride across," Liesel tells me.

Then Gerta her sister jumps in, "Remember on cold wet mornings like dis, how the dew water run down your arms as you pick?" They both shiver and laugh at the same time in this memory.

"Will you be here when we finish?" Liesel asks. When I nod, she replies, "Goot. I brought you somefing." I look back as I leave, and I see she picks like she sorts mail, her hands quick, her head forward, her eyes focusing on the next ripe bundle of berries. I know that unlike many pickers, this trio will pick their bushes completely clean of any ripe berries.

When they haul their nine full buckets up to the check-out hut, Liesel asks if anyone else is around. "Not that I can see, other than a few pickers down in the field," I answer. "Goot," she says again. As I weigh their berries and her husband pays, Liesel hurries back to their car to return with a bottle in a tall, decorated gift bag.

"Here," she thrusts the gift into my hands. "Dis is for you and Sarah. It's a Riesling, made from our family's vines back in Germany." The green glass sparkles in the sun, the wine offering small bubbles as I hold it up. I am amazed by her kindness and thank her with a hug.

Later, I sip and savor this gift that transports me across a wide sea to another farm I've never visited but somehow now I know.

Danica also has a thick foreign accent, though hers is Dutch, not German. She is a masseuse and at sixty, she looks like a forty-year-old Peter Pan with short auburn hair and lithe body. She comes often, usually by herself, and picks steadily, breaking only to drink water. When I pick alongside, I ask about her work, her dog, her own fruitful garden.

"I don't know, Jim, but I think I'm getting old," she tells me. "I get worn out now after giving five massages in a row."

I stop picking and just laugh, a hard, too-much-sun kind of laugh.

"Why you laugh at me?" she asks with a smile.

"Danica, you're complaining about getting worn out after giving five massages back-to-back. I'm younger than you and I get tired after twenty minutes of rubbing Sarah's back. I can't believe you!"

She just smiles wider, keeps picking, and says, "Well, it's true."

On one visit, Danica asks Sarah how many berries we freeze for the two of us. When Sarah says 125 to 150 pounds, Danica considers this for a moment, and then says, "That sounds like a good number. I think I'll pick that many, too." And she does, all by herself, taking at least three or four long days to reach this goal.

To be honest, I wouldn't mind if she picks three times this many. Early on we work out a barter with her, berries in exchange for massages. I know already her soothing touch, her ability to find the pressure points, to work out the kinks, to ease the pain. And each time I visit her massage table, Danica always says, "Every morning I eat my blueberries and yogurt and think of you two." And every season, we look forward to her welcoming hug.

One morning, Louise, Martha, and Danica all pick near each other. Even though each woman lives within ten miles and has come often to our field, they are strangers to each other. Like always, Louise introduces herself, asks where the others live, makes connections. They talk about flowers and vegetables and all three have deer-in-their-garden stories. Danica offers her latest fencing success. Then Louise realizes that Martha, like her husband Fred, is also a school board member, just in a different county, so the two talk about politics.

By late morning, Louise is about finished topping off her last bucket for the day. She turns to the others and says, "It was nice meeting you'uns, but I need to head home to spray Roundup on my flowers—the weeds are so bad this year."

The other women can't believe this. "Why pick these organic berries?" black-haired Martha asks. Danica tries to talk her out of spraying, explaining that "it stays in the soil a long, long time," her Dutch accent drawing out the longs.

But Louise, unflappable school secretary that she is, just says, "It might stay around longer than I do, but I've got to save my flowers from the weeds."

The other two realize Louise's stubbornness and don't push any further. Then Martha asks what the others plan to do with their berries. Danica says she freezes them all and eats them on her homemade yogurt every morning, a cup a day.

Louise explains, "I take them home and wash them first."

"Why? They're not sprayed," Danica asks, again incredulous.

"Well, birds and bugs might dirty them."

"You would see the bird poo poo."

Louise ignores and continues, "I don't want to take any chances. Then after I wash them, I roll them in sugar and that way they're ready to use when you take them out of the freezer."

"You roll them in sugar!?" Martha rolls her eyes, smacks her forehead. "I can't believe this. These berries don't need sugar; they're sweet already!"

Louise replies, "Oh, I sweeten everything, even Frosted Flakes."

Chapter 40

❦

Pursuing Art

A few years earlier, in the winter of 1996, Sarah and I take a Master Gardeners class at the nearby ag school. We figure we might learn something and meet some like-minded, dirty-fingernailed folks.

We have a hard time, though, with the name. Every time we make the hour-long drive to the weekly class, I always wonder about the *Mistress* Gardeners. "What about them?" I ask.

But Sarah's too busy singing the theme from *Superman* and slipping in her own lyrics. "Jim's a Master Gardener," she croons in her mock-deep voice, "here to save the world. Ask him your gardening questions, and he'll give it all a whirl." I take my hands off the steering wheel and throw out my arms, straight in front, leaning this way and that, flying with my cape fluttering in the wind. Sarah doesn't lose a beat, grabs the wheel, and keeps on singing, making up more silly verses. We even contemplate getting our own blue T-shirts with the Superman shield in yellow on our chests, but instead of a huge "S," ours would have a giant "M" for Master Gardeners.

During class, we hold in our smirks and diligently take notes. At the end of the semester, we officially pass, but the work isn't over. In exchange for all of the information, the program requires that each student complete so many volunteer hours. On the list of options and projects I see, "Write a gardening column for the local newspaper." The instructor says the last person moved away, so the need definitely exists. Most of the other options consist of forking mulch and pulling weeds in various public gardens in the region, two activities my body is already doing too much of in our blueberry field. So I write a sample column on how to choose and plant blueberries and send it in. To this point in my life, I've only had a handful of other essays and poems published, and only a few of them made money or reached more than a very small audience. I don't expect the newspaper to pay, but it could reach a crowd of 20,000 readers, something I hadn't even thought possible.

Two weeks later, I find an envelope in our cavernous mailbox and in it a kind letter from the editor saying she loves the blueberry article. Would I like to write more and become a regular columnist? she asks. And can she send a photographer to take photos of us in the field? Of course, to both questions I say yes.

So our goal of pursuing art while also running a berry farm starts to articulate itself, starts to feel a little more real, a little more possible. And while I write my monthly nature and gardening column, Sarah also pursues her own art as well as other off-farm work to help cover our living expenses and pay the berry-field bills. In 1998, she takes a part-time job at a women's shelter that has its own in-house school, a modern version of the old one-room school where every grade is taught. Here, Sarah helps teach reading to first graders and multiplication to older students, along with a variety of other subjects. But always, underneath every lesson she tries to provide security to these often abused children shocked to no longer live in their now unsafe homes.

Sarah works out the stress of this job by keeping busy at home. The half-day position gives her time to prune the bushes and always attempt to control the weeds, millions of weeds under our 1,000 bushes. And, thankfully, she develops her other talents besides pruning and wielding a hoe. As I grade freshmen essays in the living room of our tiny house, she hooks rugs, knits sweaters, or weaves baskets in the upstairs workroom.

The basketry comes, like many gifts, unexpectedly. A few years earlier, we heard that a woman down the road from us died. We never knew this neighbor who kept at least thirty goats chained around her house. We hardly ever saw her and simply called her the Goat Lady.

Another neighbor buys the property and by chance I drive by when I see him cleaning out the run-down house. He's already hauled three loads of furniture and bags of clothing to Goodwill. "But they don't want the rest of this junk," he tells me. "Especially these," he holds up coils of dyed basketry reed.

On the mound of trash that he plans to burn I see half-finished baskets. "I didn't know she made baskets," I say.

"Me, neither," he replies. Then he looks at the bundles he holds. "You want'm?"

I take the coil of reed, turn it in my hands, and then look at the piles of colors scattered everywhere. The thin slips look new, most of them dyed in rich shades—robin's egg blue, deep-hued magenta, and dark cobalt, all of them bound and labeled. I've never made baskets, never known anyone who has, and I'm pretty sure Sarah would say the same. But I'm also pretty sure Sarah could learn.

"Why not," I answer. We pile all that will fit, boxes and bundles stuffed to the ceiling in the car.

"That ain't even half of it. Come back and get the rest in the upstairs. It'll help me clean out this sucker," my neighbor says, nodding to the tarpaper-covered house. I say I'll be back in an hour with the truck.

Ten minutes later, I shout for Sarah as I get out of the car. "Come look what I brought you." My excitement doesn't transfer.

"What's this?" she asks as I hand her a string of odd-shaped oak handles.

"Basket-making material. For you." Then I explain where I found it and that "there sounds like a whole room still full of it, all for free."

"But I don't know what to do with it," she tries.

"You'll learn." And with that I shove a box into her arms and together we start making a pile in the garage.

We return in the truck, and true to his word, our neighbor takes us up sagging stairs to a room overflowing with basketry supplies. Hundreds of handles cover two walls and underneath piles of boxes full of reed. We realize there is more stashed here than any healthy person could use in a year, let alone someone dying with cancer. "Maybe she kept buying materials,"

Sarah whispers, "believing she would live long enough to weave all of these reeds into baskets."

This quiets us all.

Then I say, "We gotta save these."

Sarah reluctantly goes along with my plan, but keeps asking questions. "Where will we put it all?"

"In the storage room above the root cellar," I reply. "I'll even build you some shelves."

"How will I learn?" Sarah asks on the umpteenth trip back in.

"You're good with your hands; we'll find some books, maybe some classes. You'll learn." I hold up a bundle of round hoops of different sizes, all of them smooth and sturdy oak, all of them full of so many possibilities.

For a year, the bulk of the basket stash waits in a little shed. But in that time, Sarah reads anything we can find on how to make baskets. Then she ventures to a folk school in the mountains of North Carolina where she learns more, begins to perfect her egg baskets and the two god's eyes that join every rim to handle.

By the time we open the field in 1997, Sarah has a few market baskets for sale. When I start heading to the farmers market a year later, she has expanded her repertoire, the variety of handmade, beautiful baskets lining both my market table and the berry hut.

I keep writing also, and I even get a few fan letters and earn a little money. The strings of words, the strands of reed, help us weave together this dream of homesteading and art, and though neither talent makes much money, they both make better people as we work toward this goal of independence.

Chapter 41

Thursdays with Brian, Fridays with Chico

Like he promised, Brian, the mad mulcher, returns. And like the first time he saw our berries right after we planted them years ago, Brian takes his long strides into the field, his bushy head of black hair now the only thing visible above the plants. "These have really grown!" he exclaims as we try to keep up.

Brian brings his partner, Lizzie, a small woman with long hair and long face. Her calmness balances Brian's energy. The two of them, along with one or two others, pick for their intentional community, filling freezers with enough berries to feed several folks for the whole year.

Then the next week, Brian and company pick for the local CSA, a community-supported agriculture farm on the other end of the county. Earlier in the year, he had called to make sure we didn't mind if they did this. "We want to offer the members a fruit-share, and figure they'd love your berries," he offers.

"Sure," I say, "same price whatever quantity and whatever you do with them afterward." We don't mind if they resell them, we're just thrilled to have this many berries guaranteed to come off the field every Thursday through June and July.

.   .   .

Usually, a rainy day during the season means a catch-up day, a day to shift focus away from the field for a moment, to maybe even write a poem or make a basket. But not on Thursdays. When all the sane pickers stay inside because of downpours, Brian and company show up by 9:00. They have to pick and fill the promised, already paid-for fruit share for that week, whatever the weather.

I pick along with them. We usually have bulk orders to fill or there's always market looming just a few days away. I'll pull out a wool sweater from the winter stash in the cedar chest, and then don slicker and gum boots. Brian and Lizzie also wear wool sweaters, but no slickers and no boots, usually just worn sneakers or sandals, and one of their cohorts always goes barefoot. And to be honest, after a half hour of picking in the pouring rain, I'm as soaked as they are, my slicker having sprung a leak, my feet squishing in the ponds of water collecting inside each boot.

"Maybe we should just pick in the nude?" I joke, but the rain is so heavy that no one hears me, even though they stand just five bushes away.

And that's how picking in the rain is—so cold, so miserable, so sopping, you can't complain, for what's the use, everyone's equally miserable. You and your companions might make halfhearted jokes, but really, the pounding water blurs your vision, drowns any desire to talk, and forces the picker inward. But even then, it's just a short journey, the mind too numb to focus on coherent thoughts. Just move fingers and arms. Just shake water from hands every other handful of berries. Just reach for that next blueberry.

Once the rain slows to a drizzle, strands of mist float over the bushes. The world softens, the harsh pounding of a million patters ceases, and you can hear the individual drips as water falls inside each bush from leaf to leaf. I inhale that rich smell of drenched soil, and I still shiver, here while wearing a wool sweater in the middle of July. My fingers have numbed so much that the berries feel like cold marbles, and I keep dropping too many.

Finally, when my second bucket seems to hold as much water weight as fruit, I hike up to the shelter of the shed. Brian and Lizzie have already taken over the table where they pour their sopping berries onto a towel, and then back into a dry bucket for me to weigh. The blues get towel dried once more to prevent mold before a final pour into the waiting quart clamshells.

"Well, we needed this rain," Brian says as he readies to leave. "Let's just hope it doesn't snow next Thursday." He grins and then carries several flats of filled containers to the car. The rain has picked back up, and he tries to hurry, half jog without spilling his precious cargo. When they all pile in, the car instantly fogs up, and I can just barely see them through the wipers waving good-bye.

Like Brian, Chico comes once a week, usually on Fridays. And like Brian, Chico brings a picking crew to fill as many containers as fast as they can in order to resell our fruit to restaurants and other markets.

But where Brian leans over everyone with his lanky frame, Chico is compact, quick, a Costa Rican firecracker with hair pulled back into a ponytail. He can pick as fast as he talks, and he sells all he can pick, if he doesn't first make it into jam for himself. Chico lives part of the year at Left Bank, a hippie community, looser, even hippier than most of the others in the county. His crew consists of anyone he can rouse by 7:00 on a Friday morning. Sleepy Latinos like Pancho or bearded whites like Mike spill out of the orange van, yawning and scratching their tangled hair. Young women with infants strapped to their chests, and Dawn, a tall, smooth-skinned local, also join this crew. She is, we think, Chico's latest. Many of these folks are artists and musicians from thousands of miles away who have never seen a blueberry before. Chico teaches them quickly, the Spanish rapid, and they settle to work a bed. Usually he can only roust four others to come with him, but once he brought eight, the swarm of them overwhelming any other nearby pickers.

When possible, I pick near Chico, try to learn a little Spanish, or at least hear his stories of traveling. Every winter, he avoids our snow and heads back to the equator where he buys Peruvian sweaters, tiny Andean dolls, and other handmade items from Central and South America. During the spring and fall, he then visits a circuit of East Coast colleges where he sells these wares. He mentions baskets, and I ask him to bring them the next week.

The crew always spreads their grub over the picnic table at lunchtime, the kids crawling underneath or hording piles of pinecones. When Sarah heads to the house for a break and to bring back a sandwich for me, Chico brings out his baskets. I want to keep them a secret, a surprise. He has several—huge oval potato-gathering baskets and round hampers—but I settle on the set of nesting baskets made of pliable grasses. There are five of them, the largest the size of my palm, the smallest the size of the end of my thumb, all of them with bright strands of red, and all of them with perfect fitted lids. I pay Chico in berries, of course, and then stash this gift for my own basket-weaver under the car seat. Sarah won't see these baskets until Christmas.

Chico and his crew keep their full boxes of berries in the back of our shed until they finish picking for the day. We label them with CHICO on a slip of paper, and carefully stack one flat of blue perpendicular on top of another. At check-out time, he watches closely as I weigh and total each container. He keeps a mental tally, and he always tries to beat his previous picking record. Regularly his crew picks 75 pounds, and the one time he brings a van-load of eight people, they go home with 125 pounds.

Usually he pays for his berries with cash, but one time he pays with a check. I'm surprised and glance at the upper corner. Then I look more closely and see his signature also reads Juan.

"No Chico?" I ask.

He smiles bashfully. "That's my nickname; Spanish for 'little.'"

Even though he is forty years old, travels the world, and can skillfully boss a crew, he will always be Chico.

Chapter 42

❧

Scars

Right index finger, between first and second knuckle. The white ghost of a slice, now a rib of tissue where the scythe slipped as I sharpened it. Witnessed the white of bone. Should've had stitches.

Left index finger, near third knuckle. Another braid of white, again deep enough for stitches. This one from butchering my first deer, a doe shot at back edge of field.

Right ear, boom-scar from gun blast, same deer.

Right hand, first two fingers, second knuckles. Handle of wheelbarrow pinched and scraped both fingers against corner of shed. Didn't spill load of mulch but sucked blood all day.

Little finger, right hand, first knuckle. Swollen with arthritis from who knows what—too many pruner cuts, too many weeds pulled?

Left hip, deep in the muscle, no sign. Felled a tree at field edge to bring in more light for bushes. Then when dragging the top into the woods, I tumbled backward hard onto log. Even had a CAT scan and physical therapy for that one. Years later it still flares when overworked.

Right shin, scar only in memory. Fang marks from copperhead.

.   .   .

Sarah?

Right knee creaks by fourth week of season from the thousands of squats done to pick the millions of berries.

Right hand, all knuckles ache halfway through month of pruning from so many hand-squeezes of pruning shears.

Both knee and hand ease to normal when season and pruning finish. So, no scars, yet.

Both of us, all four eyes, outside corners. Wrinkles from too much sun, too much squinting for blue.

What other scars lie hidden in our bodies, lining skin, joining buried fractures? How else has this land shaped us as we have shaped it?

Above my writing desk, I keep a photograph taken in Pennsylvania woods, at least fifteen years ago. It is one of the first of Sarah and me. We have been cutting firewood with my parents, splitting the wheels of oak and cherry, chunking it all into a beat-up pickup. We wear flannel shirts and knit caps. The leafless trees of autumn form the backdrop.

We stand side by side, facing camera, sideways-hugging, forcing back grins. I grasp splitting maul in gloved hand, hold it up by my side like a pitchfork. Sarah does the same with the ax. Our youthful, woodland version of American Gothic.

We are twenty-three. Our skin is smooth, our faces unwrinkled.

What will we look like after fifty years of this, of pruning bushes and picking berries, of splitting oak rounds, stacking cherry, feeding the fire every morning, shutting it down every night?

And how long will our own fires burn?

Even if we die with no memories of this farm and this field, our bodies will never forget.

Chapter 43

❧⁂❧

End of a Season

I dream of picking blueberries. My hands reach out and I watch fingers, *my* fingers, pluck berry after berry after berry.

I stand in the middle of a field, our field, our creation, and I am alone. No one has picked yet, the branches arch with so much ripeness—prime picking, we call it. I should fill one bucket from just one bush, yet no matter how fast I pick, the pail is always empty.

We have no berries picked for tomorrow's market, so I hurry, the fireball of sun a poor companion in this vast field. For a moment I rise like a bird and look down on my own blond head, my moving hands, and then I can see the whole field, the rows and rows of bushes leading to beyond the horizon.

How will I ever pick so many berries?

And then my hands twitch me awake.

By early July, I have this dream at least twice a week. By the end of the season, it feels like I wake with a handful of blues every night. Sarah, too, suffers from these dreams. Sometimes her twitching hands wake me, and I gently hold her till the shaking stops.

. . .

We wake to a tiredness ten days of sleep cannot relieve. All of the hustling and phone calls, all the picked pounds of blueberries, all the hours of wearing a "perma-grin," of tending people as well as plants . . . all of it we know, thankfully, will soon have an end. We just have to figure out when to close for the season—too early and you waste fruit; too late and you frustrate pickers. But then one morning we walk the field and realize only Berkeley has any berries, the other varieties already picked over and empty. We set this weekend as our last day open for the year, and then call the gleaners.

They come from nearby towns, the four of them part of a network of volunteers organized by a Catholic group. They gather what farmers miss after a harvest, to glean a field and take these gleanings to local soup kitchens. The leader, a thick-haired man with black-rimmed glasses, thanks us for giving them these last berries, and then admits that none of them has ever picked before. They've harvested corn and tomatoes, but never blueberries.

I take them to the bottom of the field, to the late-ripening Berkeleys. These bushes usually grow from only one or two canes as opposed to the other varieties that put up fifteen stems each year. And the Berkeleys bend at odd angles, framing their inner air in funky borders and edges. They are beautiful bushes and always remind me of bonsai trees.

But they are also some of the hardest berries to pick, hiding their treasure inside several layers of leaves. So I part the branches, show the gleaners where to look, and tell them to peer into each bush from many angles. They'll still miss a few, but the birds, those evolutionary gleaners with wings, will take care of the rest.

While they pick, I sit at the picnic table with calculator and notebook, our blue-covered record keeper of the field's progress. For every berry picked by every customer through all of the five-week season, we write on its blue-lined pages, a daily tabulation of years of work. It becomes our log-book, our memory bank of names, dates, and amounts, our ledger of income for this field into which we have invested so heavily.

I swat at a fly buzzing my head as I flip pages, punch in the weekly sub-totals, check my numbers. Then I write 6,123 and circle it several times. Here in 1999, the field's fourth year, it yields over 6,000 pounds, three tons. I slap the table with a happy "Yes!" because this target number means the plants have matured. All of our work getting them established, mulching and fertilizing and watering and pruning, all of it finally "paying off" with a good crop. We have 1,000 well-tended and happy babies producing what the manuals say they will, at least as a good target early in their lives. Will they produce more, even double this amount, like some manuals predict, or is this it? Who knows, but to be honest, they appeared so loaded in June that I can't imagine them bearing much more.

Then I look at the other number, the money amount—$7,955. That's respectable, I think for a moment. We can go out to a few expensive restaurants and celebrate with that amount of income. But then I remember I have to deduct the season's expenses. And I remember how last year the accountant deducted depreciation on the bushes, the tractor, and all our other long-term expenses—great for saving on taxes but not for showing a profit, not for making enough money to live off of. Then it settles in again, like it did last year—the realization that it will be a long time before we break even, let alone have enough to even pay one of us a salary. My exuberant "yes" fades to nothing.

The gleaners slow-walk up the steep field, each looking tired but content. They've been at it two hours and have only found a bucket of berries each.

"I wish you could've picked more," I apologize.

"Oh, no, this is terrific," the leader replies. "Such a peaceful place; we really appreciate you letting us come and pick." They say they'll take the fruit to the local soup kitchen and know the diners will enjoy.

I weigh their berries, add the small poundage to the field's total, but add nothing to the money column.

Part IV

Prune

(2000)

a round door that mirrors
the round O of my mouth
so a door into me swallows a door into the world

Chapter 44

❧

Pruning

Over the years, Sarah has become an expert at pruning. She's been at it the longest, with weeks of hours alone in the field tending these plants. So, in the few seconds it takes her to walk from one bush to the next, she can see where the new one needs to be cut, which canes should stay and which come out. Even though each differs from the last, Sarah with her quick vision can see what each blueberry needs to become.

She kneels in the spring-wet mulch before a plant, leans in to part the canes, and separate the one to cut. Right hand holds pruners that snip soft cane; left hand pulls out the spent fellow, untangles the red and yellow stem from its remaining brethren.

"You want a balance of the old and new growth," Sarah tells me when I try to pitch in to help.

I know that, I think to myself as I kneel and stare into the snarl of canes. Then I add, "You make it sound easy." Sarah doesn't hear my low whines, just works ahead, and I try to catch up.

I count the lichen-covered older stems and cut out one bent and another broken. On the last I have to use the bigger, two-handed pruners, the gray wood thick and resistant. When I lean in to make a cut, branches scratch my shoulders, brush my cheeks, tap my head. "I know, I know," I whisper to myself and to the bush. "Don't take too much." The thin, young canes slice easily, the inner wood a white eye of circles, growth rings counting years. When I add the spent to the pile, this eye looks out onto the world for the first time.

And finally, when I forget about keeping up with Sarah, when I just focus on the plant and lose myself, I, too, begin to imagine what each bush needs to become, begin to see what to cut and what to keep.

Snip, snip, dead and broken stems first. Pause and look. Concentrate on what is and what could be. Then work to bring some openness to the berry bush's interior. Try to imagine a space in its heart large enough for a sparrow to fly through. Create that space, and then move to the next.

What do I need to cut . . . what do I need to keep . . . to allow a sparrow to fly through my heart?

When the work flows, when the pruning comes easily, the mind can roam, can wander through its many fields, some blue, some not.

One field it returns to often is this: Why have we struggled so to find friends, to feel like we belong here in this place, this county? For the five weeks of high summer when the blueberries roll off of this field and all the pickers roll in, we are overwhelmed with people, many of them becoming friends for an afternoon. But in my journal at the end of one season, I write this short poem:

> We grow blueberries and a little more.
> I want that more to grow more.
> I want to find wholeness, but instead find
> a taillight, an empty bucket, the end of the season.
> We grow a community that reshapes itself each day,
> then disappears.

And for the forty-seven other weeks of the year, we are alone, in this field, in this life. Often, we like it that way—the meditative quiet, the richness of birdsong.

But not always.

In a sense, we are pruned because of what we value, what we've chosen, and where we live, because of what we do and don't do, because of who we are in our oddball lives. Just as we spend months of afternoons in this field intimately pruning each bush, we, too, are pruned by these blueberries.

What to cut, what to keep?

We prune in the dormant season, usually starting in October and hopefully ending by bud burst in April. We never prune when the thermometer reads 32 or below, though, cutting in colder weather risks injuring the bush, so say the books. Besides, the fingers stop working well when it turns too cold.

Sarah averages 3 minutes per plant, her actions steady, her pruners swift. I'm lucky to get a bush pruned in 5 minutes. That's 3,000 to 5,000 minutes per year, 50 to 80-plus hours spread out over sunny afternoons when Sarah comes home from her part-time job, or on weekends when I can help.

And here in this dormant season when no berries need to be picked and no leaves shade a bush's inner air, in these moments I come closest to realizing a fantasy I had before we ever bought a single blueberry. Back then, I thought maybe I could know each of these plants, could recognize them individually, could even greet them by name. Such a foolish idea. The volume of work and the quantity of 1,000 bushes quick-cuts this fantasy from my mind, prunes out that sucker of wasteful energy. But still, now as I lean in to take a cane from a Bluecrop, I recognize for just a brief moment the bush as a bush and not just a small part of a larger field.

And I say hello.

The textbooks all say that cutting old canes encourages new growth, to prune in order to promote health. But the plants teach us what this health looks like. I see last year's cuts heal over and then sometimes sprout new growth where we don't want it. Or other times, the bush behaves as we envision. So much depends on the variety, the sun and rain and fertility of the soil, on this history of cutting. And so much depends on the cutter, how well we listen to each bush, how much we learn from these professors in this school of blueberrying.

Given proper pruning, how might our own lives grow and become healthier? What fruit might we both bear? Maybe Sarah's right—maybe we should just be happy hermits. We have this field, we have our dogs, our art, this meaningful work, and we have each other. Maybe that is a sufficient grace.

We pile the pruned branches at the end of the beds and then fork the heaps into the back of the truck. I climb on top and tramp down this airy mass, bounce the whole pickup with my jumping. Down the hill we unload, fork out all that we forked in, sweep the bed clean of these now dead sticks. With each trip, the pile grows to the size of a garden shed, Thoreau's cabin, a hippo waiting to swim in the nearby pond.

When the weather is right, we wad the news, stuff its black print into the pile of grays, yellows, and reds, and then flick the match to burn any pests that might survive winter. The dry canes flare to a moving curtain of blues and reds, cane colors consumed, transformed into these other brilliant shades by the flicker of flame. The heat warms us on this spring afternoon, even makes me sweat as the pile slowly falls into itself. I rake the half-burnt ends back into the hot center, then lean again on the handle, out of the smoke, to watch the spents disappear.

The flames die down, and the hippo becomes just a circle of ash and embers. Into these glowing coals, we push our "hobo-dinners"—potatoes, onions, and carrots that steam in the foil.

And in so doing, the bushes, one more time, feed us.

Chapter 45

A Different Dream?

During the winter holiday of 1999–2000, Matt and Melanie and their two kids, Savannah and Everett, visit us on Berry Hill Road. They are Sarah's brother and his wife, and their children are our only niece and nephew. Since we don't have children, these two youngsters are the closest we'll ever come to such a thing.

They plan just a daytrip to see us and hike around the berry field, but it starts snowing even before they arrive. By the time the kids jump with a shout from the van, two inches cover the ground, with at least another four inches predicted. These, our kinfolks, live near Charlotte, 150 miles south, where snow of any amount is a rarity. The thrilled munchkins run around trying to catch falling flakes on the tips of their tongues.

In the house, Melanie stands drinking tea and looking out, white flakes sifting along the windowsill. She has a dimpled smile that creases deeply with pleasure as she watches her family through the glass. Outside, Matt builds a snowman with Savannah, who is six, and Everett, four, their shouts and squeals muffled by the falling snow. Everett tries to keep up, rolling his own ball while Savannah's grows bigger and bigger. Matt runs back and forth between the two of them, and when he sees us watching, he makes a snowball and throws it at us. "Guess that's his invitation to come play," Sarah comments.

As we pull on our winter coats, Melanie asks, "What do you think of letting us spend the night on the floor?"

We say yes, of course, and offer the sleeper-sofa.

"No, we'll have a campout under the dining-room table, if you don't mind. That'll just add to the fun they're having."

Soon we're all bundled up, including our four visitors who wear any and all of our extra coats, caps, and mittens. I shovel clear the shed door and haul out the sleds. Savannah has her mother's light blue eyes and spiritedness, and though she's never ridden a sled before, she wants to jump on immediately. "Slow down, kiddo. I have to make a trail first." I sit and glide, lean my body to the right and yell "yippee" as I make a long sweeping curve through the meadow. After I climb back up the hill, Savannah wants to go solo, but Matt insists they take the first ride together. She screams with delight the whole way down.

That night, after the kids fall silent in their sleeping bags, we four adults drink beer and talk in the next room. Matt has his father's quietness, his blond hair cut short, his carpenter's hands calloused as he holds the bottle. He and Melanie have visited us in the past, especially Matt who has hunted this land and helped build our berry hut and repair the root cellar. They know how much of ourselves we've invested in this farm, and they also understand our struggles both to find community and to somehow balance teaching, farming, and our desire to create art.

I've been around Matt enough to recognize when he has something important to say. Usually he just likes to work, letting the task at hand fill any silence. But now, I watch him slowly pry the label off of his beer bottle, keeping his eyes focused on his fingers. Melanie talks about the kids' schools, but all of us wait.

Finally, after a pause, Matt starts. He says he's tired of his construction business and wants to find a new job, something with benefits and a steady income. And they've been thinking about moving to the country, selling their place.

Then after another pause, he adds, "We were wondering if you two would want to join us?"

Sarah and I are both too shocked to say more than "Whoa! Where did that come from?"

Matt tells of how they realized driving up here that the four of us together could buy a huge parcel of land and share it. "We'd be neighbors," he adds. And we all understand that means we could be more involved in Savannah's and Everett's lives.

"We never thought about leaving this place," Sarah finally replies. She looks at me, searching my face, and I smile and shrug.

"Maybe this could work," I add. "Give us a few days to think about it."

Matt's question forces open a door we thought we had nailed closed forever. Sarah and I had planned on spending all of our lives on the banks of Lost Bent Creek, planting our own roots right along with the roots of 1,000 blueberry bushes, having our ashes spread here on the pond's still waters. How could we leave this homestead, this blueberry dream?

And how could we not? I remember my own childhood, my great love for my grandparents and uncles and aunts who all lived within walking distance. Given this chance to have family for neighbors like I did and to be a part of our niece and nephew's childhoods, how could we not at least consider the options?

So, tentatively we agree and say yes to this hard-to-fathom idea. "But this new place has to be absolutely beautiful, far better than our blueberry farm," we add as a contingent. They understand we could stay where we are just fine and so they start searching.

Through that winter, we spend several weekends with their family, exploring back roads and valleys we've never visited, even sections of our own county we thought we knew. We climb to the top of Will's Ridge for an amazing view, but the terrain is all steep, all wooded, and all rocky rough. We journey to other counties, other mountain land that has been subdivided into a fragmented development, or another with a cutover forest, the ground covered with a maze of tree tops, all the destruction hard to walk through, let alone live in.

And then in the spring, through the Internet, Melanie catches a glimpse of a landlocked farm located 75 miles from our berry farm. I'm away at a conference, so the next weekend Sarah meets Matt, Melanie, and the realtor to have a look. Within five minutes, as the realtor drives them to the top of the high knoll with its 360-degree view, all three know this is the place. They trade glances when the realtor isn't looking, Matt even pretending to reach from the front seat into the back for a snack, just to give a secret thumbs-up. So the whole two hours as they drive over the many fields, ford the stream to another hilltop, journey through this farm's 200 acres of woods and meadows, the whole time their bright eyes say yes, while their quiet mouths say only maybes. They don't want the realtor to know how stunned they are by this place, so they question the lack of clear right-of-way, the steepness of the roads, or the price.

But all I hear later, over and over again, is how beautiful it is.

I am doubtful. How can something be better than this blueberry farm, this Eden we've created? The next weekend, Sarah takes me for a tour on a cold clear day in April, the sky so blue I feel we have entered a domed cathedral. We want to see the land on foot, so we hike through hidden coves and narrow valleys, by quiet streams and a giant sycamore. We wander through woods covered with cohosh, bloodroot, and other forest medicinals, plants that could heal us simply with their beauty. On an open knoll, we sit to take in the long view of Iron Mountain to the south, and other mountains we can't name to the west and north. And as we rest there on that grassy slope, we watch a figure fly across that ceiling of blueness toward us. It is an osprey gliding so low over us, I see the yellow of its eyes. It sweeps the surface of our faces with its white wings, and all I can say is yes. Maybe there are other lives to live, other Edens to find, other dreams besides blueberry ones.

We call Matt and Melanie to say yes. Then we make an offer, draw up a contract, and wait. This new farm has far exceeded our restrictions, but now our business partners have a contingency of their own—they have to sell their home in North Carolina first.

A month later, after countless would-be buyers walk through their house, Matt and Melanie have to tell us that no one is even close to a final deal. Our joint contract and offer on the new farm in Wythe County falls through and all four of us try to forget it, try to move on.

Another month after this, in early June, Matt tells us he's been hired by the Charlotte fire department. He's found his ideal job, which also means they plan to stay in that area. All four of us realize that any chance of buying land together has disappeared.

And besides, Sarah and I have a field of ripe blueberries to harvest.

Chapter 46

❦

Uncle Nathan

Every Christmas, I sign cards to relatives and friends with COME VISIT! But seldom do I expect anyone to take up this offer. We live too far away, in the middle of nowhere, and everyone is always too busy.

Except for Uncle Nathan. He is my oldest uncle, a bachelor who ran the dairy farm for over two decades, who struggled with depression all those long years, who sold the cows and now works as a night watchman at a factory. He takes some of his vacation days and drives the 300 miles to spend four nights on our sleeper-sofa.

Nathan barely fits on this lumpy bed. A big man, both round and tall, his graying curly head hangs off of one side while his massive feet dangle off of the other. And always, Nathan has been slow. Not dumb, just slow. He graduated from college, but didn't really survive student-teaching, so he tried office work, only to get laid off. That left the farm where he lived with his parents and took over the daily running of the small dairy, improving the herd and fields, but always at his own pace.

As a child and then a teen, I worked for Uncle Nathan, putting up hay, feeding the cows, building a huge shed. Always Nathan didn't really walk but instead shuffled his feet, moving from cow to milking machine where he poured in the gallons of milk, then moving on to the next cow, all of it to the rhythm of the slow-pulsing milker, a *thump-thump, thump-thump* that filled the warm, white-washed barn. Like his mother, he loved feeding the calves and cats, and always, at some point in the milking, he poured warm, fresh milk into a huge pan and called, "Kitty, kitty, kitty." The cats would circle and hunker down, a ring of calico around a circle of white.

The only time I ever saw Nathan hurry was when a gate busted and the cows headed toward the busy highway. Nathan trotted then, sneaking around the herd to push them back to safety. And afterward, like so often, he bent his head to the side and scratched behind his ear before glancing up with a smile and saying, "That was close."

So when Uncle Nathan comes to visit our blueberry field in Virginia, we try to have a list of to-do jobs to keep him busy and entertained. The first year, he comes early in the season, before we are overwhelmed with berries, and the two of us fence in our half-acre yard to keep the dogs safe. He taught me how to build a fence around his Pennsylvania pastures, but here on our farm, he just follows along, does what I ask, unrolls wire, holds posts while I pound. And I realize then how much he has always been content to follow, how much of a burden all the decisions of the farm must have been, how he has never acted like the oldest son that he is, always deferring to my father, the second-oldest.

The next year Uncle Nathan comes later, right at the peak of the season, and so we have smaller jobs. And besides, we realize he is in his late sixties, not in the best of health. Instead of building fences, Nathan helps me make deliveries. We haul our blue pints to two grocery stores in the county, and I give him a tour of the small town that serves as the county seat, complete with its singular stoplight, famous for being the only one in the whole county.

And always, Nathan picks blueberries every day of his visit. Some he takes home to freeze in his apartment refrigerator, and others he donates to our cause, knowing we seldom have enough for the weekend market. He might see us hauling in four buckets to his one and comment on his slowness, but I shrug it off, say he's here working on his vacation, say we appreciate any he can pick for us.

In the evening, after Sarah's special blueberry slump for dessert, we sit on the porch in the lightning-bug-lit night. Uncle Nathan knows our family history, knows generations of relatives before even he was born, so I always try to learn the family tree, all of Grandma's nine siblings. And I ask him about the blueberries that Grandpa planted, what varieties he chose and how he planted them.

Or I ask Nathan about the family barn that burned before I was born, how it started with a broken electrical wire, how Grandma grabbed the red-hot chains to release her cows, how the cinders smoldered for days after, and how all of the neighbors pitched in to rebuild. I want for a while to feel this sense of community that once embraced Nathan and me and our whole family, this sense of community I miss now even with so many people coming to pick our berries. Like those burn scars on Grandma's hands, this history, this sense of community I want to hold on to, want it to burn into me.

Chapter 47

What Else?

The April-time accountant confirms my summertime figures: here in the year 2000, five years after planting, the farm isn't making enough money. When you throw in all of our unavoidable expenses, including tractor, bushes, and the land itself, we are making zip, zero, zilch. No, worse. We are making *negative* zip, zero, zilch. We're in the hole, and if we don't want any trench-coated IRS people to come knocking, we need to make the money figures change for the better. But how?

If we want to keep at this and really make a life as well as a living, we need to expand. We need to sell other things.

Throughout the season pickers often ask, "What else do you sell?" We might point to a few drinks and even a locally published blueberry cookbook, but usually we mumble, "Just blueberries," unable to meet their expectations for more. Their questions, though, make us realize we have an audience, captive even—so why not build on this expectation?

And this leads us back to our art. I have no books to sell—yet anyway—just a few pieces here and there, a regular column, and a huge pile of rejection letters worth negative zilch. Sarah, though, has begun to excel at her newest art that might make a little money. Ever since childhood when her grandmother taught her to knit, Sarah has worked with her hands, making scarves and sweaters, then hooked rugs, and now baskets. After we stumble on a stockpile of free supplies, Sarah spends a week at a basket-weaving "camp," coming home with five beauties she made there. I know without asking she was the top student in her class.

So through the fall, winter, and spring, Sarah spends all her afternoons either tending the blueberries or making baskets. Her father constructs hat trees that she hangs her finished artwork on—egg baskets, wall pockets, birdhouses, and market baskets of all sizes. Our workroom overflows with coils and handles and piles of finished woven containers. Some winter days when snow closes all schools, I sit at the computer writing while Sarah weaves strands through spokes and handle. The tan reed makes a hissing sound as she draws it through the weavers, and then the end flies out and taps the floor, a quiet dance to a percussive song. Sometimes the reed flings out to tap one of our sleeping dogs, making him jump. Sarah always coos, "I'm sorry, little Grover," and the mutt flops back down to soon sleep again.

We plan to sell these baskets in the check-out hut, a hat tree full of them right beside the scales, and I'll take a bunch to market as well. Folks will recognize their beauty and utility and buy a bunch—we hope.

I also spend the winter developing a new product: shiitake mushroom logs. I hear about another farmer in the Midwest selling already-inoculated logs, and think, *I can do this*, I can become a mycology salesman, a "fun-gi," even! I've already inoculated oak logs for our own mushroom eating, so why not do it for others?

I order more spawn and head to the woods. The mushrooms colonize and grow on logs, preferably oak. I cut and drag out fifteen small logs, all short and skinny enough for an average person to carry and move. In the garage, I drill each with a series of holes, and then Sarah taps in the spawn plugs and seals them with wax. The logs will sit in the shade till summer, the mycelium or fungus "roots" spreading throughout the wood. During the season I'll take a few to market and in the field we'll lean two or three by the berry hut door. I have no idea if or how well they'll sell—or how many people in our rural part of the country even can say the word "shiitake." But I figure it is all worth a try on a small scale.

. . .

And then there is the idea of expansion, which leads to the question, Is this right? Do we really want to grow more blueberries? I have to keep remembering the goal in all of this as I grade another stack of essays through the long winter. The teaching is supposed to fund the blueberries, which eventually should provide enough income for us to quit teaching, stay home, and pursue our art. But what if that plan won't ever work? What if the means obliterate the ends?

Already, I've felt the lack of time to write during the summer. Before the blues, we went on vacations to the beach, and I'd often spend days in our cottage pouring out words held back by a year of teaching. But now we don't ever vacation, and worse, I have little time to write. Will enlarging the blueberry field solve this problem, or just compound it? Will that sparrow even find my heart in all the tangle?

And that gets at a deeper fear: What if we fail? What if we stop growing blueberries, stop being blueberry farmers? What then?

I try not to dwell too much on this last question—it is too unsettling. Instead, I plod on with carrying out our plans to expand, filling up the remaining cleared half acre with long rows of dreams. With Sarah's help, I lay out new beds and figure we can put in 200 more bushes. No double-rowed beds, though, that make the picking and mowing difficult. We've learned that much at least.

I plow up the dozen beds, the tractor straining against the earth, the soil turning over in rich, brown furrows. Then I haul out fifty-pound bags of sulfur. In the six years since we cleared all of the pine trees, the soil has "sweetened," has become more neutral. The sulfur will acidify the soil, bring it back to what the berries like, but it takes a year or so to work, a year at least before we can sock any new bushes into this new ground.

Every soil amendment has its own texture and odor. In the main field now, I spread dried pellets of chicken manure as fertilizer, most of the odor baked out of it in the drying process. We first used cottonseed meal, the green powder having a tang to it, not pleasant, but bearable. The worst fertilizer, though, was the fish meal we tried one year, a gray, flaky powder that knocked me back every time I ripped open a bag. And, of course, the worse the smell, the more the dogs loved it. As I spread this fishy-stench of a dust, the two mutts would tag along behind, licking the ground as fast as they could before I chased them off. We never used fish meal again.

But this sulfur packs more nose-whacking thump than the fish meal. It makes me remember a spring my family used to visit back in the Pennsylvania mountains when I was a child, a seep of water we had to hike two miles to reach. It had sulfur water that stank so much that my cousins and I dared each other to just sip it. We might pretend to swig from our cupped hands, but only my great-aunt Hazel seemed to really drink, seemed to think it improved her health.

So I open a bag and smell concentrated rotten eggs. Think a whole, hefty sack full of them. Think a whole pickup load. Nothing to do but wear a face mask, rip a bag, and sweat through the stench. All around me, the dust rises and hovers in a copper-colored cloud. And this dust cloud follows me, sticks to sweaty skin, creases along my neck, overpowers even my own body odor. The dogs don't even think about licking any of this, and when I call them for a petting, they run away. And they usually eat rotten eggs.

I roll up the last empty sack and drive the long road home for a shower, the fresh air through open windows cutting some of the sulfur stench. All the while I wonder if this is the smell of more blueberry dreams.

Chapter 48

✿

Hired Help

We hire Katie to pull weeds with us from the bases of bushes where the weed-eater can't reach, and the three of us crawl on hands and knees into the jungle of ripening green. We hire her to squish bugs, especially Japanese beetles and earwigs, and Sarah and I try to help her perfect the quick-catch and pinch needed to dispose of the fast insects. But mainly we hire Katie to pick and sell berries. We want to try a bigger market, and though I don't know Katie outside of the classroom, I'm sure she can handle these tasks.

Of all the thousands of students I've taught in twenty-plus years, Katie is the only one to write a truly comprehensive exam, tying together Thoreau and O'Brien and a slew of other authors into a coherent, brilliant essay. It is an exam I still read and use as a model. Add to these smarts a responsible, conscientious, hardworking, outdoor-loving personality, and you have the ideal employee. We are thrilled when she says yes to our offer.

Her genius hides behind an open face, round with pale blue eyes all framed by long hair. And this openness also describes her personality, which is another way to say that despite her academic brilliance, Katie is gullible. I can tell her an outright absurdity, like blueberries evolved from monkeys, and she'll believe it, at least for a few minutes, before saying, "No way!"

In the field, on a Wednesday before we officially open for the season, the three of us pick for market and for our own freezers. The early varieties have started to ripen, bluing up like the sky above us. A midnight storm with its giant broom swept out any remaining clouds to leave us with one of those sun-bright, blue-struck days too beautiful to imagine. It is a grand way to start the season. Though the field hasn't yet reached "prime picking," we find plenty and find again that familiar soft patter as berries fill empty buckets. And now we have a third companion to ease the load and share stories.

We work Bed 1, and Katie tells us of picking huckleberries in the woods of her childhood on the Chesapeake, "but they were never this big or easy to pick!" When I lend her a belt to hold the bucket at her waist, she remembers tactile lessons in physics from her father who sometimes spanked her, but always first let her choose the belt. As a child, it took her a while to pick the right one. I remind her that my picking belt is a loan, that I need it back, and she says, "Oh, you don't need to worry about that." She has no fondness for these leather straps.

While we pick, Katie talks about her anthropology studies. "I'm finally doing something that I've been reading about for years, now," she jokes. "I'm becoming a hunter-gatherer!" Yet she's serious, too. She talks more about "walking in the work of ancestors," of "how the hand and body seem to know how to do this picking automatically." I have to admit that I've never thought of picking with such a long view.

But Katie also has a short perspective. She sees a whole cluster of ripe berries, a rarity this early in the season, and she shouts, "Wahoo! This is like playing the lottery. Like how you never know what you might find with the next bush or the next ticket? Well, I just won." She holds up eight plump blues all from one bunch, all of them picked in one hand, in one swift motion.

Despite her lottery find, Katie doesn't have Sarah's quickness for picking. As the day wears on, though, she shows a steadiness and endurance. She tells us of her adventures hiking the Appalachian Trail, of squirrels raiding her food cache, and of hiking too many miles to find a dried-up spring. That kind of endurance I see now as our backs tire of the bending. The pull of blue weight restrings tired muscles, and the sun penetrates the wide sky to paint our bare necks red.

When we break for lunch in the shade, Katie's openness gives us a new light into her life. She tells us of her boyfriend, of how they've been together for eight years, yet no matter how much she tries, he still doesn't communicate, except in fits of anger. He sounds like someone not nearly good enough for this sweet woman, but Sarah and I only speak of this to ourselves later.

Instead, I shift the conversation and ask Katie more about her anthropology fieldwork. She says that while picking this morning, she remembered a Pentecostal preacher she interviewed a few years ago who liked to say, "higher briars, bigger berries."

"He'd repeat this after any accomplishment, large or small," she speaks in a quiet way. "And I always thought he was right, you know? The deeper the thorns gouge you, the greater the reward."

Then she waits a long moment, looking out over the field. "But this morning as I watched how easily you two work together and talk with each other, I realized maybe the preacher is wrong, maybe life can be sweet without the cuts. After all, blueberries don't have thorns."

None of us say anything for a long time. We finish our meal and stretch our tired bodies before refastening bucket and belt, and heading back into the patch.

A few weeks later, Katie brings this boyfriend of eight years to the field. She has already picked and sold well over 200 pounds, and despite the backaches and sunburn, she has fallen in love with this field. She wants to share it, and us, with him. But when they first drive into the field, he doesn't come to meet us. Instead he slips into the dense greenery of bushes while Katie walks up the shed steps to say hello.

Later we find him, his broad, tattooed shoulders hunched to a bush, his brick-laying biceps thick. We introduce ourselves, but the brief conversation makes me realize there is no way into the walls he creates. As I walk away, I hear him say to Katie, "I've had enough of this." Then, as he picks up his bucket, "Who needs so many berries anyway?" Katie hangs her head and just stands there.

He waits in the truck while Katie slow-walks to the shed to check out and say good-bye. She who last week picked eight pails in a day only has had time to fill a half bucket this morning. She had hoped to make jam, but she looks at her berries and knows it is not enough, not enough even to bother with freezing.

Before she walks out the shed door, she apologizes to both of us, her eyes dull with the knowing of what we've witnessed. Sarah simply says, "You deserve better." From Katie's half smile, we know she knows this, too.

But like us, she also knows the power of dreams, whether they are for an ideal partner or an ideal way of life that revolves around a blueberry field. And all three of us know how hard it is to let go of such dreams.

It takes Katie another year to finally let go of this person who has dragged her down so long. And it takes Sarah and me that long to also real- ize that maybe blueberries do have thorns.

Chapter 49

❧❧❧

Regulars

When we open the field on the first day of the 2000 season, we find a car jam. So many people hear of our blueberries that the parking area overflows with twenty-five cars. "Hope we have enough berries for everyone," Sarah whispers to me during a mid-morning break. We have just checked out a long string of people, and in the lull we look out the window of the berry hut and both wonder this same question.

"So far, no problems," I finally reply, and look back inside at the piles of labeled and full boxes already lining the back walls. Many of our regulars have returned, so as we shuttle people and berries up and down the field, we also visit, try to catch up with these folks we haven't seen in a year.

One of the first pickers to arrive this morning is Ruby, Ruby with round glasses and curly, dark hair, Ruby who went berry-spying with us before this field even existed, Ruby who now is a widow. Her husband Rudolph had a stroke during the winter, and now her shoulders seem a little more rounded, her step a little slower. For many years, she and Rudolph worked in the local elementary school, she as a teacher's aide, he as the school custodian. But really they were the resident grandparents, knowing every child, doling out candy and hugs as well as scoldings and reprimands.

Once, while Ruby was Sarah's aide, the class slowpoke, a five-year-old named Aaron, kept dillydallying with his coat. He didn't seem to mind that the rest of the class had already left the room and walked the long hallway to find their buses. Aaron just kept fiddling with his pockets, emptying contents into his lunchbox, humming his own little tune. And Ruby kept prodding, kept saying, "The buses are going to leave without you, Aaron." She did this at least a dozen times, her temper brewing, patience disappearing. Finally, they both heard the roar of all the bus engines starting up, the sound funneling down the hallway, and Aaron realized he'd better move. He slung on his coat, grabbed his lunchbox, and scurried out the door with Ruby right behind him. But then he stopped five steps down the hall and turned to her, "Which bus, Ruby?"

Ruby just threw her hands into the air and yelled, "Any bus, Aaron, the first bus, the middle bus, or the last bus. I don't care which one, just get on a bus and *go!*"

When she walked back into the classroom, Ruby chuckled and admitted, "I probably shouldn't have said that, but it just came out." Sarah just grinned and agreed with an oh, well.

In the field, Ruby has brought along her son, Josh, a teacher at the local community college. He, too, has the sloping shoulders, a certain sadness hidden by wit and chuckles. Ruby thankfully has held on to her rich humor; her first words to me as she gets out of the car: "I'm still here. The vultures haven't come, and I still haven't sung yet." We both laugh, and I'm glad to see her head-tilted-back, mouth-full-open, joyous release—she still has that laugh hidden within. One of the first times I ever met her was in the school parking lot. I joked about the long day finally ending, and Ruby replied, "Oh, no, it ain't over till the fat lady sings. And I haven't sung yet!" Then she tilted that head back and cackled. It is a joy to see this again, and later, to hear it across the field as she settles in to pick our berries.

An even earlier set of pickers is Amos and Pearl. A month ago, at the end of May, the couple called just to check, just to make sure we'd let them know when the berries were ready. Hard of hearing, Pearl yelled into the phone, while I listened to Amos in the background telling her what to say.

A muffled, "Ask them if we can come early like last year."

Then so loud into my ear I have to hold the phone a foot away, "Can we come pick before eight in the morning, like we done last year?"

"Sure, Pearl, we'll call you when the berries are ready and you tell Amos the gate will be unlocked." Because of their age and their aversion to heat, we let them come early, which means 6:00 A.M., two hours before everyone else.

So when we drive up this morning before the crowd arrives, there sit thirty pounds of already-picked blues, six buckets lined up on the bench waiting for us to weigh and check them out.

I yell out a hello and set about opening up the check-out hut, putting out buckets and drinks. I glance down into the field to see round Amos has already sweat-soaked his T-shirt, and Pearl sits on a stool. They work a bush together, one on each side, talking soft to each other, but sounding loud to us. I hear Pearl ask if he finished that last bush. Then after he says yes, "Well, you missed some." She stands back up to hobble over and pick a small cluster.

I head to the first bed to check on them. As I near, I hear Amos talking over the bush about the upcoming Galax Old Fiddler's Convention. Pearl turns to me, says, "Amos's famous. This will be his thirtieth year at the festival, camping the whole week."

"Oh, really, Amos? I didn't know you played bluegrass. What instrument do you play?"

And without slowing his hands as they fill another bucket, Amos looks up, smiles, and quips, "The radio."

Long-necked, exuberant, goofy Laura is another regular, another picker who returns at least once a season, usually more. A single mom, she lives on a farm across the ridge, where she raises ponies and two sons in a house as old as ours. She has wide eyes that act like the dots under the exclamation points that end just about every one of her sentences.

"Oh, Jim and Sarah! Guess how many bats live in my house?" she sparkles as she climbs out of her pickup truck.

"Forty," I venture with a smile.

"Oh, no, double that! The boys and I count them every evening at dusk. We stand there in the yard and out they come, squeezing through the gable vent and swooping down over our heads. Quite a show!" And on the word *swoop*, she waves her hands all over her head like she's swatting a thousand horseflies.

"And these bats are wild!" she flings her long ponytail behind her. "They sink into the walls beside my boys' bedroom and then they make noisy love all night. We can't get any sleep!"

Later, with her two buckets overflowing, Laura begins hiking out of the field, but she can't, she keeps stopping to pick one more berry here, and then another there. And then she lets out a loud, "Oh, you poor bush!" She stops by a plant so loaded that its canes arc to the earth under the weight, berries dragging the ground. Laura shouts to us on the other side of the field, "Jim and Sarah, I'm going to report you! Berry neglect! Berry neglect! You could go to jail for this abuse."

I hurry to see what she's yelling about and find her kneeling by the bush saying, "Here, sweet baby. Let me pick just a few from this clump and maybe that'll help."

Another regular who greets us with a hug is Tessa, tall with short, gray hair and a smile like she knows some secret. She, too, has a keen sense of humor, though more subtle than most. She might shoot a sideways glance after a sly comment, checking to see if we catch the joke. Usually though, she just looks the other way, holding in her chuckle. And usually the joke targets Simon, her husband, who has his own badgering talents.

They live along the Parkway where they retired from upstate New York, Tessa's native ground. Simon, though, has an accent that warbles of his French homeland. He is a small, wiry man who wears his own specially designed straw hat. "I like your hat," I tell him the first time they come to pick.

He grins and pulls it off to show me. "Zee rim shades my eyes." He gestures, one hand holding the frayed hat, the other pointing to sweat-stained rim, the hands making small, quick movements like chickadees. "And I cut zee top off to vent my head, to get zee air moving," and with this, he waves his free hand in circles above his curly red hair.

"I bet it works well," I comment. "I think I might need one."

"Oh, oui, oui, you do! Just find a cheap one and cut away." Then with a flourish, he pulls it down tight over his eyes, jiggling the two crow feathers that jut straight up like weather vanes.

Once they settle to filling their buckets, Sarah and I make bets on how long Simon will last. He usually tires of picking, and sure enough, an hour or so later, I find him at the shady picnic table smoking one of his hand-rolled cigarettes. We don't allow smoking in the field, but for Simon, I don't mind; I love his proud accent, love to hear his words flow like a calm wave.

I sit down beside him, pull out my lunch, and offer him some chips. He takes one and then another, kindly nibbling his way through a whole bag. When he finishes, I offer him a few carrots, and he munches through them as well, talking the whole time. I hold in my grin; I want to see how much food he'll eat, but I also want to hear his stories.

Between bites, Simon tells of coming to America, meeting Tessa at work, and marrying her in a big church. "And zat, I'll have you know, made me a French Yankee!" He slaps the table in laughter.

After lighting a new cigarette with a puff of smoke, he adds, "Then we moved here to zee south and now"—pause and a puff—"that's made me an official French hillbilly!" Again, a slap and a big grin.

I ask about his childhood, and he shares stories of searching for truffles and picking berries in the Alps, the whole village hiking out on certain days every year to fill their pails. He leans in close, scrunches up his eyes in quiet rapture. "My relatives zere, zey make zee best blueberry liquor. Oh, my, so good. And from a secret recipe," he whispers, then smacks his lips and rolls his eyes remembering the potent sweet taste. "Everyone zat come to visit has to taste. You should go, you should go!"

When I finish *my* half of *my* lunch, we both walk back down to check on Tessa and her picking. Sarah joins us and tells Simon she studied French in school years ago. He grins when she breaks into the French national anthem, and he hums along, swings his arms to direct the band as she joyously sings this march. When Sarah finishes, we all clap and Simon takes off his straw half-hat and bows to her, saying, "*Merci*, Madame Blueberry. Beautiful! Your teacher taught you well . . . especially—how do you say?—the nasal intonation. Not many Americans get zat. I'm impressed!"

Then Sarah remembers French Christmas carols, and she begins singing them. Simon again hums along to "Silent Night" and "O Come All Ye Faithful." But one tune, "Bring a Torch, Jeannette Isabella," shocks him; he's never heard it before. "Imagine!" he exclaims. "I'm sixty-five and never hear zis song until today. I have come all ze way to Virginia to learn a French carol from a hillbilly!"

Later, when Tessa and Simon come into the hut to check out, we almost make the mistake of combining their berries. "Oh, no," Tessa says, shoving Simon's one bucket away from her three. "Weigh his separately, and definitely don't put them in the same container." She looks around, makes sure Simon is listening. "Look, honey, if you had picked more we would have at least another bucket, maybe two."

He just waves his hat like he's heard it before.

"Why do you keep them separate?" I ask.

"Oh, I have to freeze his in their own container. Look at the difference! See how many leaves and green berries are in his bucket?!" And then, without saying more, she tilts the two buckets forward to compare. In his, I see slips of leaves and twigs along with mashed berries, green berries, and a few nice blueberries. Then in Tessa's, I see only blue, nothing green and nothing pointy like a leaf or stick. When I look back into her face, she only smiles and shrugs.

When I look at Simon, he just waves his hand and scoffs. "See what I put up with?" he asks.

"Yes, see what I put up with?" Tessa echoes. They both hold back smiles as they argue, and I can tell by their half-grinning eyes that this tired argument only fuels their love.

We carefully pour their blueberries into separate dishpans, and then after a slight bow to Madame Blueberry, Simon, usually the gentleman, grabs his container and heads out the door, leaving Tessa to carry her three full pans. I go to help, but she says, "No, you have other things to do. I'm used to this." Then in the doorway, she turns to add, "He'll get his share of these, too. I just want to make sure he appreciates them." With that, they get in their car and drive away, silent at least for the first few miles.

❀ BLUE INTERLUDE ❀
Blue Lit

The blueberry hasn't reached the apple's fame in our literature, and thank goodness for that. Who would want to have "mal" as part of its Latin name, permanently labeling it as a "bad" and "evil" fruit? No, the blueberry hasn't received such infamy, but it has been picked by some outstanding writers, showing its blue face in prose and poetry.

One of our country's best nonfiction writers, John McPhee, captures the life of Pineys and blueberries in his famous book *The Pine Barrens* from 1968. The author tells the story of one of the domesticators of blueberries, Elizabeth White, serving the New Jersey transportation officials tea and blueberries. Afterward, she asked them to plant this native luminary along the state's many highways. How could they resist this charismatic woman? So today, blueberries line Jersey pikes.

McPhee also writes about the people bused to the Pine Barrens from Philadelphia to pick these Jersey fields. The "real stars" of this troop earned good money for a day's labor. But these busloads of pickers also included folks just wanting a day in the country, drunks who passed out between bushes, and whores who lured men into the nearby woods. On the trip home, the bus drivers sold the tired pickers cheap wine cut with soda water.

So the Pineys, those denigrated souls, appear better than the city folk recruited to pick. And the blueberries just offer a stage for our many human stories.

Of course, the most famous literary debut our hero made came as Mark Twain's *Huckleberry Finn*. And like so often the case with our protagonist whether blue or huckle, he was chosen because the name implies humbleness. As Twain once purportedly said, "'Huck Finn' was all that was needed to somehow describe another kind of boy than 'Tom Sawyer,' a boy of lower extraction or degree."

In poetry, the blueberry also fairs well. Diane Lockward in her "Blueberry" poem, calls it a "[t]iny paradox, tart and sweet, homely / but elegant. . . ." Laid out on her counter, they become "strands of blue pearls." This fruit transports her back to childhood, where her mother made blueberry pancakes, the "blueberries sparkling / like gemstones, blue stars in a gold sky, / the universe in reverse, / the two of us eating blueberry pancakes." The blueberry triggers this memory and saves this moment of bliss.

Another poet, Amy Clampitt, in "Blueberrying in August" describes picking wild berries on an island, the berries "sea-spray-fed chromosomes / trait-coded, say, for eyes / of that surprising blue. . . ." This blueberry also carries her to other people and places, but in the end she returns to this particular moment of picking. And after the last berries are picked, "living even so, minute to / minute, was never better."

Pulitzer-prize winning poet Mary Oliver falls asleep in a berry patch and describes the moment she wakes in "Picking Blueberries, Austerlitz, New York, 1957." A deer interrupts her nap, a creature "so busy with her own happiness" that she "stumbled against" the sleeping poet. And in that moment of the deer's "stalled breath of . . . curiosity," Oliver sees the animal's "flower of . . . amazement" and holds onto that memory for over thirty years.

So the blueberry, for Oliver, acts as a portal, a place "to be absent again from this world / and alive, again, in another." No wonder the poet ends by asking the deer: "Beautiful girl, / where are you?"

Finally, there is Robert Frost and his praise for this humble native fruit in his poem, "Blueberries." Here the speaker finds in a nearby pasture,

> Blueberries as big as the end of your thumb,
> Real sky-blue, and heavy, and ready to drum
> In the cavernous pail of the first one to come!

The speaker and his friend remember other times, "How we used to pick: we took one look round, / Then sank out of sight like trolls underground. . . ." They pick for hours, competing with birds, moving from bush to bush away from each other. Then one picker, thinking he has "wandered a mile" from the other, gives a shout for his companion. He's surprised when his partner stands up beside him.

Frost understands this language of blueberries, the dew of the morning, the soft *thump* of the filling bucket. Like all of these writers, he helps us know this berry in a different way and leads us to a field full and waiting where the "blue's but a mist from the breath of the wind, / A tarnish that goes at the touch of the hand. . . ."

Chapter 50

᯼ᘏ᯼

Buckets

One nests inside the other, holding the shape of itself.

Upside down, the stack of buckets rises, a pillar of plastic, a column of contained air spilling onto the floor.

In May, I load the pickup truck with these stacks of red and white, and haul them to the house. One by one I hold them in the tub and let each bucket become a vessel of suds. Once scrubbed, the containers dry on the porch, each a barrel of sun.

At the berry hut, a stack always sits beside the door, like wallflowers at a dance, waiting to be picked. The lucky ones slide away from the crowd to swing on their partner's arm, promenading through the patch. They square-dance their way through the bushes, making their own music, the lolling low timpani of just-picked berries.

They are hungry dancers, wide-mouthed and in love with the taste of blue. They lip and swallow each tender globe. As they swirl among the other dancers, do-si-doing a bush, they fill and pitch and roll and slow till they have become an overflowing tumbler of midnight wine.

Their partners carry them then, like heavy sacks, up the hill and into the shade of the shed to rest. Like yesterday, like tomorrow, they are emptied, they are cleaned, they are stacked to wait for the next dance.

Chapter 51

❦

Variety

As the seasons and years progress, we learn which catalog description turns true and which so long ago sold us glorified flops. Bluecrop, for instance, lives up to its reputation as the industry standard. This variety gets planted in the greatest numbers throughout the country, and for us, it and its cousin, Blueray, yield the most, at least seven pounds per bush, their fruit-laden canes bending with sapphires. They grow vigorously, prune easily, and taste great. I sometimes watch pickers disappear into the jungly bed to pick a full bucket in just one spot.

Of our two early season varieties, Spartan yields especially good tasting, large berries on an upright, easy-to-tend bush. It quickly becomes our favorite both to grow and eat, though we never tell customers, of course. If they pick often enough, they usually come back to these bushes on their own. Before too many customers clean them, we try to fill our freezer with these, one of our sweetest and largest berries. Patriot, our other early bush, bears well also, but nothing like the sweetness of Spartan. Neither Patriot nor Spartan yields as heavily as Bluecrop or Blueray. And despite our loving care, for some unknown reason, Spartan seems to wither away as the years pass.

Our two late season varieties, Nelson and Berkeley, only have timing in common; they differ in just about every other way. The Berkeley grows upright, sometimes only on a single cane as thick as my wrist. This definitely makes for easy pruning, but not always easy picking. The large, sweet berries often grow up under the bush's canopy and require extra searching during picking time, but oh, are they sweet! Several customers specifically request Berkeley, passing up the early varieties as they wait for these to ripen.

Few customers, however, request Nelson. I know of three in all of our years who specifically return to pick this, the one variety we regret planting. Again, we never reveal this mistake, never share how hard we have to prune this bush's dense thicket of canes. Instead, we talk about its uniqueness. It makes good pies and wine, we say, never mentioning its tartness.

One Saturday, though, Sarah and Donna, a longtime customer, walk the field, tongue-testing their knowledge of the varieties. They pick a few from each kind, and then give a different sample to the other person in random order. Sarah, who knows these berries best, gets stumped on one berry, its sweetness a sharp surprise. Donna knows our dislike of Nelson and laughs when Sarah discovers that this is the berry she has just eaten.

We learn then, that any berry, if it hangs long enough on the vine, will give of its sweetness, if we only have patience.

❧ BLUE INTERLUDE ❧
Blue Movies

Our hero was actually a cowboy hero once, in a movie, even titled *Blueberry*. Mike "Blueberry" Donovan rides out of a comic strip and into this French, psychedelic movie set in the American West. Of course, he saves his girlfriend and rids the town of the bad guy.

Then there was *My Blueberry Nights*, that drop-dead nonthriller starring drop-dead gorgeous Norah Jones. So much for this blues singer's movie debut. Blueberry pie is what no one eats in Jude Law's bakery. Yet he keeps making it, hoping for someone to take a bite. Along comes Jones, who feels sorry for herself and the blueberry pie, so she takes a piece. Jones admits later that if she were addicted to anything, it would be blueberry pie. In the end, she falls asleep on the counter, after eating her pie, and Law bends over to kiss the crumbs from around her lips. So our hero the blueberry acts as the love potion, the sweetness that draws them together, the excuse for a kiss.

Probably the cutest role our hero has had in the movies is in *The Sound of Music*. Maria has fled the von Trapp family, afraid that she is falling in love. But all the children miss her, so they go searching without any luck. When they return, their imposing father greets them in the yard and asks where they've been. They pause, seeking a believable alibi, when finally Friedrich, the oldest son, says, "We were berry picking!" The others chime in, saying there were "thousands of them" and the youngest shakes her head and says, "Yes, we were picking *blueberries*."

But Captain von Trapp's half smile reveals his disbelief. "Isn't it too early for blueberries?" he asks.

Friedrich, now sensing a trap of his own making, quickly says, "They were strawberries."

"Oh, really?" queries his father.

"It's been so cold lately," Friedrich hurries, "that they turned blue!"

And with that, the children hurry inside. Our blueberry has rescued, though clumsily, this swarm of kids. And also, our hero has shown the growing softer side of Captain von Trapp. Maybe he, too, will kiss the blueberry pie crumbs from around Maria's lips.

❧❧

Chapter 52

Kids

Occasionally some picker will ask if we have kids, usually an adult from one of the fundamentalist, home-schooling clans, a parent with four or six of her own. Often these families come from nearby "villages" that they helped create, gatherings of folks from all over the country who form their own enclaves in preparation for the Y2K that never happens.

"No, no kids," I'll reply. "Just two dogs and one thousand blueberry bushes. Plenty enough. That's what we want."

Sometimes they'll look at us with pity, and to temper my temper, I've learned to change the subject. I've also learned that they probably will never understand why I might believe in helping this planet by lessening the human population, and I'll never understand why they believe in having so many kids. So talk about something else and keep the customer happy. After all, the more mouths to feed, the more berries they have to pick. So hold it in, Jim.

But I do love kids, love to witness their wide-eyed wonder, to hear how they make new meaning of our old language. Like Heather, the daughter of a colleague, who said "more" for the first time when she wanted another handful of her favorite bedtime snack, Heather who for years always called this beloved treat "blueblerries."

Or Samuel, one of the Hoover children, a Mennonite family of seven and growing. Every time they pull up, six-year-old Samuel is the first to jump out of the van, yelling, "Jimminick! Jimminick!" He runs and gives me a hug, then grabs a bucket and buckles its handle to his waist, just like me. He has to wrap his father's old belt two times around his skinny middle but there the bucket rides, and there he'll pick it full.

Samuel has yet to learn that "Jimminick" is really two words, so every time he finds something of fascination, like a delicate green lacewing, he'll cry out, "Jimminick! Jimminick! Come look at this!" Who cannot hurry to such urgent love of this world?

Some children (or is it their parents?) don't know how to channel this energy. And it doesn't matter the social class or religion—hippie, Mennonite, rich, or poor—sometimes Sarah and I have to step in to make the uncomfortable confrontation. The kids will be playing in the outhouse, pretending it is a castle as they climb on the roof, or making the shaky door creek in a constant cicada rhythm. Or instead of picking berries, they rip up our bushes, breaking branches, squishing unpicked fruit. Despite our sign (PLEASE SUPERVISE YOUR CHILDREN) and despite our tactful comments when they jump out of their vans ("We love kids, but please make sure yours behave"), the parents just gab away, ignore the destruction.

One time, my held-in temper boils over: I have watched a pair of scrawny boys run not around, but *through* several bushes, and from one hundred feet away, I can see the broken branches. Finally, when I see one child fall *into* a bush, I do my own running and surprise them by suddenly towering over them. I grab the two red-faced hoodlums by their upper arms, a pincher hold on biceps that my own mother used to transmit her anger.

"Where are your parents?" I demand.

No response, so I pinch harder, glare into their faces. One half-points to the other side of the field. I drag them in that direction, their other arms trailing behind.

I approach a woman in expensive running pants, fashionable glasses. I remember her getting out of the pricey SUV, remember her fruitless yells as her boys took off, ignoring her.

"These yours?" I am out of breath.

She nods, a bit of fear creeping into her eyes.

"They've been running through our bushes for the last half hour, breaking branches and disturbing other pickers. Either you control them or leave." And with that, I thrust the boys forward, release my grip, and storm off. I know from memory that my fingerprints will leave bruises on their upper arms, but I don't care. I leave the field and hike down to the pond, getting rid of the pent-up rage. When I return, twenty minutes later, the boys sit in their van, kicking their feet and pouting, making sideways glances of anger my way. But at least my own children, these fragile blueberries, are safe for now.

By far, most kids, and their parents, are well behaved. And most of the older generation wants their offspring to see where food comes from, to enjoy both the picking and the eating. Our doctor, Ryan, for instance, plans on coming to pick on his one day off, to bring his three-year-old son, a child with thick black hair and a pointy nose like his papa. But the doctor's afternoon off also becomes the sunshine's time off, and instead of a hot, muggy midday as usual, we have a long, cold, hard rain—good for the berries, but not for picking. Only the three of us in the whole field, we wait a while in the shed, the drone of rain on tin roof drowning out our words. Ryan and I try to make small talk and watch his son, Sidney, explore Sarah's baskets.

"This isn't going to stop, is it?" he eventually asks, and I agree.

"Sidney," he calls the boy. "Come on, we're going to go look at the blueberries." The boy doesn't understand, only sees sheets of water as his father hoists him onto hip. And out the door he runs, the now-crying child jiggling beside him. The doctor yells, "Look, Sidney, look at these blueberries! See how big they are?" They pause by a bush to pick and eat a few, but all I see is water running down the boy's crying face, and even as I stand under the rain-deafening roof, I can still hear the child's wails. Ryan keeps laughing, running from bush to bush, even belting out, "Singin' in the Rain." All the while, they both become totally drenched.

Finally, the father jogs back under the porch and puts the child down to retrieve some towels from his station wagon. "That was fun, wasn't it, kiddo?" he wipes the child's hair and face, then his own. The child just sits on the steps, sniffling and looking at his feet.

After Ryan buckles the child into his car seat, he slides a flat of berries beside his boy who has brought the gallons of rain inside. That morning, the doctor had called ahead to order ten pounds of berries prepicked, in case it rained. "Thank goodness for these," he says as he takes the second flat from me. And then to the boy, "Look, look at these blueberries!"

When given one of these edible marbles, the child with hair plastered to his forehead finally quiets and smiles.

And then there's Paul, a five-year-old who wears a floppy-eared, boisterously colored knit cap with a dangling ball on top. It only partially hides his thick curls and huge blue eyes. One sunny morning, the field full of berries and pickers, I find Paul gingerly tiptoeing into the middle of a canopy of bushes, with walkie-talkie in hand. Once hunkered down, he whispers into his little box, "Granma, Granma, can you hear me?"

Five bushes away, his grandmother pauses from picking and speaks into her walkie-talkie, "Yes, Paul, I hear you. Where are you?" All the while, she looks the other way and pretends to search. "I can't see you, Paul, you must be far away."

Then the happy boy pops out of the bushes and shouts, "Here I am!" and Grandma and parents cry out with joy. But Paul doesn't pause. He hurries to scuttle into the jungle of the next bed, and the game of hide-and-seek-with-walkie-talkies continues through the morning.

Eventually, with some cajoling, Paul abandons his walkie-talkie and decides to pick some berries, but only big berries, only those the size of nickels and quarters. The cap has come off, so now his curls bounce in the sun as he runs from bush to bush. He searches each, squatting to look up into a plant, reaching his stubby fingers in to pluck one huge globe to add to the three already rattling in his bucket.

I get on my knees to help him. "Oh, Paul, look at this one!"

He comes racing, bucket over chubby forearm, other arm pumping, his face red and sweaty. "Where?" he shouts.

"Right there," I point to a blueberry hidden at the base of a plant. "It's huge!" Then without thinking, I add, "That one's all yours; it has your name written on it, Paul."

He plucks off this blue treasure, turns it in his fingers, a furrow above his eyes as he examines the berry closely. Finally he asks, "Where? I don't see my name. Where is it?"

While we all laugh, he pops this round, nameless berry into his mouth and runs on searching for the next.

Chapter 53

❧❧❧

Spies and Lies

The spies are easy to recognize. They don't hurry into our field with their buckets like most pickers. Instead, they amble nonchalantly, trying to stay close to us as long as possible, trying to ask so many questions without appearing too inquisitive. But usually, their fifth or sixth question concerns how many pounds come off of our acre, and after I answer, I can see the calculators in their heads punching pounds times price per pound to arrive at a nice figure. Then I add, "We're still not breaking even."

But that doesn't burst any blueberry bubbles—the skin on these dreams is too thick to bust so easily. And I've had these dreams, too, know how easily they shade out any doubts. "Oh, well," I'll mutter to myself and hurry to the next customer.

An hour or so later while we weigh their berries, the spies will ask a few more questions about varieties, soil amendments, or such, pretending to want to grow for their own family. I usually counter with my own questions, "How many do you plan to plant?" or "Where do you live?" If they live far away, I relax and talk easily, but if they live nearby, my answers stay short. There exist already several blueberry growers in this region; I don't know if the market can stand many more.

But who am I to stop these dreams?

.   .   .

We still resort to some spying, too, as well as a slight deception. Before the season opens, I call two or three other growers. I've met these folks at least once, so I have to disguise my voice, give it a nasal, uppity air. "Yes, hello, I'm interested in coming to pick your berries this season." Sarah's in the living room looking the other way, but I can see her whole body shaking with laughter. "When do you plan on opening?" Pause. "Yes, and how much do you plan to charge?" The two vital bits of information secured, I quickly say thank you and hang up. We want to raise our prices, and yet we don't want to send pickers to other places with a too-high figure. So a few phone calls nets what we need.

And then there is the opportunity for fame and free publicity that calls for a little bit of lying. A large regional newspaper accepts an article I write about the field, and they even pay—a little, anyway. But the editor wants a photograph, and he wants it in early May, and he wants it to have people picking. Though the berries have another month before they turn ripe, another month of greenness, the editor can't wait.

"But," the editor tells me finally, "the photos will be in black and white. Think you can make it work?"

I catch his pass and call Donna, our curly-headed neighbor, and her two kids, Sophia and Caleb. We know her quick wit will love this minor greenberry scam, and sure enough, she agrees, driving up in her huge Ford pickup the next Saturday, a bright, clear spring day.

Soon after she greets us, Donna grabs buckets, hands two to her kids, and yells out, "Wonder how these berries taste?" We all head to a bed and gather around a few bushes. "My, look at these huge berries!" Donna exclaims as the photographer clicks and moves around us.

Donna has prepared her kids well, and they, too, join in. Young Caleb proclaims, "I've never seen such green berries!" Older sister Sophia tries to get him to eat a few, but Donna interjects, "Now, Sophia, you're supposed to look out for your little brother, not kill him."

All three smile and make the motions of parting bushes, of cupping handfuls of berries, of moving hands from plant to bucket. Donna even pretends to sample, says directly to the camera, "My, these are the best green blueberries I have ever eaten."

The newspaper comes out the next month right as the berries really ripen and we open the field to the hundreds of pickers. We have a huge stack of the issue in the check-out hut, and we pass out free copies of the story and photographs to every customer. And every time Donna comes to pick, we all laugh. Only we know of her hidden acting talent, and only she and her kids know the real story.

Later, after our season ends, we still need to do more spying. We haven't decided on what to plant in the newly laid-out beds. We know they'll be blueberries, but will they be highbush like the rest of the field, or rabbiteye, a type of blueberry recommended for farther south? Even though the literature tells us not to grow this variety here in the mountains, one farm an hour away has done so for several years. Their ad in the classifieds always pops up in early August, after our season has finished. So, would these rabbiteyes give us a season-extension boost, or would they just be harder to sell since most pickers assume blueberries grow only in the summer? And besides, by August, most families are focused on school, not blueberries.

Sarah ventures to find out, and she goes by herself. We figure she'll be more anonymous that way, since my photo appears in the local paper once a month with a column I write. No need for both of us to blatantly spy when one can do it alone well enough. So off Sarah travels, wearing ball cap and sunglasses, and she's so paranoid that when she arrives, she introduces herself by her maiden name.

This new field, Sarah finds, looks a lot like ours, set on a mountainside, looking down over a narrow valley. And the berries are plentiful and good-tasting, though smaller because of the late-summer drought. She spends an hour picking several pounds, chuckling at herself for spending money on this fruit when back home we already have a chest freezer full.

But mostly Sarah listens. She hears the owner talking with another picker about the great trouble they've had for several years now trying to get people to come. "Everyone assumes the berry season is finished when our bushes are just beginning to bear," the woman complains. And sure enough, Sarah sees a field full of berries and not many people. She decides there in that field to forget about experimenting with this new type of blueberry. We need to stay with what we, and our customers, know and expect.

Sarah pays and sneaks away unrecognized, sunglasses finally coming off, secret mission safely accomplished.

Chapter 54

❧✿❧

The Jazz of a Perfect Weed

From childhood on, Sarah and I both have been overachievers—straight-A students seldom satisfied with just the grade. We had to have the most creative papers, the best art projects, the highest A-pluses. So when we become blueberry farmers, you can imagine how well we tolerate a prickly weed or buggy berry. The jazz of the blueberry field cures us of this, in some ways at least.

Take weeds, for example. (I used to say take them all home if you want.) Every blueberry manual says berry bushes have shallow roots. Each mass of rootlets fills the top two feet of soil and supposedly doesn't tolerate weed competition. This translates from manual to Minick-head: "Absolutely no offbeat weeds allowed." So we chop and hoe and grub and pull every single mullein and thistle and slip of grass. All the while I keep hearing Joe, our neighbor, whisper in my ear, "Just a little Roundup would take care of that."

But no, we're organic, and instead of spraying, organic farmers control weeds by cultivating. So sharpen that hoe and get to it. No time to cultivate yourself when the weed seeds are about to pop and spread.

I even cut off the handle of a new hoe to shorten it for Sarah. This customized chopper allows her to get under the bushes, to root out all that flourishes in the mulch, all that sucks up the water and fertilizer intended just for berries. The too-long handle no longer whacks the bushes, but it does little to save Sarah's knees or back.

We spend the most time hacking at red sorrel, a low-growing, fibrous-rooted perennial that thrives in the same acidic soil as our blueberries. And the six-inch layer of chipped mulch that usually smothers weeds only aids sorrel. The lemony leaves form thick mats and within a season, they totally cover the mulch. "Nothing like mulching the mulch," I try to joke, try to ignore the hours spent hauling and raking, now obliterated. I pick a leaf and chew its tangy sweetness. "Hey, it's certified organic—we could sell it," I quip, knowing sorrel is edible in small quantities. Sarah just shakes her head at my halfhearted jokes.

To fight the sorrel, I buy an expensive weed-eater. With goggled eyes and plugged ears, I spend days hacking at this wicked weed with a motorized string of nylon. Always, my back burns from the slight lean forward, the weight of the machine. I move slowly, trying not to girdle any berry canes but also letting the weed-eater pulverize the mulch and soil. I want to reach the sorrel's roots, pummel them to shreds. The green growth splatters my glasses, the rocks and wood chips cut my face and hands, fly up to bruise knees. I keep my mouth shut to avoid a broken tooth.

A month later, the sorrel's red-tint carpets the ground once again. I start up the weed-eater, its noise drowning out all else, even the music in my head. Maybe one more shot will wipe out this evil, I hope, but it never does.

After the first few years I finally fathom two ironies about sorrel, bugs, and blueberries, about the music of this field. Our records show that Bed 5, the strip of land covered with the worst sorrel, actually bears the most berries. It seems the sorrel bothers us more than the bushes.

Obviously I've misunderstood this plant. Instead of an intruder, could it be a part of the band, the star trombonist and not a ragged outlaw? Why not encourage its own tune, let it grow as a living mulch, to shade the soil, feed the bugs, and spread its own fibrous root system for free?

Let it join this blues chorus of one million players; let it take the limelight even. Set up a billboard: NOW PLAYING: THE PERFECT WEED.

· · ·

And there is this: Once while weeding, Sarah finds a box turtle, tiny and just-hatched. In the dark soil, it has waited and grown, and then egg-toothed and clawed its way to light and new life.

Months earlier, its mother felt the warm softness of this soil and dug into the duff of mulch below bush and sorrel. There she laid her round, soft eggs and then covered the hole. I would guess she knew that through the summer, the eating under these bushes could not be better, the overripe fruit falling from above. She had given her offspring a good start.

The hatchling, its shell the size of a quarter, squirms in Sarah's cupped hands as she walks to find me. Together we sit in the shade and admire its orange-rimmed shell, its eyes gold-ringed and curious. The carapace flexes, tough yet tender like a fingernail. I want this shell to grow hard and smooth and blacken with age. We have found other turtles on this farm, turtles that wear carved inscriptions dating them to the 1930s. I want this newborn to furrow through the sorrel, to eat bugs and pick berries, to live long.

And then there is this irony: the sorrel in every bed crawls with lady beetles and their larva called aphid lions. One spring I mark off a square foot of weeds and methodically count; I want to see how many beetles actually live in this small space, this miniature, lush jungle. They all move, happy it seems, mating and egg-laying, and, of course, gorging on aphids and whatever else thrills them, so I have to count three times. Each time I come up with at least twenty-five: twenty-five orange-crowned creatures in one square foot, all humming and feasting and flying into the bushes to find another meal and save our berries.

I kneel there and realize I've missed this quiet music, this big band of bug and bush, predator and prey, weed and soil. And I'm part of the band, too, if only I lay down that jackhammer of a weed-eater and take off my earplugs. I've helped create this song.

So pull out your drumsticks, your trumpet, your director's baton, and play along. Let those saints come marching, praise that lucky old sun, and watch that moon stand still on blueberry hill. Play along, play along.

❧ BLUE INTERLUDE ❧
Blue Songs

For years, we humans have warbled our love of our protagonist, Mr. Berry. Johnny Mercer in "Moon River" calls his beloved river "my huckleberry friend," and he's not the first or last songster to connect our hero with love.

Take Bette Midler's "Blueberry Pie." At first, blueberry becomes the substitute for a lover who "walks on by." But soon enough, the singer realizes her profound love for blueberries, because, as she confesses, "I love you, yes I do, / 'cause, Blueberry, you're true blue / . . . so very berry blue." Her song then becomes an ode to our hero where she sings, "I love a Blueberry. I hug a Blueberry. / Oh, yes I do. . . . / Irresistible you! Irrepressible you!" Midler even turns the noun into a verb, saying "Blueberry me!" She ends this ode with "Oh, he's so necessary. He's so necessary. / Blueberry Pie!" Her love complete with a forkful.

Blueberry's love is hot and fast in The Mamas & the Papas' song "Blueberries for Breakfast." Here they sing of "blueberries for breakfast, love in the afternoon," but by the end of the song, they threaten to call the cops, "if you don't leave me alone."

But in Toby Keith's "Huckleberry," this berry's love is constant and faithful. "Baby, I'll be your Huckleberry," he sings, echoing a line used by Doc Holliday in the old western movie *Tombstone*, meaning I'll be your man. Keith continues: "We'll grow up and we'll get married / I'm gonna be your Huckleberry / Mmmmm." The ballad tells of this young couple's dating, dancing, and riding on a roller coaster at the fair. Later they steam up the car windows but then she says, "Until I get my wedding ring, boy, we can't go that far." In the end, they grow up, get married, and "now look at those three little Huckleberries. / Mmmmm."

Blueberry has been featured in a lullaby by Miria L'auroel, titled "A Marshmallow Moon in a Blueberry Sky." And as an odd contrast, our hero also was featured in a rap song by Ludacris called "Blueberry Yum Yum." Here, the singer falls in love with a special drug he calls "Blueberry Yum Yum" that he "neva would of thought that it could taste this gooood. . . ." Later, he sings "I got the ultimate Mary Jane." So this blueberry "medicine" takes him far away—no wonder he loves it so.

The most famous appearance of blueberry in song is of course "Blueberry Hill." Elvis Presley sang it. So did Fats Domino, Andy Williams, Little Richard, The Beach Boys, and a long list of others. All of them found their "thrill on Blueberry Hill" where they discovered their special lover. Because of her, "the moon stood still on Blueberry Hill / And lingered until [their] dreams came true." Louis Armstrong even added his own variation where the two lovers climb the hill. He brings along his horn and "Each afternoon we'll go / . . . Higher than the moon we'll go."

But in *all* versions sung by *all* singers the song makes a mysterious leap. Something happens and "all those vows [they] made / Were never to be." So the songster ends with "Though we're apart, you're part of me still / For you were my thrill on Blueberry Hill."

So, where did the thrill go?

Chapter 55

❦❦

The Fourth of July

For two weeks in 2000 we worry about the Fourth of July. It falls on a Tuesday, a day we normally stay open. Will people come pick on their day off, or will they all stay home and enjoy barbecue and beer and then fireworks at the ball field? We don't want to lose business by closing, but we also don't want to be stuck in an empty field. Our families live too far away to visit for just a day, so we decide to stay open. We have to pick for Saturday's market anyway, so might as well keep working for our independence.

And how is that dream of independence, that vision of a homestead built on blueberries? How is the progress toward that ultimate goal of staying home to write and to weave baskets? We can't really say, can't determine because we're working so hard at growing and moving berries. We know the field will take a few years to mature, and we know it'll probably take that long to build up our market, to have the same people come year after year. But how long till we can at least cut a few cords that tie us to off-farm jobs?

The manuals say a mature acre should yield anywhere from 6,000 to 12,000 pounds per year. Our field will be, at least in our idealistic vision, the most productive as well as most beautiful acre ever created, every bush in prime health, bearing at its peak capacity, loaded with blue. So we expect the higher six-ton figure. Twelve thousand pounds times $1.25 per pound might be enough to allow at least one if not both of us to stay at home.

But our records show the field has a long way to go before it reaches even 7,000 pounds. So we keep picking, just the two of us, our full buckets parked under a shady bush at the end of the bed. I try to keep up with Sarah, my bucket belted to my waist, its weight adding pain to my back. Kneeling helps ease the deep throb for a while, but I can only reach so many berries from such a low spot. So back to standing with a permanent bow, a constant reach, a continuous coiling ache. Sweat seeps into eyes, soaks shirt and shorts, coats bare legs. Bits of bark mulch stick to my knees along with the smear of smashed berries. The humidity and the heat bend us, make us pliable as melted wax. We say little, especially by mid-morning when we realize no one is coming to pick. We, too, should've celebrated our nation's birthday; we, too, should have taken the day off. Instead we're shackled to this field and its demands.

Three bushes ahead, Sarah climbs out from between a tangle of stems, carefully settles her third full bucket on the ground, and then sits down under the scant shade the plants provide.

"I feel like that woman last week who had to change in the shed," she says between guzzles of water, referring to a customer's menopausal hot flash in our field. "And I'm not anywhere near menopause."

Then Sarah takes off her floppy hat and pours water over her head.

"That looks like fun."

"Try it." She points to my own water bottle.

"Can't. Empty already." I put down my almost full bucket of blueberries and sit down beside her.

"You know, this just isn't right. We're here working our butts off in this ninety-five-degree heat and everyone else is out having a good time."

"I know what you mean." I swig the last drops from her bottle. Through the long last hour of picking, we both have thought this, both not wanting to whine, but finally, there it is, the truth of our sorry state.

"Let's go swimming," Sarah says, the spark of an idea burning out some of her tiredness, her hazel eyes getting a little glint back. Our swimming hole of pond is just 200 yards away, the shine of its water barely visible through the trees.

"Sure." I warm to the thought of a dive into cold water. "Let's go skinny-dipping!"

"No way. What if someone comes? Let's just go in these," she says, point-ing to our cutoffs. "Can't hurt anything." Then with a jump, she takes off, yelling, "Last one in's a rotten berry!"

And off I go chasing her tank-topped shoulders, her smooth, tanned legs. We head for the shortcut, a narrow, root-bound path that cuts through the woods. She's already through the thicket of maple, disappearing into the rho-dodendrons by the time I enter the forest. I want to run faster, but I've already fallen on this path just walking, so I don't dare more than a trot, especially in loose sandals. I turn a corner by three huge pines, and see that she's already made it to the road, and I've only gained a few steps. I leap down the bank onto our lane, and sprint the last fifty feet, but she's already close to the wa-ter's edge. When she turns to see me, she yells, "Na-na-na-nanny boo boo," and runs into the water, the waves rippling, the small roar of splashes echoing down the hollow. A few steps out she dives under and then a moment later her head surfaces in the middle and she whoops at the shock of cold. "Come on in!" she yells after shaking her long hair. "The water's fine." And I know she is lying, see her already beginning to shiver.

I slow to a walk, grab the two inner tubes hidden in the rhododendrons away from pickers, and throw them out into the middle of the pond. Then I, too, wade in, hoot as the cold water envelopes my ankles, thighs, torso until I lean forward and swim toward my sweetie.

The pond is twelve feet deep, its dam our main access road to the field on the ridge above. Pickers often stop on the dam to admire the reflections of blooming rhododendrons, the stillness of water.

But often in summer, the top layer of water has a thin film of scum on it, so I dive below. And beneath the surface, the sun's heat never reaches, so the deep springwater stays its eyeball-numbing cold. I surface and scream with the sheer joy of shock. Sarah's already stroked out to one of the tubes, and I watch as she dives to surface into its middle where she leans out over a side. She kicks her feet to spin her tube to face me, her hair slicked back, her face a wide grin. I swim to the other tube, while Sarah scrambles on top of hers to stretch out and dry in the sun.

The most relaxing position on an inner tube comes when you lay on your back with only your hind-end in the water. We call this the butt-cooler position, the sun on your face and chest and legs, the hot rubber heating the backs of your thighs and neck, and then that ice cube of a pond balancing all this heat by chilling your buns. Sometimes a bluegill even nibbles at your fanny, goosing you with the hard rim of its mouth, keeping you from dozing too deeply.

We slow-float this way for a long timeless moment, the sun curtained to a red glow behind the lids of our eyes. I listen to a pileated woodpecker cackle from the ridge and trail my blue-stained fingers in the water.

Then we both hear it, a distant whine of a small car.

"Sounds like they're coming up our lane," I mumble.

"Don't they know not to pick in the heat of the day?" Sarah complains.

We both begin to paddle to the shore, but before we can reach the shaley edge, a little red car drives up onto the dam, and there it stops. I recognize the car, know the slicked-back head of silver hair, know we're in for some ribbing from Joe, our neighbor.

"Well," he yells as he slams the car door. "Look at you! I thought you were working, and here you're taking a swim. I even felt sorry for you over here picking in the heat of the day, so I thought I'd come check on you . . . but nooooo, you're floating like a big fat goose. My, oh, my."

He leans back on the fender, crosses his arms on his overalled belly, and spits a brown goo of tobacco juice into the grass. He wears worn sneakers, never tied because of his sore feet, and he loves fatback and bacon and all the grease you can use to fry ham. His shoulders have slumped from so many years of hoeing strawberries, and he complains often about his back. He used to preach, though he always corrects me if I call him a preacher by saying, "No, I just played the piano, sang, and testified." I've heard him get wound up and know he can roll out a sermon if he gets a chance, and it is always full of sharp wit, a tongue that spares no one, not even himself. But what a fine target he sees now as he watches us get off of our inner tubes, wade and drag them ashore, twist and shake out water from our clothes.

"You've really outdone yourselves, Jim. I just can't think of anything that tops this." He smiles sardonically and claps his enthusiasm. "My, my, what a good show you put on!"

"We've already picked six buckets," I say, trying to slow his laughter. "And no one has come all day. No one till you."

"Your sign said open, so I just drove on up," he jibes. In the past, he's ribbed me about working for a state school, having a steady paycheck that he's never known. ("No need to worry about the farm when you have all that good state money coming in.") So today he takes up this, one of his favorite themes, "And you call this working! Whew, I thought you had it made with your feet in the state trough, but this beats all. You must really be rolling in the dough. Who's working for you up in the field? I bet you keep a truckload of Mexicans hidden in your root cellar."

"Hardly," I mutter and start walking up the road. "Come on, let's go up to the field." I want to get him off his pulpit, and I want him to see the field. Though I visit him often, he hasn't made the mile journey down his winding lane and up to our field since he helped us spread fertilizer five years ago. "I just don't get out that much, Jim," he retorts every time I bug him to come visit. "Plus you think I talk too much, and I don't want to hurt your ears." So he hasn't seen the bushes, hasn't ever picked a blueberry, and now that he's come this far, even with all the embarrassment and harassing, I want to make sure he sees our work. He drives the last steep leg to the field, while Sarah and I hike back up the shortcut.

When we reach him, Joe's already out of his car and in the middle of the bushes. "Good Lord, Jim and Sarah. These look great!" At last, the soreness from his sharp tongue-lashing begins to ease. He rubs the green leaves, parts a bush to look into the mass of green and blue berries, and even asks if he can taste. "Of course, Joe. Eat all you want. Here, I'll get you a bucket," I offer. But no, no, he's just here to "inspect." With a finger, he rakes out the snuff that fills his lower lip and spits the stray wisps of tobacco. "Now I can eat a few," he says, grinning as he wipes his mouth with a cloth hankie.

Joe's a quick study and ever curious. Even though he's "about wore out" from forty-plus years of strawberry growing, he still dreams of growing blueberries. "You know, Jim, if I was half my age, I'd put in a field of these and give you some competition." And then he quizzes both of us, "Come on, Jim, guru me! What's this variety? Do you like it? Does it yield good?" He's impressed by our knowledge, but even more by the vigor of the plants. We pick samples, keep offering him handfuls, and eventually get him to pick a few.

"Boy, now this is easy picking. Don't have to bend over like with strawberries." But still, he doesn't want a bucket. "I'm just sampling," he says with a smirk.

If other pickers ask such hard questions about varieties and favorites, I usually give an evasive answer. I don't want to bad-mouth a variety that might turn out to be a particular person's favorite, and to be honest, I want all the berries picked. But with Joe, Sarah and I are honest, complaining about Nelson's short stature and tart berries, or confessing to planting the bushes too closely together. "Looks like you might have to pull a few of those bushes if you want to keep getting your tractor through." He points to a particularly narrow aisle between Beds 5 and 6, and I agree. Even though he's never grown blues and even though he doesn't believe in mulch or what he calls our "magic powders" of organic fertilizer, he has dealt with this wild, weird world of pickers, and he knows farming, knows how to do things.

"Good Lord, you mulch all of these bushes?! Now a little Roundup would take care of these weeds just like that," and he snaps his fingers. Then he pauses by a particularly loaded bush, plucks a berry, and shouts, "Look at this one. Big as a quarter!" He holds up the blueberry between finger and thumb and makes sure we both see.

"Lots of them like that," I add. And then I can't resist, "Must be our organic fertilizer, don't you think, Joe?"

"Oh, I don't know about that." He turns and I can see he is smiling and shaking his head. "I wonder how the phosphorous is in these babies?" he says to himself, but loud enough for me to hear. And then he bends to pick another.

Chapter 56

❧

American Sushi

In the field one busy Friday morning, two young Asian couples arrive. They drive slowly, hesitantly, while in the backseat toddler boys press noses to windows and search for berries. I wait and watch them get out, unlatch the two boys, and then lock the car doors. When I welcome them, the parents nod their greetings and one of the men says a hello, but then they are silent as they listen and survey the field. They try to smile, but even this is hesitant and shy. I can only imagine what they think, how bizarre to find a crowd of people surrounded by green woods at the end of a very long dirt road, all of them speaking a foreign tongue and picking a foreign fruit. The two boys ignore all of this and tug them into the field as I hand them buckets and point them where to pick.

Later I venture down to visit and see if they need any more buckets. They smile more freely now, and shake their heads no, say they'll just try to fill the ones they have. The boys nibble berries then chase each other around their parents' legs, squealing with mooshed berry glee. I squat beside the nearest child and offer a berry. He pauses, takes it from my palm, and thumps it into his mouth, almost eating his fist with this sweet food.

When I stand back up, one of the fathers tells me that he and the other man are graduate engineering students at Tech. "This is our first year in

America," he says. He pauses, then struggling with the English, explains, "These blueberries remind me of my uncle back home. In Korea. His orchard . . . I helped harvest the persimmon and peach crop." His voice trails off, his eyes staring at the rows of bushes. When he looks back, I have to turn away, the homesickness so clear in his eyes. These berries for a moment have transported him thousands of miles away.

Soon after they come to the check-out hut, the little boys' hands and knees and cheeks covered in a mixture of dirt and mashed blueberries. I weigh the berries, and the fathers hold each child up to the circle of a window on the scales, where dark eyes peer at me and then watch the numbers roll. When they stand on the floor again, each child clutches the table and presses nose to the edge. Their wide eyes follow me as I empty each bucket, the blueberries rumbling into boxes. One boy tries to reach for another berry, but the mother gently pushes his hand back, saying he's had enough.

The parents pay and thank us with warm smiles, and then they don't leave. Instead, they stand around their car eating lunch while the boys sit on the hood, all of them sweating in the midday sun. Sarah points to our picnic table, says to please use it, and they move their plates of food to the shaded benches.

A moment later, one of the women offers us some of their sushi. We surprise them by taking two pieces out of the neat rows in a Tupperware container. Sarah tells her, "We've tried to make sushi rolls, but ours never are this tight." And sure enough, I hold a perfect roundness. A black strip of seaweed wraps chewy white rice with slivers of celery, carrot, and cucumber in the middle. But also in the very center, a surprise, some type of meat.

Sarah points to the meat and asks.

The woman replies, "Beanie weenies."

It tastes good.

Chapter 57

❧❧

What They Lacked

We sit in the shed and wait out a shower—Vada, her brother-in-law Harlan, and me. From previous visits, I know her as a widow who puts up quarts and quarts of greens, pork, and, of course, berries. This is Harlan's first time to the field. He is a skinny man in overalls with only one arm, his left sleeve pinned to his shoulder.

The two of us watch Vada shake off her clear rain cap, both of us amazed and amused by her perfect gray curls, all dry. She sees us and only smiles as we all sit on wooden chairs and look out the door at the downpour. The water hammers the tin roof, the roar so loud it forces us to yell. We shout about berries, cattle, and hay, and we also just sit in silence and wait.

As the rain slows, Harlan pulls out a pouch full of loose tobacco and a pack of rolling papers. I glance out of the corner of my eye, try not to stare. In his lap, he lays the creased paper and carefully pinches in a string of brown leaves. Next, he slides the paper and tobacco between his first two fingers, lifts it to his mouth to wet an edge, and then with his thumb, he rolls it tight. He knows I am watching but only after the cigarette dangles from his lip does he look at me. Then he smiles, nods his head, and steps out the door to enjoy his smoke under the porch roof. After a bit, when the rain stops, he stamps out his cigarette and carries his two buckets back down to the field.

Vada hangs back, pretends to fiddle with her rain cap. Together we stand in the doorway and watch her brother-in-law head back out to pick. After a pause, Vada says, "Harlan lost his arm to a cut-off saw in the 1940s. He and Alfred, my husband, were twin brothers. Alfred lost a hand in the same accident."

An hour later, Vada and Harlan both walk out of the field with tired smiles. And they each carry two heaping buckets of gleaming, wet berries.

Jeannie, Sarah's mother, can't really pick. Before she was even fully born, she suffered a stroke that paralyzed her right side, leaving her fingers curled, her foot canted inward. The doctor's forceps caused this, the same forceps that saved her and her mother.

As a young woman, Jeannie lived her life as any other person would: she married, had two kids, drove them to school and volleyball and piano, and then came home to cook supper and mow the yard, limping only slightly the whole way. But now at seventy-two, she's suffered several small strokes and has found the ground sometimes shifts under foot, this ground that doesn't cushion falls. So by necessity she's learned somehow to slow her stubbornness and let Ben, her husband, drive the car and mow the yard.

In the field, Jeannie walks hesitantly, like she should have a cane but refuses. I keep close in case she stumbles. She inspects the first bed, admires the plants' vigor, and samples a few berries. Then at her request, I pull a chair from the shed and place it in the bright, open grass above Bed 1. Here she sits to steep in the sun and the blueberries. For sunglasses, she wears flimsy plastic inserts, and she tilts them at an odd angle. "I know they look goofy," she admits, "but I'm old enough I don't care anymore. Besides, they're more comfortable this way." I settle her into the chair and go back to picking for market.

As a minister's daughter, Jeannie long ago learned no strangers exist in this world, so she becomes our official greeter, saying hello to everyone who walks to and from the berry patch. She glows in this role, warm to the sun and the passing folks. If they pause, she might comment on the pretty day, or praise all the berries the customers have picked. When she can, she always works in, "Oh, Sarah and Jim are hard workers; they work all the time," as if we've raised these bushes from scraggly stems to now overloaded sweetness. Jeannie, too, takes pride in her now-grown Sarah, and in me, and in this field.

. . .

The heat of the day has already faded as Cassie jumps down from the van, special collar around her wet nose. A sweet, young dog, this Australian shepherd has the standard gray-and-white fur dotted with black periods. Sylvia, the owner, called ahead to make sure we'd allow her dog in the field. When we realize Cassie is her helper, naturally, we say yes.

Sylvia says hello out the driver's window. She's brought along two friends but they just stand and hold Cassie's sagging leash while Sylvia shifts into her wheelchair, maneuvers onto her van's lift, and then lowers herself to the ground. When I shake her hand, I am for a brief moment penetrated by her blue eyes—they are so fine and sure and deep.

"If you haven't figured out yet, I have MS," she says upfront. "I still can use my arms and hands, but the legs are shot. And Cassie here is learning how to help me for when these go." She holds up her hands and wiggles her fingers.

"Can I pet her?" I ask, not sure of the etiquette with working dogs.

"Oh, yes, she'll love you forever for just a rub."

I crouch close by and hold out the back of my hand. The warm nose and soft breath cover my knuckles as the small shepherd scents me and our dogs on this hand that soon rubs her back, her ears, her smooth head. I scratch her chin and say, "What pretty eyes." They are different colors, one the deep brown of peat-filled earth, the other that light blue of a just-turning berry, the same light blue of Sylvia's eyes.

"Oh, she's a pretty girl, and spoiled, too," Sylvia admits. Then in a commanding voice, she says, "Cassie, take the bucket." The dog nudges my other hand and gently mouths the metal handle out of my palm. Then the picking crew slowly makes their way over the bumpy grass to the field of bushes where they disappear among the greenery. I listen to the whir of the wheelchair's motor, hear them admiring the blueberries, and after a bit, I hear the soft *kerplunk* of berries filling a dog-held bucket.

Another van carries a different picking crew, this one full of delinquent teenagers, all young women, all from The River House, a rehab for minors. They're here on a "picking field trip," to use their counselor's words. The first girl slides open the side door and jumps out, hollering to the counselors, "Can we smoke here?" But she already knows the answer.

The others climb out more slowly, reluctant to enter the afternoon heat. I count eight of them, plus the two counselors. They've come at the end of a busy day, so I wonder how many berries they'll find. But then I realize they're not here just to find berries.

I hand out buckets, and again find reluctance, some barely raising their hand to take the handle. They are so young, I think, as each begrudges the empty container I give her. They all wear jeans and light green T-shirts, uniforms of a sort. But they also have their own "uniforms": the heavy black boots, the dyed black hair with purple streaks, the piercings in noses and eyebrows and tongues. A few stand by themselves, have no tattoos, keep their hair's natural red or blond color. Most look away when I give them a picking pail, their eyes darting silver like minnows in the bottom of a creek. But a few look me in the eye, and one even tries to flirt.

What have they done to get here? I wonder, as we walk to the bottom beds. *What crimes did they commit, and what crimes have been committed against them by parents and uncles and brothers? What wounds do they carry inside?*

"Look for berries in the middle of the bushes," I tell them and part the leaves to demonstrate. "The ripe ones should roll easily into your hand." When I hold out a palm full of blue, they take and sample. One even asks, "You grew these?"

Soon I see them spreading out, some trying to get as far from the counselors as allowed, but others stepping up into a bush, looking inside, finding for a brief moment, a little something they didn't know they lacked.

❧ BLUE INTERLUDE ❧
The Benefits of Blue

At a sustainable agriculture conference, I'm invited to speak about blueberries, so I give a slide presentation on our farm. To start, I ask the room full of people a "quiz" that goes something like this:

1. What food is the number one antioxidant?
2. What prevents short-term memory loss associated with aging?
3. What aids nighttime vision?
4. What helps prevent urinary tract infections?
5. What like wine has the chemical that reduces cancer and heart disease?

Through all of this, on the screen behind me, a close-up photograph of dew-covered blueberries gives the answer to every question.

Our timing with the blueberry field seems ideal. In 1998 and 1999, as the field reaches maturity, more and more research illustrates the power of a blueberry. At market and in the field, we offer handouts with quotes from magazines like *Prevention, Health, Woman's Day, USA Weekend,* and *Cooking Light,* as well as the actual research behind these articles, many from Tufts University. One writer, Holly McCord, starts her article, "If you add one food to your diet this year, make it blueberries," calling them "the single most ferocious food in the supermarket at halting the forces that age you." Ferocious? I never thought of our berries as anything but tame. Once eaten, though, they take on a whole different personality.

Take, for instance, the blue in blueberry. Scientifically known as anthocyanins, these pigments give the berry its color and name. Researchers at Tufts University's USDA Human Nutrition Research Center on Aging tested forty fruits and vegetables for antioxidants, the chemicals that ward off cancer-causing free radicals. Of the foods tested—including spinach, kale, broccoli, and plums—blueberries far surpassed them all in total antioxidants, containing almost 40 percent more than strawberries, the next highest on the list.

So impressed by this study is one of its authors, Dr. Ronald Prior, that he now recommends everyone eat at least a half a cup of the gems daily. "With 1/2 cup of blueberries, you can just about double the amount of antioxidants most Americans get in one day," he explains. He also articulates that the current quantity of blueberries consumed by Americans only amounts to 2 1/2 cups a year. Like most of our pickers, Dr. Prior keeps his freezer full of blue.

Dr. James Joseph, another Tufts University researcher, finds still another blueberry benefit, the prevention of short-term memory loss. In one of his studies older rats puzzled through a maze they already learned. The rats without blueberries in their diet wander and get lost, like many of us in the grocery-store parking lot, forgetting where to find our cars. The blueberry-fed older rats, however, zip through the maze and even improve their skill of navigation. The berries also improve the animal's speed and coordination. As Dr. Joseph exclaims in one interview about blueberries, "These things are fantastic!" He eats blueberries by the handfuls whenever he can, saying, "I pop them like M&M's."

Many other health benefits of eating this fruit abound. For example, like its cousin the cranberry, the blueberry also fights urinary tract infections, thanks to tannins in each fruit. Researchers at Rutgers believe these tannins prevent the infecting bacteria from latching onto our bladder, helping the body eliminate any possible illness. And like grapes, blueberries also contain resveratrol, the chemical made famous in wine for reducing heart disease and cancer. Other studies in Europe on the bilberry, another blueberry cousin, show the fruit improves night vision and helps our eyes adjust to bright lights. World War II pilots reportedly consumed them in large quantities before each night mission. Lastly, each blueberry is low-calorie, virtually fat-free, and packed with fiber because of the tiny seeds. We can meet roughly a quarter of the U.S. Food and Drug Administration's recommended amount for fiber by munching on a cup of blueberries a day.

Ferocious indeed.

Chapter 58

※/⁂

A Certain Tenderness

Sarah and I still spend an occasional Sunday morning with the Mennonites. Despite our differences, we shake hands, listen to scripture, and join to sing fine hymns that spill out of the church near our farm. They welcome us warmly, invite us to dinner, and become friends.

Slowly, our lives intersect in other ways. We ask Ezra, the preacher, to make a desk and bookcases for us using our own pine lumber. In a few months, the smooth boards glow a warm yellow in our living room where they fit just right and fill with our stacks of books.

Ezra's son-in-law, Phillip, helps me replace some rotting sills around the back of our old house. He is a tall man, and he brings his two oldest sons, the three of them all with the same face, the same high forehead, the same deep creases framing shy smiles. We spend a day jacking up the structure, pounding out the bug-riddled timbers and sliding in the replacements, their work solid and sound, like Phillip's handshake when he leaves. He looks me in the eyes only briefly, though, the shyness always present.

That summer we ask Phillip and his family to help fill our market orders by picking blueberries on shares. The seven of them come on a Wednesday, the field closed so we have it all to ourselves, and I watch them spread out, teenagers and parents, to cover two rows. They've picked before, so they know how to clean a bush and how to keep the teasing constant so as to ease the labor. Phillip's quiet gentleness and easy smile emanates from each member of the family.

When ten buckets with seventy pounds of berries sit at the end of a bed, Phillip stretches out on the grass, his long legs crossed, his hat pushed back. He chews on a blade of grass, pushes up the bridge of his glasses, and asks about the work involved in tending the field. He also shares his own early days picking peaches on a different farm. The evening promises rain, we hope, and the graying clouds to the west seem to support the weatherman for a change. When a rumble echoes far away, we all gather ourselves and carry the buckets of berries, heavy at the end of our arms, and good in their weight.

In church, in the field, his wife and children and friends all treat Phillip with a certain tenderness, like they want to hold his hand, stop him from walking out the door, but know they can't. Finally, from Ezra I learn why. Phillip's liver is failing, and he's already had several close calls. For three years he has waited for the right donor, the right match for a transplant. When his doctors find one, they quickly operate, take away this vital, failing organ to replace it with a younger, healthy one. But Phillip's body rejects it, and the transplant fails. At his funeral, the church overflows and the hymns and all of their harmonies rise and fly out the open windows, but they can only carry away so much grief.

Of all the Mennonites, I feel closest to Mrs. Kutz. She hobbles slightly climbing out of the van with her daughter and grandchildren all swarming around. And always she grabs my elbow, squeezing tight when we walk to the field. Her bonnet covers the tight bun of her silver hair, and from under its shade, I still catch the sparkle of her blue eyes as she praises the beauty of the bushes, the vigor of these vines, all the while her faded yellow bonnet bobbing with affirmation.

Like my parents and grandparents and great-grandparents, and like me, Mrs. Kutz grew up in Pennsylvania, and the lilt of her tongue carries me back to all of my great-aunts with their gardens and quilts and root cellars full. As she picks our blueberries, I try to stay close, pick with her when I can, just to listen, just to remember these kinfolk long-gone—Aunt Carrie and Aunt Hazel and finally, Aunt Esther, who picked huckleberries in the mountains with my grandparents and great-grandparents so long ago.

And every time, when her buckets are full and she climbs back into the van, Mrs. Kutz always says, "Come see us."

I regret that I never do.

❧ BLUE INTERLUDE ❧
Blues Today

In 1916, Elizabeth White made a little over $200 when she shipped twenty-one bushels of blueberries from her farm in Whitesbog, New Jersey. Though wild blueberries had been sold for many years, this 1916 transaction was the first sale and shipment of domesticated highbush blueberries ever.

In 2006, according to the U.S. Highbush Blueberry Council, "[t]otal production of both lowbush and highbush blueberries in North America reached an estimated 536 million pounds" with highbush berries accounting for 62 percent of the harvest. That crop was worth over $800 million. Ms. White's 10 acres has grown to over 60,000 acres in the United States alone and her dream of trains called "blueberry specials" hauling berries all over the world has definitely come to fruit, except now the "specials" are more likely trucks.

Of the thirty-eight states that commercially grow these blue nuggets, Michigan, from where we bought our bushes, ranks first, and New Jersey, with its long history and state-fruit declaration, ranks second. But this humble fellow has become a world traveler, living abroad, and claiming residences in Chile, Argentina, Australia, Poland, China, Africa, and many other countries. It even has scientists all over the globe studying it and coming together every few years to share their knowledge.

Scientists, however, aren't the only ones who have fallen in love with this, our native fruit. We Americans love our blueberry and we love to honor our blue hero with festivals. Celebrations take place every summer all across the country. Communities gather to pick and eat fresh berries, hear blueberry folk songs and blueberry jokes, and probably eat too much homemade blueberry ice cream.

And eat we do. We Americans devour and drink over 160 million pounds of these berries every year. We love them fresh, primarily, but we also consume our blues frozen, dried, pureed, juiced, canned, and concentrated. We drink blueberry juices, blueberry beers, blueberry wines, and even, if we're lucky, blueberry moonshine. We chew our way through blueberry pies, blueberry pancakes, blueberry yogurt, blueberry muffins, blueberry cereals and health bars, and on and on. But read your labels. Once I bought blueberry bagels to find they had no blues in them at all, just blue-tinted bits of apples. There are evil forgeries everywhere.

With so much blueness the world over, and even fakeries trying to mimic this prize, I've come to question one of our abiding blueberry legends. We say Coville and White domesticated the highbush blueberry plant so long ago, but I wonder if maybe the blueberry hasn't just been waiting, has known all along what it wanted from us. Maybe in a way this blue hero, for its own purposes, has domesticated us.

Part V

❦

Harvest

(2001-2002)

a worm-house like it or not
the shadow of doubt
a bullet from the gun of God

Chapter 59

※※※

Frozen

L ate May in 2002, and I wear a winter coat on my morning walk. Last week I wore none.

Late May, and I hike to the blueberry field with dread. Last week I knew none.

Late May, and I unglove my hand, reach out to touch green berries frozen to solid deadness. Last week I touched roundness to feel a firm expectation in every one.

We have no smudge pots, barrels to hold a smoky fire to layer the field in a heavy quilt of protective smoke. We have no windmills to stir up the air and blow away this danger. We have no spray irrigation to shower the bushes with a fine mist that would freeze over each leaf and berry in a protective coat of ice. We have nothing but the weatherman telling us an unseasonal cold front barrels down onto us from the far reaches of the far north. We do the only thing we can: bundle up to worry and watch.

Blueberries are tough, I think as I hike the lane, my breath fogging in front of me. These plants are not far removed from their wild ancestors, so they can handle this cold. But it is only foolish wistfulness.

In the field, the berries hang with a different heaviness, and their color has changed from the light green of fresh peas to a darker shade, the cracked deep green of frosted grass. I pick a berry and try to pry it open with my two thumbnails, but first have to warm and thaw it in my closed fist. Inside, the seeds have already started to brown where yesterday I saw only white. And the once-soon-to-be-sweetness of flesh has turned to mealy mush.

In my junior high science class, Mr. Wilson always preached, "Air has mass," his deep voice filling the air of the room, his eyes darting to check on sleepy students. Vapor, he taught, has density, a certain inertia. It can register on a scale, its mere presence carrying a new contradiction for me. But that came from a textbook and a teacher, not the invisible air itself.

Not until today, this week. For five straight nights, that mass of arctic air the weatherman predicted drops its weight onto our region, zeroing in on our blueberry field like a bomb homing to its target. But this bomb doesn't explode all at once or with any sound. Instead it settles in silently and doesn't move. I feel its weight in my lungs, the cold detonating, trying to burst through lung walls. But I have 98-degree blood and a cavity of ribs to protect these lungs, this heart. The green berries have only a thin skin, nothing really.

For a month now the berries have slowly swelled with the energy of root and soil and sun and water. Now at 28 degrees, they swell with the brokenness of busted cells.

The next week the temperature spikes back up to the 60s and we again put away our winter coats. We walk the field to find over half of the crop has turned brown, a rust of orange. The little pebbles of wasted fruit cover the ground, the fallout of that silent explosion.

Two weeks later, we find clumps of berries still on the bush but turning suddenly blue, prematurely. I pick one to find it dimpled and dented, the damaged cell walls shriveled. I pick another and place it in my mouth. Instead of that squirt of rich tartness, this one is a dry mash, grainy, like the texture of an old rubber ball. Maybe the birds will eat these, I think, but they, too, avoid these bland, miniature globes.

Do we have a crop, do we have enough berries to even open the field?

We keep walking the grass-ways and asking the bushes, but we can't tell or hear their answers. With all that dropped and all that still hangs like deflated balloons, we estimate we've lost at least two-thirds of the crop, maybe more. The blue of the damaged mixes in with the blue that survived . . . so who can say?

And we do find some that survived, mostly at the top of the field. I pick and eat a handful and am grateful to find that familiar squirt of sugar and acid. Either these bushes are hardier or the slight difference in elevation between the top and bottom of the field created a pocket of warm air, enough to protect, enough to give us some ripe berries. Enough, we decide, to open at least a few days of the week, or maybe just one.

In farming, it seems, you make a plan and then because of the weather you forget about it. As in previous years, we mulched the field in winter, finished the pruning in March, and spread the fertilizer in April. A crop of blueberries only seems like a reasonable expectation, a reasonable sweet note, a finale to all of this work.

But now we don't know what to expect, our dreams frozen like so many of these blueberries.

✿ BLUE INTERLUDE ✿
Our Problems

Whether we farm blueberries or beans, deal with late freezes or drought, our country's problems with agriculture are amazing in their complexity and number. And because we all eat and thus are members of this culture, we all are also implicated in these many problems and necessary in their solutions.

Take our assault on the very elements that sustain us. Iowa, for example, is one of the flattest and, at one time, topsoil-richest places in the world. Now, though, it has become one of our most eroded and eroding states, all because of how we farm. Plus, all the tons of dirt that float down our rivers carry petroleum-based fertilizers and pesticides, which in turn create river-delta dead zones visible from the moon, yet too big to imagine.

So we mine the dirt, failing to replenish it with sound farming practices. Then we pollute the water and mine it as well. Irrigating desert lands to produce soybeans only will last as long as the freshwater in the ground and the petro to pump it. We're quickly running through both.

Other problems, of the many we face, include a loss of diversity in natural habitats and crop seed genetics; a loss of land to development (Virginia lost twelve acres an hour between 2002 and 2007); a loss of experienced farmers as the old retire and the young don't take their places; a loss of rightly scaled farms, replaced by factory "farms" with their pigs, cattle, and chickens no longer creating fertilizer for fields, but now industrial "waste," something once unknown on a farm; and a loss of food security as fewer and fewer farms grow more and more of our food. The 2007 USDA Census, for example, states that though the total number of all farms increased since 2002, only 125,000 farms grew 75 percent of our food. And that number was down 21,000 from 2002.

On the other end of this agriculture table are all of our health problems related to how we eat: cancer, diabetes, and especially obesity. We live in a country where it is now normal to be sickly fat, and even *Reader's Digest* has noted this. There, Andy Simmons writes,

"Americans are a collective 7,223,637,522 pounds overweight (give or take a million)."

Though few see the connection, our treatment of the soil is not separate from our treatment of our own bodies. They are the same.

Organic agriculture and local food movements are great alternatives, but still they only account for a miniscule amount of all our food.

What to do? Value health over wealth. Push for legislative change. Eat less or even fast once a week. Help feed your neighbor. Grow your own.

Chapter 60

❦

Bit

On an evening in early June, two weeks after the big freeze, the sky becomes so overcast that no last rays from the sun squeak through. I stand at the kitchen sink, washing supper dishes, listening to the news on the radio. Then I hear a too-familiar bark. It starts as a low growl, hesitant at first, and then it escalates to yowls that repeat and grow higher and higher. They come from Little B, our youngest dog, a husky-shepherd mix, and this is her signal to tell us she's cornered something that slithers, something that bites. This is her snake bark.

I run out the door to the state road that separates our house from the barns. There in the road's bare dirt all three of our dogs circle. They have become a mass of fur and edginess, hackles high, steps quick, like they're dancing around a fire. But this fire has no ashes and only one flame, a twisting body of sinewy muscle. It is a copperhead, coiled and ready to bite.

The dogs are too focused on the snake to listen when I shout their names. They scurry in a wide circle, tails rigid as they look for a way in, a moment to attack and kill. When they get too close, the copperhead lunges. The mutts leap back and the fangs grab only air. But I know this dance will not last long.

A hoe, I say to myself, *I need a hoe now,* so into the shed I go with growls and barks echoing in my head. Back outside and running to the fray, I see the copperhead lunge once more. This time it strikes flesh, and Grover, the poodle-terrier, smallest of our pack, screams a high-piercing yelp. He keeps shrieking as he runs to me. But I can't grab him, can't comfort him, not yet.

Again I yell at the other two dogs, this time a fiercer, "Git." They step back, seeing my hoe, but they don't leave. They just make a wider circle around us, around me and the snake. The viper has coiled, its tongue flicking, scenting me, searching for an escape or another soft spot to strike.

Do it quick, do it now, I whisper to myself. All I see is the snake's wavering head, its slits for eyes. All I feel is the cold heat of its fire.

The hoe has no heaviness, my arms no weight. I raise the tool and swing it down hard. As the blade arcs close, the copperhead strikes, hitting the handle. Then the metal cuts skin, severs muscle and vertebrae to *thunk* on the hard-packed dirt. And even after I know it is dead, I keep chopping, keep hacking this bloody body. The head must be severed, I think, or it might strike again, its nerves twitching, especially when another dog's nose touches it.

Then I kick it into the ditch and search for Grover.

I find him in Sarah's arms. When she hears his screams, she knows. She comes running to grab him and try to calm his shivering body, quiet his constant groans. "Call the vet," she directs, but I'm already dialing the number, grabbing my keys. We head out, the car tires crunching over the bloody spot where just five minutes ago a snake and a dog should not have met.

This is not the first time, or even the second or fourth. This copperhead bite is our seventh. When we bought the farm over a decade ago, one of our new neighbors told us to watch out, he'd seen lots of copperheads down in that hollow. Back then we shrugged off his warning. Now we know better.

The first time also happens to Grover, but the next two snakes strike Little B, and the last two bite Becca, a lab-shepherd mix. Only one of our dogs, Grace, never gets bit. All six of these strikes hit the dogs in their faces or front legs, and all but this last one happens by surprise, the dog unaware. One time Little B simply leaps over a brush pile and lands on a resting copperhead. Another instance, Becca sticks her nose down into what she thinks is a rabbit hole.

Every time, the dogs howl in pain and the injured muzzle or leg instantly swells. Every time we ride this hurried half hour to the vet's.

Grover won't let Sarah look too closely, but we guess the fangs entered his neck. On the shiny stainless steel table in her office, the vet confirms this. She parts Grover's tangled curls to give him shots including a tranquilizer to calm him. Then she gives us a slew of other medicines and directions.

"The bite won't kill him," she tells us, "but the swelling might." She fears the venom will inflame the muscles around his throat, constricting it. "The inflammation might suffocate him," she warns, so she advises us to check on him through the night to make sure he's still breathing. And she cautions that eventually his hair will fall off and the poisoned flesh will blacken and also slough away. But she, too, understands that we already know this. We have become too well known for our snake-bit dogs in this town.

But I haven't told you about the seventh bite. The time the fangs found me.

It happened sometime after the first or second dog got struck, in the summer of 1993, before we even had cleared the field or planted blueberries. I wanted to pick raspberries, like I did as a kid, and the best picking was along Lost Bent Creek. I put on old sneakers, grabbed a bucket, and headed to the upper reaches of the stream where brambles grew thick. There I slowly filled the white pail with the dark stains of this sweet fruit.

The purple canes covered both creek banks, arching over the shallow water. The easiest way to pick, I soon saw, was by wading, so into the coldness I went. The clear stream had a constant low whisper of a gurgle that filled the wooded hollow, and its wetness soaked my sneakers and pants to cool me and to make this summertime ritual even more pleasant. I worked down the branch, picking from both sides, stumbling on the slick rocks, humming while the dogs worried a bunny in the nearby brush. Ahead, a tree had fallen across the creek, a barrier between me and the other berries I could see farther downstream. No way there but to climb the steep bank and hike around the tree.

I scrambled up the shaley bank, grabbing roots with one hand while holding my bucket level with the other. And there as I worried about sliding back into the stream or worse, spilling all of these fine raspberries, I felt something at my leg.

It didn't really hurt. It felt, instead, like a giant bee sting. When I reached a level spot, I looked down, expecting to see some yellow jackets around my calf, but spotted nothing. I looked over the bank, and again nothing—no snake, no swarm, not a thing except my trail and the rippling water below. Then I lifted my pants leg and there on the shin were two puncture wounds, small pinhead-sized holes about an inch apart. *Definitely copperhead,* I thought, as once more I searched the steep bank. I never did see the snake.

So what next? I said aloud. Where's the incredible pain I've read about and witnessed in my dogs? Where's the swelling? And why doesn't this hurt?

I hiked back home, put the berries in the fridge, grabbed the newspaper and an ice pack, and sat on the porch. I figured if it hadn't swelled yet, I must've somehow got lucky and I'd be all right. So I propped my leg up on the banister, wrapped the ice in place, and read the paper. Every ten minutes or so, I checked the two fang marks, mainly just to make sure they existed. I still had trouble believing all of this.

A half hour later, Sarah drove home from school, and as soon as she saw me, asked, "What's wrong?" She could tell something had happened, so I told her my story. Like a good wife, she panicked. "Let's go to the doctor's *now*. You should be there already." I tried to protest, but she called our physician and he said yes, he'd wait an extra few minutes past closing time just to see us.

When I sat on his examination table, the spectacled doctor looked at my leg and nodded. "Yep, that's a snake bite for sure."

"But why so little swelling and hardly any pain?" I asked.

"Must've been a dry bite."

I said I never heard of such, and he explained that after a poisonous snake has struck and just eaten, it often takes a while for the venom to refill the little sacks behind the fangs.

"So, if it has to strike again before these sacks are replenished, it's called a dry bite. Which means that you, my friend, are very lucky."

He gave me a tetanus shot, told me to never pick berries there again, and sent me home.

So ten years later, we once again have to keep Grover by our bedside at night, confine him to the bathroom during the day, dope him up on pain-killers and antibiotics, and wait until his immune system slowly dissolves the copperhead's venom. We take the other pooches for our evening hike, staying on the road, keeping them out of the brushy areas near the stream, the places the snakes seem to like.

And since last month's late freeze, we also avoid the field. Who wants to see again the ground littered with the waste of our fruit? That image already has slipped into our sleep to never leave.

Instead, we sit by the pond in the quiet of the day and try not to think about copperheads and blueberries. The sunset's glow soaks into every nook of this world: the soft leaves, the surface of the pond, the air itself—all of it hums. This glow even seeps into us, into the corners of our eyes, into our stillness.

Sarah glances at me, then stares back at the pond. Finally she interrupts this blue reverie. "You know, Jim," she says. "I've been thinking."

I stop rocking, wait for more.

After a pause, she asks, "Do you ever wonder about that place?"

I am stilled by her complete and sudden confession, by this recognition of a door that has stood ajar for both of us despite our efforts to close it.

And I, too, touch the latch of that door with the simple reply, "I think about it all the time." About its hill covered in trillium and the heart-shaped deer tracks that dimple the trails. About its streams, how they join to form a giant Y visible on any topographical map I search. About its long views of whole mountain ranges, and its close views of miterwort and hepatica, plants I never knew until I hiked that land we had hoped to buy with Matt and Melanie, our kinfolk. And always, I remember that first time Sarah and I sat on the hill together, that cold day in April, the clear sky holding nothing but a single osprey gliding over us, marking us with the shadow of its wings.

"Yeah," I repeat, "I think about that place all the time."

"We could buy it on our own, you know," Sarah says after a long silence, and I nod my head, thinking the same. "And I could go back to teaching full-time." This surprises me even more, makes me realize how much she, too, has been bitten, not by any poisonous snake, but by a love of this new place and by a chance to dream again.

That night, almost a year after we last looked at this land, we call the owner. He tells us that the property has gone through two other failed contracts, and yes, it is still for sale. The next day we call the banker and lawyers, and a month later, we own a new farm.

Chapter 61

❦

Still They Come

Those first years we had it easy. No bugs, no freeze, no critters. And we didn't even realize it. We wasted our youth on hand-weeding sorrel, an impossible task on an acre, futile and needless. At least we've learned that much.

Today, just this season's third day open, over thirty cars of pickers come, many moms with kids, but also regulars like Chico, Danica, and Louise. In previous seasons these folks—who Sarah and I call serious pickers—have carried hundreds of pounds of blueberries off this field in a single day. Chico's group alone boasted 125 pounds in four hours, a record he always tries to break.

But today, by 1 P.M., we are picked out. Chico and crew cruise the field and leave after an hour, only a few buckets in hand. Same with Eileen and her kids, those two youngsters who each picked a whole bucket last season for the reward of ice cream and swimming. But this time, the three of them can't fill a whole bucket together. Even Eileen's youngest, little Sarah, tells me, "These bushes are green, but they're empty of blue."

I can only nod and say, "You're absolutely right."

As Eileen drives out, her kids buckled in and waving from the backseat, she leans out of her car window and says, "I hope some damn moron doesn't buy this place and spray it to hell." I just smile and nod my head. Beside me stands a potential buyer waiting for a tour.

Later, after the last stragglers give up searching and after the land-looker heads home as well, I tally the half day's picking. I expect a dismal return but still am surprised by the number: 175 pounds. Thirty cars, at least 50 pickers, and only 175 pounds. For the first time we learn what "crop failure" really means, not some abstraction in the newspaper, but this, an empty field, an empty cash drawer, and a row of empty buckets.

Early mornings, when I open the gate to the dewy field, I still have doubts, still have those faithless moments. I see the empty parking space, the rows of so many plants, and I wonder if people will come. Will they negotiate our steep road, find our isolated farm to fill their pails with summer sapphires?

And even now, with a puny harvest, still they come, still they are happy. We've warned them in our e-mails, describing the hard, late freeze, the severely damaged crop, and they come anyway and sympathize. We decide to open just on Fridays, one day a week instead of our usual five. After three consecutive Fridays, the same folks have returned two or three times. A woman from Woolwine, her third visit this season, has to bring her husband, to show him our bushes. And though she knows she won't buy this farm, she still loves it, visits her own blueberry dreams.

So this year, with no advertising, no phone calls, and really, no berries, people come to spend a happy day in the field. They crave the quiet, a day in the country, the idea of procuring their own food. Not necessarily the reality, but the idea. We've known this for years, that they come for the *experience* as much as the berries. But now with a bumper crop of nothing, we see this experience part more starkly. You can make a good life off of this experience, but not a good living.

A new picker and her six-year-old daughter drive all the way from Boone, North Carolina, three hours away. I point them where to park, and before the car even stops, the mother yells out her window, "We're reading *Blueberries for Sal*, and we had to come see your blueberries!" The buckled-in daughter waves to me and then keeps pointing to the bushes and pickers. I can't tell who is more excited.

When the girl prances out of the car, she holds up her purple tin pail. "See," she exclaims, "my picking pail is just like Sal's." Both mother and daughter have short blond hair, just like Sal's, and together they carry their pails through the bushes, hurrying from berry to berry, the child, like Sal, sampling the three in her pail before picking more. As I turn to park another car, I hear them both sing out, *"Kuplink! Kuplank! Kuplunk!"* their song echoing the soft rumble of their berries. They are content to travel so far just to see a blueberry bush, just to imagine a mother bear and her cub nearby, just to sing this picking song.

After an hour or so, they climb the check-out hut steps to weigh their berries. The little girl lifts her knees high for each step and she holds her miniature pail in front with both hands.

"Did you see any bears?" I ask her, and her eyes widen.

"No," she whispers, "but I think I heard a cub rustling nearby."

"Oh, my! Did it try to eat any of your mother's berries?"

"No," she sighs, "Mama wouldn't let it."

When I place their precious fruit on the scale, I realize the pair has only picked one and a half pounds. For a moment I wonder if I should even charge them the two dollars, they've had such fun, such a fine day, but the mother already has the bills in my hand before I can say no.

❧ BLUE INTERLUDE ❧
Listening at Whitesbog

Though Elizabeth White died in 1954, her legacy lives on, thanks to the Whitesbog Preservation Trust. This organization, based in Whitesbog, New Jersey, holds an annual blueberry festival to commemorate White and our blue hero, and also "the history, culture, and natural environment" of this small village. The trust is recreating this company town to help visitors understand the significance of where White and Coville first domesticated blueberries, and where both cranberries and blueberries once required whole villages of workers to harvest.

The Whitesbog Preservation Trust has also restored Elizabeth White's house, Suningive, a building she designed. She situated the house beside her blueberry field and with a view of the cranberry bogs her family had farmed for several generations. White appreciated how humans could work with the land to create a crop and a livelihood. But she also appreciated the natural beauty of that land and those plants. She wanted to live not in the town where she grew up, but there in the bogs that so nourished her.

Another remarkable woman also nourished by the plants she loved was Barbara McClintock. In 1983, when she won the Nobel Prize for her work in corn genetics, she claimed she "listened" to the corn. As Linda Hogan writes, McClintock's method was "to translate what the plants spoke into a human tongue." This scientist "came to know each plant intimately" and her approach "crossed over boundary lines between species." This radical method "astonished the scientific community," which took decades to recognize and accept her conclusions.

I often wonder if Elizabeth White had a similar relationship with blueberries because her writing and work illustrate a curiosity beyond the normal. Did she listen to the blueberry? What did she hear and learn from such a humble fruit? What can any of us learn if we only open ourselves?

❧

Chapter 62

Critters

Something is eating our blueberries, something other than humans and bugs and birds. These somethings came last year at the end of the season and ate hundreds of pounds of berries, maybe as much as a ton. Now by night, when we tuck ourselves into bed a half mile and a hill away, they return to obliterate what few berries survived the freeze.

And they don't eat gently. They break branches, twist tops, even pull down the stout trunks of our oldest bushes. They not only harvest this year's crop, but their destructive habits kill the next several years' crops as well. What something is this, we don't know. Coon or bear, we guess. A mile away, one of our neighbors spots fresh bear tracks, but we try to keep that news, that fear, to ourselves. The bears that eat berries in *Blueberries for Sal* are cute, the cub even smiles. But beyond the romance of this children's book, what brave customer will pick in a patch sporting a resident black bear?

Early June, the berries just turning, Sarah spots the first broken branch in the top row of bushes. That evening, I slip up to the field with my rifle, climb the ladder into a hunting perch high in a tree, and wait. I lean against the big pine, my feet dangling twenty-five feet up in the air. In my arms, I cradle a .22 that my grandfather gave me, a .22 he once used to kill groundhogs in his own blueberry patch. If it's a coon carousing in our field, this small rifle will work. If it's a bear, I'll just have to watch through the scope and then call the game warden after it disappears. Hopefully it'll be frightened enough by shouts to run; otherwise I might be sleeping in this roost. One way or the other, I want to know what critters lurk here.

At dusk, I hear some rustling behind me. I slow-turn my head to gaze at a raccoon rounding the corner from behind the berry hut. It waddles its fat body across the parking area to the first bed. In no hurry, the animal follows its snout to a sweet supper, the striped tail lifted just above the grass. I watch in the scope. When it pauses to scratch an ear, I pull the trigger and the rifle's crack breaks open the field's quiet. The coon slumps, doesn't move. I hurry down the ladder to make sure it's dead. Kneeling there beside it, I admire its delicate claws, touch its coarse coat. Then in what I hope is a gesture of warning to other coons, I heave the dead weight into the woods.

The warning isn't heeded. The coons keep coming, even returning on that very night I kill one. The next evening, I sit in the tree stand again to watch the sun settle behind Pond Hill. By full dark, I see nothing, hear only the wind in this giant tree, and I know the coons have already learned to wait.

So I wait. The following night, I head out at 9:00, full dark, and I don't walk, but drive the pickup to the field. As soon as I come out of the woods, I see their bright red eyes shining in the headlights, their masked faces unable to hide their identity. I stop the truck and, with a flashlight, spot a fat one halfway up in a bush. The whole plant sways with its weight as it scrambles to escape. I try to hold flashlight and rifle at the same time, try to aim both at this moving target, but I can't. The flashlight falls onto the truck's floor and the coon scurries off.

These coons, though, keep waddling back, keep climbing, breaking branches, and looting, keep destroying so many years of work and crops. We grow more desperate and call in local coon hunters. One night we stand at our living-room window and watch their tiny headlamps. They release their baying beagles and start hiking up the hollow to the field. We listen to the yips and barks, and hear, eventually, some shots. Later, they tell me they treed and shot four animals, but the blueberry branches keep breaking, the berries disappearing. None of this killing slows the marauding, the midnight berry raids.

Every morning we find fresh, purple scat at the end of the beds, their thank-you notes for another night of delicious dining. Like they want to make sure we know they've been here. Like they want to rub in how much they've outwitted us. We collect the broken branches, and I remember one of our families of pickers named Looney. One time last season, the father, mother, and teenage son worked a string of laden bushes. When I asked again their names, the father joked, pointed to his wife, and said, "*I* didn't have a choice, and *my son* didn't have a choice, but she *chose* to be loony!"

I feel like that father, that son. Loony by default. Loony to imagine ten thousand coons surround us, snickering from the safe portals of their tree dens.

When I tell Joe, my neighbor, he just sympathizes and explains, "You kill one coon, and a thousand come to the funeral."

And, of course, he's right.

Chapter 63

❧❧

Joe's Blues

Earlier in the year, Joe had what probably was a mild heart attack. "My arms tingled and I had a little pain in my chest," he tells me later, "but I just sat here and eventually it went away. Nothing much, and not enough to call the doctor." He didn't even call his son and daughter-in-law who live nearby. Only after they checked in the next day did he mention what he calls "the episode," and only after they insisted did he go to the doctor.

"He gave me all kinds of pills." Joe holds up a baggie full and points. "One for my heart, another for sugar, and another for my high blood pressure. One for cholesterol and an inhaler for my emphysema." He pauses to suck in on the tube. "And this one," he says, rattling another blue bottle, "this (rattle) single (rattle) pill (rattle) is in case I have another attack. It must be a helluva pill, don't you think, Jim?"

I nod, empathize, and offer to help where I can: clean dirty dishes, bring him some water from the kitchen. But I'm also here to break some big news.

After he sips on the water, he reaches into his overall bibs and pulls out a small gray container. "Can't give up this, though," he says, holding up his canister of snuff. "Don't care what the doctor says." When he fills his lip with the little spoon full, I see it's time to tell.

"We're selling the farm." I let it out with a deep breath. "Moving to another farm in Wythe County."

He is uncharacteristically quieted as he puts the spoon back in the canister and screws it shut. But only for a moment.

"It's a bad year with that freeze and all, I know, but Jesus, Jim, I didn't expect this. Is that it? The freeze?"

"Partly," I say, shrugging, "but not really." And here in my head I go through the many reasons, trying to decide what to say.

"Was it because of the neighbors?" He grins, pointing his thumb at his chest, but I know he's also serious.

"No, no, I'm going to miss this neighbor the most." I nod my head at him.

"Well, why then, Jim?"

"A bunch of reasons," I finally begin. "I'm not finding any time to write, because of the blueberries, and they were supposed to *give* us more time, not take it. Plus, we're putting in tons of money and work, and they're just not paying off like we hoped. And then this new farm is just so amazing. It's huge and healthy," and I realize I had better stop for fear of somehow insulting this farm, his place, unintentionally.

"You need to come see it," I say hurriedly, but realize he doesn't get off his farm for his own groceries anymore, let alone travel seventy-five miles to hike on some land that doesn't really have any good roads.

"You know," he finally says, "I thought you might stick. That house has had at least five different owners since I've lived here, and I thought you might stay, outlast me, even."

"I'll come back to visit, you know that?"

He nods and we both are silent. He hits the volume button on the remote so we can listen to the weather forecast. His Chihuahuas nestle around him, perched between his hips and the recliner's armrests. Cricket, the oldest, with silver hair sprinkled like salt over the pepper-black of her snout, snores and yips in a dream.

After the weatherman ends his forecast, I speak again. "Your garden looks good."

He hits the mute button, says, "Oh, it ain't much now, is it? Doctor didn't want me to have one at all, but I gotta have something. So Joey worked up that little plot."

Little it is, especially compared to his patches from previous years. Instead of a half acre of vegetables out in a field behind the house, this ten-by-ten stamp of a garden sits in the front yard, beside the sidewalk.

"Shoot, Joe. I saw beans and mustard greens all ready to pick, and your tomatoes are loaded."

"Did you see what was *behind* the tomatoes?"

I shake my head and he just grins wide. "Up, up," he commands, tapping the dogs. "Come on now, let's go outside." The dogs yap and scamper down their special ramp from chair to floor. Joe works himself to the front of the chair, and then with a heave, onto his feet. He uses a cane now, and when he stands, he leans forward, the pain in his back hunching his shoulders. But once moving, he's out the door after his pups, and I have to hurry to catch up.

"I sit on that bucket to hoe every morning. Then I move from bucket to bucket," he says as he points to the scattered upturned containers. "Only way I can keep up with the weeds." He loosens the wire gate, and the two of us slip through the fence. "I expect to eat my first beans any day now, and those peppers are coming on early, just like my cucumbers."

He sits on one of the buckets and points his cane. "Now Jim, go around these tomatoes and tell me what you see."

I scoot by him, around the staked row of six tomatoes, and there find eight blueberry plants against the fence. "Well, looky there, you've planted blueberries!" I say with a grin.

He nods and tells me Joey, his son, bought them at a local nursery. "Couldn't let you have all the fun, now, could I?"

We talk varieties. Four of these we grow, but four we don't. "You'll have to tell me how they taste. But remember to pick the blossoms off this first year."

"Yeah, I know," he tells me. "I've been reading those manuals. But I might leave a few blooms . . . can't hurt too much to sample."

I touch a leaf, part the branches. "They look good and healthy," I compliment. And then silently, with mock seriousness, the grin only in his eyes, Joe raises his cane and points to the corner of the garden. There I see a bag of 10-10-10 fertilizer, opened, slouched, half empty.

I remember all the years of his biting jabs about my organic beliefs and practices, and I just shake my head at his huge lopsided grin.

"You just can't win, Jim. You know that."

And yes, I think, with you, Joe, that's all right.

Chapter 64

Why Move?

hy move? Why leave these blueberries?" We field these same questions through the last season of coon-damaged, frozen-fruit dol-
drums, through the eight months we have the farm for sale, for the rest of
our lives, really.

"Gosh, this is the most beautiful spot in the world," one picker comments.
"I couldn't imagine leaving it."

Well, imagine, I think to myself, and then I turn away, pretend to not hear
so I don't have to deal with her words.

"Why move?" Like I did with Joe, Sarah and I both stumble through an
answer to this question. From pickers who know us, who know how much
labor we invest every year into this soil, we find an understanding that we
might want to try something else. Though reluctantly—they worry about
their future supply of blueberries. But they have a hint of an idea of how
hard we've worked to create and maintain this place.

From new pickers, and especially from potential buyers of this farm-
now-for-sale, we have to be more tactful. "Nothing negative," Sarah and I
say to each other, a mantra we repeat every time we give another tour of
the old house, another drive-around of the farm, another walk-through of the
field. "Nothing negative."

Don't mention the house's odd layout and small rooms, or the windows' habit of letting in cold air. Don't recall all the times you had to bundle up in negative-umpteen-degree nights to crawl underneath this house built before plumbing, you with flashlight and hair dryer to blow hot air on a pipe until it thawed, the frozen ground against your back, the insulation in your face, all of it making you feel buried in a too-soon, too-cold grave. Don't talk about how after a blizzard knocked the electricity out for five days, one neighbor told you, "The best neighbors take care of themselves." You just stood there dumbed into silence by this very contradiction of the word *neighbor*. Don't remember the other winter the pipes froze and this time busted, *fsss*ing into the living room, and Sarah home alone. No neighbor would come, even when asked, so she pulled her claustrophobic self together and slithered into the dank bowels of the crawl space, that dark cave of insulation and brown recluse spiders, to shut off the valve.

Don't mention the spiders, either, or the copperheads. Nothing negative, now.

In the field, don't mention the grass aisles too narrow to mow because you planted the bushes too close, or the coons and their masked thievery, or the picker who came with his pistol. Don't mention the freeze, or the flood that blasted all of the pipes and ruined the irrigation, or the need for a fence. Only after they ask, give them the numbers, the economics of this field. Let them realize those figures don't include expenses. Or count your labor that you have so freely given for so many years. Don't mention how you fear that this field might someday turn so sour by its so many demands, its so many hours, that your own blue-flavored dream might curdle in your mouth, make you feel like you're traveling to Eden in a handbasket.

When you stop by a bush, don't mention how you remember these plants when they first arrived, so small and spindly, so pot-bound. Don't tell of how you had to break their roots, rip their tendrils like muscle cleaving from bone, so that these roots would spread out, stop circling, stop being confined by their potted past. Don't admit that you fear you might become like these plants so long ago, pot-bound, root-bound, bound to choke on the confining demands of the pot of this place.

Don't mention these fears or any of this.

Nothing negative, remember?

.   .   .

This nothing-negative mantra forces us to focus on all the positives, and there are many: the storied house with its attractive roofline, the blueberries already established, the raw land to expand the planting, the pond and the acres of fine trees to enjoy.

But we know it will take a while to sell this unique place, to find a certain someone willing to tackle this business and to live in the small dwelling. The months of continual house cleaning, of answering the phone to silly questions (like "What's a holler?" our dialect for a mountain ravine throwing off the California caller)—all of it drags on. We question if we should have tackled this by ourselves, our FOR SALE BY OWNER Web page getting fewer hits each week, but then we get another call.

His name is Xander, short for Alexander, and he calls from Floyd's only motel.

"I saw your place on the Web, and it looks great. Tell me about it." I describe the terrain, the house, the blueberries. I answer his questions about roads and water and neighbors. Finally, he says, "I'd like to come see it, but there's one problem. I don't have a car. Could you come to Floyd and pick me up?"

This silences me. I have a zillion chores to do today and this guy wants me to drive a half hour to get him, drive another half hour back to our place, give him the two-hour tour, and then spend another hour on the road after this?

He fills the silence by explaining that he doesn't own a car, hasn't needed one for years since he lives in New York City. "But I'm tired of the city, ready to leave that all behind."

Something in his voice, in his questions, tells me that Xander is odd enough that he might be our man, so I quell my disbelief and offer him a compromise. "You get yourself here, and I'll drive you back."

"That'll work," he says.

Two hours later he shows up on the front steps. He's tall, long-haired, and wears worn sandals. And he's walking. Floyd County has only one taxi and it had already headed in the other direction, he tells me. So he started hitchhiking. He caught a ride to within two miles, and then hiked those last two up and over Pond Hill.

I'm impressed by his perseverance. And on how well he seems to already fit into the county's alternative community. He's only been here four days, and, as I give him the tour of the house, he rattles off names of folks I barely know after living here for over a decade.

But Xander's young, and unemployed, so I wonder about money. He senses this concern and alludes to a rich uncle who is an art dealer in Europe, an uncle who he's worked for and who favors him. I just keep quiet and show him the root cellar, the catfish-filled pond, the 1,000 blueberry bushes.

He's studied agriculture in India, he tells me, and there they just throw out the seeds and let nature do her work—no plowing, no tilling, no mulching, no weeding. Just food.

I try to hold in my disbelief, say that's interesting. "I don't know if that'll work here, but you can try."

When we finish the farm tour, we stand at the top of the field, under the berry hut's porch, and look down on the blueberries. We're quiet for a moment, taking it in, and I can see in Xander's dark eyes that he, too, is enough of a romantic to make this his, to pursue his own blueberry dreams.

I drive him back to the motel, and that evening, when Sarah comes home from work, I tell her I think that this is the one. She says I'm crazy to believe in a man who doesn't own a car, has never lived in the country, and knows little about blueberries, but eventually, Xander proves me right and buys our blueberry farm.

But before we sign the final contracts, I tell him all of the "negatives." I want to be honest, want to make sure he knows. So I go through the list of snakes and spiders and freezing pipes. Afterward, he says, "That's okay. I still want to buy your farm."

"But why move?" we keep getting asked through that last season of blueberries, that last season of pickers coming to harvest. And we continue to fumble our answers. "I want time to write," I might offer, or "We thought we were going to be closer to family," but that leads to too many other tangents.

Finally we settle on *the* answer: we're moving for beauty. We tell the askers that we fell in love with another farm that just has so much splendor that we can't leave it, can't give up the chance to live there. I get a few odd looks from pickers when I say the word *beauty*, but I let it pass. I'm beginning to learn from this field of berries that sometimes beauty and business don't mix, that maybe our highest human achievement isn't monetary wealth but creative joy. I had hoped to find that creative spirit here in this field and I did for a while, but something in me missed that opportunity, something in me and the larger world demanded the blueberries turn an economic engine more forcefully than an artistic one, if they could, if such a thing exists. If a garden like this even should have an engine.

And then I remember Thoreau. At the end of *Walden*, he, too, faced this why-move question, asked it of himself. And like him, as he shut the door of his shack by Walden Pond, I find I, too, have "several more lives to live."

I want to go live them.

Chapter 65

❧✿❧

PA Picking Again

Because of the bustedness of this season's blueberry crop, I journey back to my childhood home in Pennsylvania. In the decade that we've been in this berry business, I've returned often to Newburg and to my grandfather's old patch of blueberries, just never during July, during the height of season, never when before we had so many berries and customers of our own. But now we only open one day a week.

I call Aunt Kim. She tells me the Pennsylvania patch didn't suffer from a late freeze like our Virginia one did. Then before I can ask, she invites me, saying, "The berries are plentiful, come pick."

For the two decades since my grandparents died, Aunt Kim and Uncle Pete have tended this patch, pruning bushes, picking berries, and shooting groundhogs. They've carried on what Grandpa began. Unlike our own blueberry farm, my aunt and uncle and their two daughters do most of the picking, not allowing many customers to pick-their-own. "Less hassle," they tell me, though we all know the immense amount of hassle involved in filling orders and keeping up with picking a quarter acre. But this is their last season "running" the Minick planting, a fact that relieves Aunt Kim and Uncle Pete immensely.

Like our own farm, this one in Pennsylvania is also changing hands.

Marie, one of my cousins, and her husband Evan have bought these ninety acres, the two-story house with its thick brick walls, the barn and pond, and the blueberry patch. The two of them live and work in Georgia, but in a few years they plan to build a new home and retire here.

By luck, we all visit Pennsylvania at the same time, and so Mom, Dad, and I meet them in the patch one evening, along with Marie's sister, Renee, and their dad, Uncle Wayne. Pete and Kim's daughter, Kay, sees us all pull up, so she walks over from their house bringing her five-year-old daughter, Willa. Suddenly we have a picking party of nine people and three generations.

Of course, everyone picks the first few handfuls for the belly, to taste this sweet, old fruit, to use the blue sugar as energy to fill our buckets. Willa tells us she's picking to help her grandmother (Aunt Kim) fill an order.

"How many quarts does she need?" someone asks.

"At least twenty," Kay sighs. She has been doing this all of her twenty-five years. She, too, will be glad not to have to help her parents tend this patch.

"Well, let's all pick for Aunt Kim," I suggest, and we do, grazing a little, and slowly thudding berry on top of berry in the quieting pails.

In the past year we've lost two of our clan, Aunt Betty, Marie and Renee's mother, Uncle Wayne's wife, had a heart attack in the spring. And Uncle Nathan never recovered from a car wreck in the winter. He was the oldest of the four Minick brothers, the one who ran this farm for two decades, the one who came to visit us in Virginia. So for a moment, I realize this is the first we've all been together since those funerals, and I'm glad, truly thankful, for the solace of picking with kin.

The child leads us. Willa, with her big brown eyes and her bigger imagination, points to the nearby cows and names each one. "I talk to Julie Anne every day," she informs. "But Frances, that black one, she gets jealous and has to come talk, too." I goad her along, ask what they tell her. "Oh, nothing much, just how the grass tastes or why they wish the darn flies would leave them alone."

Then she finds a bug and carefully gathers it into her fingers. She tries to sneak it into her bucket, to take it home with her berries, but her mother knows this trick, says, "Now, Willa," and the child just holds it cupped in her palm.

From the next row over, my dad asks what I've also been wondering, "So, Evan, how's it feel to be a berry-farmer?"

And before Evan can answer, Uncle Wayne, who inherited most of my grandfather's gruffness, harrumphs and says, "Evan don't know squat about berries."

Luckily, Evan has married into this family long enough to know how to handle the snips. Plus, he and Marie have a certain sauciness to their marriage, a bantering playfulness full of wit and bite.

"That's why I want to hire you as our farm manager," Evan shoots back to his father-in-law.

"Yeah, right," Uncle Wayne responds.

I watch and listen, and as the heat of the day evaporates into the clear sky, I realize that despite her cow-talking, bug-collecting distractions, five-year-old Willa is picking more blueberries than fifty-year-old Evan. She might roam from bush to bush, but she grabs handfuls at each and only eats a few. Evan, on the other hand, picks the berries one at a time, and most of them find their way into the slot beneath his mustache.

"So how many times have you picked blueberries, Evan?" I ask.

And this makes everyone laugh.

"He doesn't really like to work," Marie chides. "He'd rather play golf." Then she steps beside her smiling, silent husband and tilts his bucket. "See," she holds her half-full container next to his. "You haven't even covered the bottom of your bucket."

He shrugs. "I grew up in the Midwest. We didn't have blueberries there," he admits while dramatically popping another berry into his mouth. "Plus I want to *retire* here, not work *more*."

Marie asks about our field, about the amount of work, about how to plant these bushes. She's considering expanding this patch in a few years, after they move here. And in the meantime, she tells me they've found a person interested in managing the blueberries, someone other than Aunt Kim and Uncle Pete who will tend the patch, pick and sell the fruit, and give Marie and Evan a small part of the profit.

I'm glad they've bought this place that has raised five generations of our family, glad they're willing to try to keep the land as farmland, even if they don't know themselves how to farm it.

And I'm glad they're willing to give these fifty-year-old blueberry bushes another decade or three or five of life. Give another generation or two a chance to know the sweetness of this family's fruit.

.   .   .

After we fill Aunt Kim's order and then pick some more to take home, the crew splits to head separate ways. But I stay. I want to hike out the lane to the pond. As a child I traveled this quarter-mile to bring in the cows, fish for bluegills, haul in loads of just-baled hay. The slivers of shale are a comfort under my feet.

While we picked, Marie used the phrase "hobby-farm" to describe what she and Evan plan to do here. Like a splinter under the skin, those words work to the surface of my thoughts. I have used this label to scorn the many sub-divided "farmettes" that sprout like weeds to cover once productive farms. Both "hobby-farm" and "farmette" imply a certain luxury, activities done in the spare time afforded by wealth made at some off-farm job. For years I knew I did not live on a "farmette" and I was not a "hobby-farmer."

But as I hike, another splinter surfaces. Once in our field in Virginia during the height of blueberry season, I worked in the check-out hut packing berries. My father sat outside at the picnic table, taking a break, and talking to a new picker. When the stranger realized who sat beside him, he asked my dad more questions about the field and us.

"So does Jim do this full-time?" the picker asked and nodded to the field.

"No," I heard my father reply. "This is a hobby they do in the summer. He and Sarah both teach."

Out of sight, I kept pouring berries into pints and held in my anger. How dare he call all this sweat and energy a "hobby," I had thought. And he's labored here, too, helped make this field produce with his own sweat.

Yet he defined me thus. And I had said nothing.

Now here on a different farm with years separating me from that moment, and more years gone since the first sprouting of this blueberry dream, I realize that maybe my father is right. Maybe like Cousin Marie, I've always just been a hobby-farmer. Aunt Kim and Uncle Pete seemed to know this, both of them working full-time elsewhere. Even Grandpa who started all this blueberry business worked full-time as an electrician, only piddling in his blueberries.

And even though our acre field is four times larger than this Pennsylvania one, it still is not enough. We needed at least four acres of blueberries, I realize now. Four acres to provide enough income to stay home, work where we live, and be real farmers. That size of a dream I never had imagined, never planned for, never knew we needed.

❧ BLUE INTERLUDE ❧
Costs

Every January, I tally the expenses for the previous year, all the fuel and fertilizer, repairs and supplies, insurance and taxes, the numbers filling blanks, filling columns, filling forms. I give these records to the accountant (another cost), and he performs his mysterious totaling, adding certain figures, subtracting others, all under the obligations of Uncle Sam. Then the accountant works through his magic formula for depreciation, that strange number I never fully fathom, that predicted wear and tear over years for our tractor, road, and so much else, including all of the 1,000 blueberry bushes.

What do these numbers mean? I have eaten from the bush of life, and found it good, yet I can't truly account for this nourishment. Who would dare pay the real value of such fruit, those hidden costs?

Yet maybe Sarah and I have paid part of this expense, and maybe we'll continue to pay it for a long time. I've begun to understand that value, to feel the slow grind of so many days piled on days, another tallying we call a calendar, a sheet that doles out the seasons, fields of empty squares that record the years. My neck and back hold the decade of stooping. My left knee creaks after the first five years of pruning and picking. The other knee joins it the next year, the two of them a duo of complaint. I realize I am depreciating.

And now that we're moving from this farm, who can tally the other costs, the wounds unexpected, the losses of leave-taking, of what's left behind? The annual hugs from Danica and Liesel. The laughter of Simon and Tessa. The graves of our dogs, Grover and Grace. The beaver in our pond. A neighbor like Joe. And the memory of the field so laden with berries. So much we lose when we leave a place well loved.

Blue is the only color we feel. No yellow emotions, no red notes. Just blue inside. My favorite musicians, Miles and Louis knew this.

And now I know it, too.

Chapter 66

❧❧

Searching for a Single Berry

We open one more day, the fourth and last of this abbreviated season, and again, the people show up, but the berries don't. The morning becomes more of a farewell party than a business day. Even strangers give us hugs. A group of five spends an hour in the field to come back to the check-out stand with one full bucket between them. Normally each person would have filled two buckets. I tell them this and about the late freeze, and the leader, a woman with short hair who reminds me of a benevolent nun, spreads her arms to embrace me. I return her hug quickly.

Louise and Danica show up as well. "Seen any snakes?" Louise hollers like always as she slams her car door.

"Not in the field," I reply, honestly, though I remember the garter snake at the edge of the woods where pine duff meets orchard grass, and the other one, a black racer that slithered in the shed's attic right above her as she checked out two years ago. "No, not in the field."

Louise came last week, so she knows she won't be yelling for me to bring her more buckets. She picks up two anyway, saying, "Just in case." We both know she'll be lucky to fill one.

In her sweet Dutch accent, Danica tells us about her strawberries. "I sprayed every evening during that freeze, every night for a whole week, and it worked. The water froze over my plants and the strawberries survived. I picked twenty gallons last month! But all the while I sprayed, I kept wondering about you and your blueberries. I hoped they survived, but here I see they didn't." She, too, is an optimist and takes two buckets.

No one stays for long. Everyone roams the field in search of a single berry. Everyone leaves with maybe a few handfuls and several empty containers.

The last picker is Beth, an art professor at the university where I teach. Though she lives a few miles away and I've long admired her paintings, I've never had the chance to talk with her. So there on Bed 8, the sun past high noon, my stomach hungry for lunch, I actually sit in the grass and visit while she picks what berries she can find. All the other pickers have gone home, all the berries that could be harvested have disappeared, and I can actually begin to relax. No need to hustle 'cause there's nothing left to hustle.

Beth tells of her travels, her dimples framing her smile. Every summer she heads to a different country where she volunteers with an organization called Earthwatch. She's helped on archaeological digs in Peru and Thailand, studied caterpillars in Costa Rica, and counted butterflies in Vietnam where "some of the butterflies were the size of small birds." She becomes even more animated as she talks, but she still searches, still finds a berry here and there.

"On a project in Brazil with bats and amphibians"—she swats a fly and keeps going—"I didn't have to handle the snakes, but I waded in the river up to my neck in water lilies. And *then* they told me about the anacondas!"

I laugh, and pick a stem of grass to chew.

"You don't need to be an expert, they'll train you," she says. "You just pay to go work, listen to many excellent lectures, and then also see that part of the world in a unique way." She plans to head out next month for Mexico where she'll help trap and monitor small mammals like ocelots, coati, and opossums.

I lean back on the grass and take in her amazing stories. *We could do this,* I think as I listen. Sarah and I could actually travel some summer when we no longer are blueberry farmers. What a bizarre notion. We have so many more worlds to see.

Again by 1:00, we pull shut the beat-up gate and put up the CLOSED sign. Then after lunch, Sarah takes a well-earned nap, and I tally the numbers for the whole season. I flip the pages in our spiral notebook, the columns filled with fractions—"1/2 pound, 3/4, 2 1/2"—and the pages themselves only a few in number. Usually, by the end of a season we fill up one whole notebook, but now I see more blank pages in this binder than ones we've used.

After a few minutes I check and double-check the final red number in the calculator's window. It reads 650 pounds. I have to sit there and repeat that number aloud before I realize that's the total for the whole season. Six hundred and fifty pounds. That means 90 percent of the berries disappeared, vanished, shriveled to nothing because of the May freeze and hungry coons. That leaves us 10 percent of what the field offered in its peak season, what the field should yield for the next fifty years.

Six hundred and fifty pounds.

With that number rolling in my head, I slip out for my last chore of the day, of the season, of my career as a blueberry farmer, really. In the garage, I grab one more sign, a wooden placard we use once at the end of every season, the one that says, SEASON'S OVER. I place it on the ground and kneel beside it. Underneath these two large-lettered words, I tape cardboard over another string of blue letters outlined in yellow, covering what Sarah painted so many years ago. I watch my hands position the pasteboard, smooth down the tape, hide these words she dipped her brush to before the first picker even came to this field. And before I carry this sign to our gate and place it beside the CLOSED sign, I watch those words disappear.

"There," I say aloud, rocking back on my heels. Now, no one can read, SEE YOU NEXT YEAR.

Epilogue

What is the sum, the total
of this field, these people,
this story?

This soil—paper.
This berry—ink.

Take, eat.

The Pickers II

⁑⁂

The catalogs all say six blueberry bushes should be enough, plenty to
feed the average family. So on our new farm miles and hours away from
the past, we shoot for a dozen plants, twenty-five at most. "Why be average?"
we both agree.

But so many varieties sound so grand. Our list grows, and I tell Sarah we
could plow up another row below the garden, which we do. We keep our
favorite varieties from the field and then add a half dozen more: Duke, No-
vember Glow, and one of the oldest, Jersey.

In the end, our patch of blueberries intended just to feed us grows from
six bushes to fifty. "At least it's not a thousand," Sarah says, to which I give
an amen.

It takes this newly planted patch a while to bear. So a few summers after
we move, I return to the blueberry field in Floyd. We need the berries for
our freezer, and besides I'm curious—I want to see how the land and bushes
have fared with a new owner. I wait until the end of June when the picking
should be prime and drive back along the familiar roads.

But these familiar roads can no longer take me back to Joe—Joe, who
wrote me hundreds of letters after we moved away, Joe, who was my best

neighbor and friend, Joe, who now rests in his own grave. He died the previous year, taking with him so much.

I don't turn up his driveway, but head to our old blueberry field. I should not have come. The lane to the field has rutted deeply from recent storms, with briars and tree limbs hanging over, slapping the car, sometimes blocking the windshield. The field itself tangles thick with half-mown grass. In years past, we'd be hitting peak picking about now, the lane busy, the parking area full of cars, the beds full with at least thirty people, especially this year with its ideal weather and no late freezes. But as I get out of the car, I see only five other pickers, and no hints of blue poking from beneath green leaves.

Like mornings past, I walk the beds. This time, though, I feel like someone who shouldn't be here, a trespasser. The bushes don't help. They should be loaded, canes drooping with the weight of berries, ripe and unripe. Instead, it seems like the field has already been picked. But when I look closely, I see none of the signs of pickers: no paths into the bushes, no squished berries on the ground, no stems still on the bush where berries once clustered. And not much blue anywhere.

I hike through the thick grass and keep coming across rows of bushes, empty, dead, and dying. These plants haven't been pruned since we left, it seems, and two of the varieties have more dead bushes than live, like they gave out and gave up on life after only ten years, when they should live another forty.

And then there are the weeds: four-foot thistle prickling any passerby, brambles and poison ivy vining into bushes, and right in the middle of several beds, rooted deeper than the bushes, whole fifteen-foot-tall trees.

I feared this, expected some of it, but still am overwhelmed. From his occasional e-mails, I know the new owner, Xander, has a good heart, but it seems he loves the idea of being a blueberry farmer more than the reality and all its demands. In my head I list what's missing: no pruning, no weeding, little mowing, and less than little mulching. By the number of dead bushes and the small size of these berries, no fertilizing. Probably no advertising, no phone calling, and by the note in the check-out hut, no daily 8:00 to 8:00 tending of pickers. $2/QUART, the paper taped to the table reads. PLEASE PUT MONEY IN JAR.

The new owner has his own blueberry dream, I begin to understand. By not doing these many tasks, he loses income but saves energy and gains time, hours and days to be with his new wife and baby . . . or simply time to ruminate, to sit in the quiet of the day and look over this field.

I slip into the middle of Bed 5 and settle beside a row of Bluecrops to pick what berries I can find. And I keep pondering over our own time here, our own blueberry years.

The dense foliage rubs against my bare arms, and I gently part the canes in search of fruit. As I pluck a berry, I realize these bushes have taught us that it's all right to fail. Or maybe *quit*'s the better word. It's okay to quit a cherished dream, especially if quitting opens such a wide door to more time to write and to hike the wooded hills that surround us on our new farm.

And it's all right to be alone. Sarah and I have so much—one another and our new place—that any loneliness eventually passes. I still wish we had more friends, but I think that lack comes in part with living in the country. And I don't want to live anywhere else.

After an hour of wandering this old patch of blueberries we planted so long ago, I realize I don't want to stay here any longer. From what used to be 1,000 bushes, I pick one and a half pounds of berries, less than two quarts, enough just to cover the bottom of my bucket.

I say a good-bye to the hooded warbler who still sings from the woods, then I leave this field a last time, and head home.

The next day, Sarah and I crouch to pick from our new planting. These young bushes haven't yet sprawled and bent over with the weight of heavy fruit, so we only spend a few minutes at each, only pick a handful of blueberries and then move to the next.

Like in other years and another place, we face each other, one on each side of the row. I already told her all about the old patch, and the images of its neglect have made us both quiet. So we keep picking, finish the top row, move to the bottom.

Jake, our new bruiser of a young shepherd, comes barreling down the aisle, eyes happy with finding us "hidden" in the bushes. He sits and we toss a berry that he leaps to catch, slobber flying.

Little B, our other dog, also finds us, though in her own slower, old-dog trot. This husky-mutt knew the other blueberry field, knew our first dog

Grover, and learned from him how to pick her own berries. I watch her sniffing around the base of a bush. She finds a cluster and then delicately bares her teeth to pick off the ripest berry.

And I realize I've never done that, never eaten a blueberry straight from the bush. I find a cluster, eye the ripest berry, then bend in an awkward pose to reach it. I miss the first time, tugging at a green berry that won't come loose. So back up I stand to refocus and bend again, and this time my lips know the softer globe, my teeth tug, and this ripe jewel falls onto my tongue.

When I stand back up, I see Sarah, hand on hip, face scrunched in a question. I can tell she's wondering about my sanity and weird contortions. So before she can ask, I tell her, "I'm eating like Little B." Then I grin and scratch the dog's ears. "We're picking like bears, aren't we, Little B? Teeth and lips only, no paws, no hands." Then I look right at Sarah and dare her. "Try it."

She hesitates, thinks me literally going to the dogs, but shifts and kneels to find a cluster of all ripe berries. Then with her typical quick-bodied ease, Sarah swoops down to grab one with her mouth. When she stands up, she grins and holds a nickel-sized blue globe between her teeth.

"You made that look easy," I say, and bend again to pick another, and then another. No sweat or oil from fingers here, I think, only straight-to-tongue, unadulterated blueness. Sarah, too, resumes this odd dance, these odd kisses of fruit. A few times I hold my hands behind my back, but most berries require hands on ground or stretched out for balance.

Then my hands go around to the other side of the bush, and I realize I'm hugging this creature, holding on to all the loss and joy, all the bushes and pickers and years in our field, and all the bushes and years before that in Grandpa's patch, and all the years before that with Elizabeth White and Frederick Coville, those domesticators of this wild fruit, and before them Thoreau who loved this "unforbidden fruit," and before that, all the people all over this continent who bent to pick and eat a wild, sweet, sky-colored berry.

I hug all of that and taste again this simple fruit.

ONE FINAL INTERLUDE

❦

From Louise Dickinson Rich's 1942 Maine homesteading classic, We Took to the Woods:

[N]owhere else are there blueberries like the blueberries of Prospect, which are what you go there for in the first place. They grow as large as your thumb nail, and have a peculiar dull black luster under the bright surface bloom, as though soot from the old fire still stains and sweetens them. There are acres and acres of them, and no matter how long and fast you pick, working in the ceaseless wind that blows across the barren from the lake, loud with the lovely sound of water lapping on stones, you can no more than scratch the surface of the plentitude. We come home, wind-burned and juice-stained, with forty or fifty quarts; but no one could tell we had ever been there.

At night, after being at Prospect, I lie in bed and see great clusters of berries slide by endlessly against my closed lids. They haunt me. There are so many of them yet unpicked, so many that never will be picked. The birds and bears and foxes will eat a few, but most of them will drop off at the first frost, to return to the sparse soil of Prospect whatever of value they borrowed from it. Nature is strictly moral. There is no attempt to cheat the earth by means of steel vault or bronze coffin. I hope that when I die I too may be permitted to pay at once my oldest outstanding debt, to restore promptly the minerals and salts that have been lent to me for the little while that I have use for blood and bone and flesh.

BLUEBERRY RECIPES

Quick tips for blueberries from our market handouts:

1. Freeze unwashed blueberries for year-round enjoyment. Toss a handful at a time into recipes to bring back that summer sunshine, or eat them like candy.
2. Stir berries into yogurt for breakfast or a snack.
3. Sprinkle them over hot or cold cereal.
4. Spoon them over ice cream.
5. Mix with cottage cheese.
6. Add blue to a fruit salad.
7. Serve in a cantaloupe half, and top with a dollop of yogurt.

❧ SARAH'S BLUEBERRY SMOOTHIE

1 cup low-fat vanilla yogurt or ½ cup of tofu
¾ cup low-fat milk or rice milk
1 tablespoon honey
½ tablespoon cinnamon
2 cups frozen blueberries

In a blender, combine all ingredients. Blend until smooth.

YIELD: **2** SERVINGS

VARIATIONS: *To the above, you can add:* A sliver of ginger for zip; flax seeds or soy powder for the health benefits; or ice cubes if berries are not frozen

❧❧

❧ COLD BLUEBERRY SOUP
From Beth, our last picker

I have a recipe from a store owner in Ann Arbor, Michigan. I've long forgotten his name, though.

Buttermilk
Orange juice
Fresh blueberries

Mix equal parts buttermilk and orange juice, and liberal handfuls of fresh blueberries. Chill and serve. Great for hot days when you don't want to cook.

VARIATION: I've extended the recipe to make tofu smoothies. Add a package of tofu and blend in blender or food processor. You can add other fruit, but just blueberries and buttermilk and OJ are good, too. I pour it into a covered pitcher and it keeps for two or three days. It gets better the second day, but shouldn't be kept too long. This is my favorite blueberry recipe, even though I don't like buttermilk, and the combo of buttermilk and OJ sounds terrible at first.

❧❧

❧ MOM'S BLUEBERRY BUCKLE

On the back of the recipe, Jim's mother wrote, "I've made this since I got married— over 50 years ago! You may remember eating this—I used to make it rather often."

TOPPING

⅓ cup sugar   ⅓ cup flour
½ teaspoon cinnamon   ¼ cup butter

BATTER

2 cups all-purpose flour   3 teaspoons baking powder
½ teaspoon salt   ½ cup shortening
½ cup sugar   1 egg, beaten
½ cup milk   2 teaspoons lemon juice
2 cups blueberries

Preheat oven to 350°F, Grease a 9×9×2–inch baking pan. Combine topping ingredients in blender until crumbly. For batter, sift flour with salt and baking powder. Cream shortening and sugar for batter until light, add egg, and beat until smooth. Add dry ingredients and milk, beating well. Pour into pan. Cover blueberries with lemon juice and then spread over batter. Cover berries with sugar-cinnamon topping. Bake 1 hour or until done. Serve warm or cold.

YIELD: **9** SERVINGS

🌸 ANN PENDRAK'S BLUEBERRY BUCKLE

From one of our exhuberant regular pickers

BATTER

2 cups all-purpose flour

2½ teaspoons baking powder

¾ cup milk

¾ cup sugar

¼ cup vegetable oil

1 egg

2 cups fresh blueberries

TOPPING

½ cup sugar

½ teaspoon cinnamon

⅓ cup all-purpose flour

¼ cup butter

GLAZE (OPTIONAL)

1 tablespoon butter melted

1 teaspoon vanilla extract

2 cups confectioner's sugar

2 tablespoons warm milk

Preheat oven to 375°F. Grease a 9×9×2–inch baking pan. Mix topping and set aside. In a separate bowl, mix vigorously all ingredients of buckle, adding blueberries last and gently, *gently*. Spread in pan. Sprinkle topping over batter in pan. Bake 45 to 50 minutes. Mix glaze while buckle is cooling. Drizzle glaze over warm buckle. Oooo Yum!

YIELD: **9** SERVINGS

🌸 BLUEBERRY SAUCE

From Susan Minick (Jim's mother)

This is one of our favorites that Dad often pours over his ice cream.

½ cup sugar

2 cups fresh blueberries

1 tablespoon lemon juice

2 teaspoons cornstarch

½ cup water

Dash of salt

Mix all ingredients well. Cook over medium heat in a 2-quart saucepan un-til just boiling. Chill. Use on ice cream, custard, waffles, pancakes, etc. Also a good pie filling.

YIELD: 3 CUPS

MORE MAMA MIL'S BLUEBERRY MUMBLES

A bar cookie from writer Heidi Hartwiger

This is good with a blend of summer berries. In the winter, use dried fruits.

FILLING

3 cups blueberries (fresh or frozen)

¾ cup sugar (or to taste)

¾ cup water

2 tablespoons fresh lemon juice

1 4-inch cinnamon stick or 2 teaspoons ground cinnamon

1 teaspoon freshly grated nutmeg

Mix all ingredients in a 2 quart-saucepan. Bring to just a boil, reduce heat, stir, and mash the berries. Cook the filling until the berries reach a jamlike consistency. Set aside and prepare the crumb mixture.

CRUMB MIXTURE

¾ cup soft butter

1 cup packed brown sugar

½ teaspoon salt

1¾ cups unbleached white flour

½ teaspoon soda

1½ cups old-fashioned rolled oats

½ cup finely chopped almonds (optional)

Mix butter and sugar, add salt and flour, and then add oats and almonds. Firmly press half the mixture into a greased 9×13-inch baking pan. Spread the blueberry filling. Pat on the remaining crumb mixture. Bake at 400°F for 25 to 30 minutes or until the crust is lightly browned and the filling bubbles. Let cool completely and cut into bars.

YIELD: APPROXIMATELY 15 BAR COOKIES

❀❀

❀ BLUEBERRY GRUNT
From picker Kathleen Ingoldsby

Kathleen provided this story: "Years and years ago, when we lived in Massachusetts, my husband and I would drive to Dogtown, a long-abandoned colonial settlement on Cape Ann in Gloucester. There we picked both high and lowbush blueberries. The trails wandered for acres up and around a hill, long overgrown with brambles. Every so often we stumbled upon a single granite boulder carved in uppercase with one of these Franklinian inscriptions: COURAGE; IDEAS; HELP MOTHER; KINDNESS; LOYALTY; IF WORK STOPS, VALUES DECAY; INDUSTRY; INITIATIVE; INTEGRITY; KEEP OUT OF DEBT; STUDY; TRUTH; PROSPERITY FOLLOWS SERVICE; INTELLIGENCE; NEVER TRY/ NEVER WIN. We learned later that the eccentric Roger Babson hired Finnish stone carvers during the Depression to carve these maxims.

"The sweetness of the blueberry is, ever thus, permanently etched in my heart." Later Kathleen sent this as an explanation of this dessert's name: "Grunts or Slump—Early attempts to adapt the English steamed pudding to the primitive cooking equipment available to the Colonists in New England resulted in the grunt and the slump, a simple dumpling-like pudding (basically a cobbler) using local fruit. Usually cooked on top of the stove. In Massachusetts, they were known as a grunt (thought to be a description of the sound the berries make as they stew). In Vermont, Maine, and Rhode Island, the dessert was referred to as a slump. From http://whatscookingamerica.net/History/CobblerHistory.htm."

1½ cups water   Large lemon
¼ cup sugar   3 cups fresh blueberries

1 cup all-purpose flour   ¼ teaspoon salt (optional)
3 tablespoons wheat germ   1 egg, beaten
2 teaspoons sugar   ⅓ cup milk
2 teaspoons baking powder

In a deep 9-inch skillet, combine water, sugar, half a large lemon, thinly sliced, and simmer 10 minutes. Remove lemon. Add blueberries, simmer 2 minutes. Meanwhile mix flour, wheat germ, sugar, baking powder, ¼ teaspoon salt (optional). Add to this, barely incorporating, the beaten egg and milk to make dumpling batter. Gently plop batter over as much of the surface as you can manage. Cover and simmer 15 minutes until done. Serve with berry sauce on top of biscuit dumpling.

Good for breakfast.

YIELD: **9** SERVINGS

MOMMA'S SCRUMPTIOUS BLUEBERRY ICE CREAM
From Camelia McNeil Elliott

2⅔ cups sugar
1 12-ounce can evaporated milk
1 can sweetened condensed milk
8 ounces whipping cream
16 ounces fresh blueberries, chopped in food processor
1 teaspoon vanilla extract

Mix all ingredients well. Pour into ice cream freezer. Add additional milk to fill line or fill bucket within 1½ inches of top. Freeze and delight your guests.

YIELD: **1** TO **2** GALLONS

❧ LEMON-BLUEBERRY CREAM CHEESE PIE

From picker Sharon Okie

This recipe is especially good on a hot summer day!

CRUST

  2 cups crushed graham crackers
  ¼ cup butter, melted with 2 tablespoons honey
  ½ teaspoon cinnamon
  Dash of nutmeg

Press mixture firmly into sides and bottom of an 8-inch pie plate. Reserve a little for the top of the pie.

FILLING

  8 ounces softened cream cheese
  ½ cup firm yogurt (we use plain or vanilla)
  ¼ cup honey
  1½ teaspoons vanilla extract
  Grated rind of ½ lemon
  1 cup fresh blueberries

Beat all filling ingredients except blueberries with electric mixer until well-blended. Gently stir in 1 cup blueberries and spread into shell. Top with reserved crumbs from crust. Chill for at least 3 hours.

YIELD: 1 PIE OR 6 TO 8 SERVINGS

❧☙

❧ LEMON-BLUEBERRY POUND CAKE

From picker Sharon Okie

  1 pound sweet butter
  3 cups sugar
  6 eggs

4 cups unbleached white flour

1 tablespoon baking powder

1 cup milk

The zest of one lemon

1 teaspoon vanilla extract

½ teaspoon lemon extract

1 teaspoon butter flavoring

2 cups fresh blueberries

Cream together butter and sugar with an electric mixer at high speed, until light and fluffy. Add eggs, one at a time, beating well after each one. Set aside.

Sift together flour and baking powder. In separate bowl, mix together milk, zest, and flavorings. Add wet and dry ingredients alternately to butter mixture, beginning and ending with the dry. Use a rubber spatula or wooden spoon and mix thoroughly, but avoid excess beating.

Gently stir in blueberries.

Pour into buttered and floured Bundt or tube pan. Preheat oven to 325°F and bake in oven for 1 hour, or until toothpick inserted into center comes out dry. After the cake cools 10 minutes, turn it out onto a plate. Let it cool completely before slicing (even though it is hard to wait).

YIELD: 10 TO 14 SERVINGS

BLUEBERRY COFFEE CAKE

From Kimberly Carter

COFFEE CAKE

¼ cup butter, softened

¾ cup sugar

1 egg

½ cup milk

2 cups all-purpose flour

2 teaspoons baking powder

½ teaspoon salt

2 cups fresh blueberries

Topping (recipe below)

TOPPING

½ cup sugar	½ teaspoon cinnamon
⅓ cup all-purpose flour	¼ cup butter

Preheat oven to 350°F. Grease a 9-inch square cake pan. Cream butter and sugar; beat in egg and milk. Sift flour, baking powder, and salt together; combine with butter mixture. Add blueberries carefully. Pour into prepared pan. Make the topping: combine sugar, flour, and cinnamon; cut in butter with pastry blender. Sprinkle topping over batter and bake for 35 minutes.

YIELD: **9** SERVINGS

✾ BLUEBERRY AMBROSIA

From *The Blueberry Connection* by Beatrice Buszek, Nimbus Publishing

1 cup pineapple, crushed or chunked
1 cup fresh blueberries
1 cup grapes, halved
2 cups diced marshmallows
2 tablespoons sugar
1 cup sour cream
1 cup peaches, cut in small bits
½ cup shredded coconut

Drain pineapple, then combine all ingredients in a bowl. Chill at least an hour.

YIELD: **6** SERVINGS

VARIATION: Omit sour cream and marshmallows and add 1 cup white wine. Add coconut just before serving.

❧ BLUEBERRY ROLL

From Hazel Robertson, Jim's maternal grandmother

1½ cups all-purpose flour
2 teaspoons baking powder
½ teaspoon salt
2 tablespoons sugar
5 tablespoons shortening
1 egg
¼ cup milk (approx.)
1½ cups fresh blueberries
½ cup sugar

Sift flour, baking powder, salt, and 2 tablespoons sugar into bowl. Cut in shortening until mixture resembles coarse corn meal. Beat egg slightly with a fork in cup; add milk to make ½ cup in all. Blend well. Add to flour mixture and stir quickly with fork until just mixed. Turn onto lightly floured board and knead gently about 10 times, until outside looks smooth. Roll or pat into a rectangle, approximately 8 × 10 inches.

Cover dough evenly with berries (all but 1 inch on sides). Sprinkle the ½ cup sugar over berries. (If using frozen berries, don't thaw before use.) Roll like a jelly roll. Place on greased shallow pan. Preheat oven to 350°F and bake for approximately 25 to 30 minutes, until golden brown. Cut in slices and serve hot.

YIELD: APPROXIMATELY **10** SERVINGS

❧

❧ BLUEBERRY CRUNCH

From picker Ruth Yoder

1 cup all-purpose flour
¾ cup old-fashioned oatmeal
½ cup brown sugar
½ cup butter

1 teaspoon cinnamon
½ cup granulated sugar
2 tablespoons cornstarch
1 cup water
1 teaspoon vanilla extract
4 cups fresh blueberries

Mix flour, oatmeal, brown sugar, butter, and cinnamon till crumbly. Put aside. Then, in a saucepan, combine granulated sugar, cornstarch, water, and vanilla, and cook until clear. Press half the crumbs into greased 9×9–inch pan. Add blueberries. Pour cooked mixture over blueberries. Top with remaining crumbs. Preheat oven to 350°F and bake for 1 hour.

YIELD: **9** SERVINGS

FRESH BLUEBERRY PIE

From picker Ruth Yoder

8 ounces cream cheese
8 ounces sour cream
¾ cup sugar
14 ounces nondairy whipped cream
4 cups fresh blueberries
2 graham cracker pie crusts

Beat together cream cheese, sour cream, and sugar. Fold in whipped cream and blueberries. Pour into the 2 graham cracker crusts. Chill till set and serve.

YIELD: **2** PIES

❧ WILD BLUEBERRY PRESERVES
From Dana Wildsmith, poet/writer

6 cups fresh blueberries   1 3-ounce pouch liquid pectin
7 cups sugar   ½ teaspoon cinnamon

Layer the blueberries alternately with half the sugar in a large pan. Gradually heat until the sugar dissolves, stirring constantly. Add the rest of the sugar, heat until it dissolves. Bring the mixture to a full rolling boil, stirring constantly. Add the pectin, all at once, while stirring. Boil, stirring constantly, for 1 minute.

Remove from heat. Stir in the cinnamon. Skim off any foam. Allow to cool for 5 minutes to prevent floating fruit. Ladle the preserves into hot jars; wipe rims and seal.

YIELD: SEVERAL PINTS

❧ GRANDMA HANSON'S BLUEBERRY CREAM PIE
From Pam Hanson, writer

Pam's great-aunt Lou's homemade pie crust recipe follows, if you want a great recipe.

1 unbaked 9-inch pie crust, frozen or homemade
4 cups fresh blueberries
⅔ cup sugar *or* ⅔ cup Splenda
4 tablespoons flour
½ teaspoon cinnamon
Pinch of salt
1 cup soy milk or evaporated skim milk

Preheat oven to 400°F. Place blueberries in crust. Stir together remaining ingredients and pour over berries. Bake at least 45 minutes, until mixture is bubbly. Let cool before slicing.

YIELD: 1 PIE OR 6 TO 8 SERVINGS

❧ GREAT AUNT LOU'S HOMEMADE PIE CRUST

From Pam Hanson, writer

1⅓ cups all-purpose flour
1 teaspoon salt
⅓ cup vegetable or canola oil
3 tablespoons cold milk

Mix flour and salt, add the oil and milk. Roll out between two pieces of floured, waxed paper. Fit into pie plate, fill, and bake at 425°F for approximately 12 to 16 minutes. (Pam likes to very lightly prick with a fork on bottom and sides, not going all the way through, when making juicy or cream pies.)

YIELD: 1 PIE CRUST

❧ BLUEBERRY CLUSTERS

From Leigh Limerick Rosenecker

2 bags semisweet chips
3 tablespoons solid vegetable shortening
1 pint fresh blueberries, washed and allowed to dry completely
    (remove any soft, mashable berries)
Coated paper or foil candy cups

Melt chips and shortening together, either in double boiler or in microwave at a medium-low setting, stirring occasionally. Remove from heat and gently stir in blueberries until all are coated. Using 2 teaspoons, drop spoonfuls of the mixture into the cups. Allow about four or five berries per cup and plenty of chocolate in between. Chill until solid. (Note: They're extra nice if you melt a little white chocolate in a bag and drizzle over.)

YIELD: 12 TO 24 CLUSTERS

❧ BLUE BACARDI

From *The Blueberry Connection* by Beatrice Buszek, Nimbus Publishing

My sister serves this pretty in a martini glass, and she even pierces a few blueberries on a stick and serves them in the drink as you would olives in a martini.

Juice of half a lime
2 ounces blueberry juice
1½ ounces Barcardi rum
Dash of Grenadine

Combine all ingredients in a cocktail shaker. Shake with fine ice and strain.

YIELD: 1 DRINK

❧ BLUE NOSE

From *The Blueberry Connection* by Beatrice Buszek, Nimbus Publishing

2 cups clear, cold blueberry juice
½ cup rum

Combine ingredients. Mix well. Serve over crushed ice in frosted glasses. Garnish with mint sprigs.

YIELD: 2 DRINKS

APPENDIX OF SOURCES

OUR HERO

Fernald, Merritt Lyndon. *Gray's Botany of Plants*. 8th ed. New York: American Book, 1950.

Gleason, Henry. *The New Britton and Brown Illustrated Flora of the Northeastern United States and Adjacent Canada*. Vol. 3. Lancaster, PA: Lancaster Press and New York Botanical Garden, 1958.

Gledhill, D. *The Names of Plants*, 2nd ed. Cambridge: Cambridge University Press, 1985.

Thoreau, Henry David. *Wild Fruits*, edited by Bradley P. Dean. New York: Norton, 2000.

LATIN LAUREL HELLS

Bailey, L. H. *How Plants Get Their Names*. New York: Dover, 1963.

Benson, Lyman. *Plant Classification*. Boston: Heath, 1957.

Coté, Gary. Personal communications. February–April 2009.

Fernald, Merritt Lyndon. *Gray's Botany of Plants*. 8th Ed. New York: American Book, 1950.

Gleason, Henry. *The New Britton and Brown Illustrated Flora of the Northeastern United States and Adjacent Canada*. Vol. 3. Lancaster, PA: Lancaster Press and New York Botanical Garden, 1958.

Gledhill, D. *The Names of Plants*. 2nd ed. Cambridge: Cambridge University Press, 1985.

Jaeger, Edmund. *A Source-Book of Biological Names and Terms*. 3rd ed. Springfield, IL: Charles Thomas, 1955.

Kell, John. Personal communications. April 2009.

Thoreau, Henry David. *Wild Fruits*, edited by Bradley P. Dean. New York: Norton, 2000.

Vander Kloet, S. P. "On the Etymology of *Vaccinium L.*" *Rhodora* 94.880 (1992): 371–73.

NEW FARMERS AND FAILURE

Stam, Jerome. "Are Farmer Bankruptcies a Good Indicator of Rural Financial Stress?" Economic Research Service, USDA. Agriculture Information Bulletin No. 724-06, December 1996. Accessed January 31, 2007, http://www.ers.usda.gov/publications/AIB724/AIB72406.PDF.

Stam, Jerome M., and Bruce L. Dixon. "Farmer Bankruptcies and Farm Exits in the United States, 1899–2002." Economic Research Service, USDA. Agriculture Information Bulletin No. 788. March 2004. (24–25). Accessed January 31, 2007, http://www.ers.usda.gov/publications/aib788/aib788.pdf.

BLUES IN HISTORY

Richards, Rebecca T., and Susan J. Alexander. "A Social History of Wild Huckleberry Harvesting in the Pacific Northwest." USDA Forest Service. General Technical Report PNW-GTR-657. February 2006. 9. Accessed July 2, 2009, http://www.fs.fed.us/pnw/pubs/pnw_gtr657.pdf.

Thoreau, Henry David. *Wild Fruits*, edited by Bradley P. Dean. New York: Norton, 2000.

WHAT WE FEAR

Cartwright, Duncan, and Sally Hughson. *Exploring Loneliness: The Experiences of Rural and Metropolitan Australia*. Lifeline Pamphlet. Profile/ 03. July 7, 2005. Accessed Jan. 31, 2007, http://www.lifeline.org.au/__data/assets/pdf_file/0018/31941/LifelineCalls3_ExploringLoneliness.pdf.

Robbins, John. *Healthy at 100*. New York: Random House, 2006.

WORKING OFF OF THE FARM

Allen, Rich, and Ginger Harris. "What We Know about the Demographics of U.S. Farm Operators." Agricultural Outlook Forum 2005. National Agricultural Statistics Service, USDA. February 25, 2005. Accessed January 31, 2007, http://www.nass.usda.gov/census/census02/otheranalaysis/demographicpaper022505.txt.

Fernandez-Cornejo, Jorge. "Off-Farm Income, Technology Adoption, and Farm Economic Performance." USDA Economic Research Service. Report Number ERR-36. February 1, 2007. Accessed June 18, 2009, http://www.ers.usda.gov/Publications/ERR36/.

Hoppe, Robert, and Jim MacDonald. "America's Diverse Family Farms: Assorted Sizes, Types, and Situations." USDA Economic Research Service. Agriculture Information Bulletin Number 769. May 2001. Accessed January 31, 2007, http://www.ers.usda.gov/publications/aib769/aib769.pdf.

Jones, Carol A., Hisham El-Osta, and Robert Green. "Economic Well-Being of Farm Households." USDA Economic Research Service. Economic Brief Number 7. March 2006. Accessed January 31, 2007, http://www.ers.usda.gov/publications/EB7/EB7.pdf.

ROOTS AND FUNGI

Coté, Gary. Personal communications. February–April 2009.

HOMESTEAD HINTS

Homestead Hints. Ed. Donald J. Berg. Berkeley: Ten Speed Press, 1986.

MEDITATION ON ORGANIC
"Industry Statistics and Projected Growth." Organic Trade Association, 2008. Accessed June 18, 2009, www.ota.com/organic/mt/business.html.

PICKING WITH HD
Thoreau, Henry David. *Faith in a Seed,* edited by Bradley P. Dean. Washington, D.C.: Island Press, 1993.
———. *Wild Fruits,* edited by Bradley P. Dean. New York: Norton, 2000.

FREDERICK COVILLE
Coville, Frederick. *Experiments in Blueberry Culture.* Bulletin No. 193. Washington, D.C.: USGPO, 1910.
———. "Improving the Wild Blueberry." *Yearbook of Agriculture, 1937.* Washington, D.C.: USGPO, 1937. 559–74.
"Frederick Coville." Obituary by The National Geographic Society. *National Geographic Magazine* 71:5. 1937. 662.
Hancock, James F. "Highbush Blueberry Breeders." *HortScience* 41:1. February 2006. 20–21.
Kearney, T. H. Untitled Obituary of Frederick Coville. *Yearbook of Agriculture, 1937.* Washington, D.C.: USGPO, 1937. 560.

ELIZABETH WHITE
Bolger, William C. "Elizabeth C. White (1871–1954): A Biographical Sketch." Presented to the National Organization of Women, Moorestown, NJ, March 12, 1997. Accessed February 3, 2007, http://www.whitesbog.org/elizabethwhite.html.
Ehlenfeldt, Mark. Personal interview. April 7, 2009.
Rose. Philip S. "The Blueberry Queen." *Saturday Evening Post.* September 12, 1942. 18–19, 52, 55.
White, Elizabeth. "The Blueberry Grower: The 25th Anniversary of the Beginning of Blueberry Culture at Whitesbog, New Jersey." *Cranberries: The National Cranberry Magazine.* Five Installments. May–September 1936. Given to author from Mark Ehlenfeldt's personal collection, March 2009.
———. "The Development of Blueberry Culture." Address before the Philadelphia Society for Promoting Agriculture, April 17, 1934. Given to author from Mark Ehlenfeldt's personal collection, March 2009.
———. "Development of the Cultivated Blueberry." 1920 Pamphlet. Given to author from Mark Ehlenfeldt's personal collection, March 2009.

BLUES EVOLUTION
Coté, Gary. Personal communications. February–April 2009.

THE BENEFITS OF ORGANIC
Curl, Cynthia, Richard Fenske, and Kai Elgethun. "Organophosphorus Pesticide Exposure of Urban and Suburban Preschool Children with Organic and Conventional Diets." *Environmental Health Perspectives* 111:3. March 2003. Accessed March 14, 2003. http://findarticles.com/p/articles/mi_m0CYP/is_3_111/ai_100730739/?tag=content;col1.
Edwards, Rob. "The Natural Choice: Organic Food Has More of What It Takes to Keep

Appendix of Sources

You Healthy." *New Scientist* 73. March 16, 2002. Accessed March 9, 2003, http://www .newscientist.com/article/mg17323341.000-the-natural-choice.html.

Kingsolver, Barbara. *Small Wonders.* Waterville, ME: Thorndike, 2002.

Schlosser, Eric. *Fast Food Nation: The Dark Side of the All-American Meal.* New York: Perennial, 2002.

Smith, Bob L. "Organic Foods vs. Supermarket Foods: Element Levels." *Journal of Applied Nutrition* 45:1, 1993. 35-9. Accessed March 9, 2003, http://www.soilandhealth.org/ 01aglibrary/Arun/Organic%20vs%20supermarket–element%20levels.pdf.

Worthington, Virginia. "Nutritional Quality of Organic Versus Conventional Fruits, Vegetables, and Grains." *The Journal of Alternative and Complementary Medicine* 7:2, 2001. 161–73. Accessed March 9, 2003 on Organic Trade Association's Web page http://www.ota.com.

NEW RELIGION

Pollan, Michael. *The Omnivore's Dilemma.* New York: Penguin, 2006.

EATING LOCAL

Adams, Katherine L. "Community Supported Agriculture." ATTRA—National Sustainable Agriculture Information Services, 2006. Accessed June 22, 2009, www.atra.ncat.org.

"Farmers Markets Growth, 1994–2008." USDA Agricultural Marketing Services. September 22, 2008. Accessed June 20, 2009, http://www.ams.usda.gov/AMSv1.0/ams.fetch TemplateData.do?template=TemplateS&navID=WholesaleandFarmersMarkets& leftNav=WholesaleandFarmersMarkets&page=WFMFarmersMarketGrowth& description=Farmers%20Market%20Growth&acct=frmrdirmkt.

BLUE LIT

Clampitt, Amy. "Blueberrying in August." *Eat, Drink, and Be Merry: Poems about Food and Drink.* Ed. Peter Washington. New York: Knopf, 2003. 78–79.

Frost, Robert. "Blueberries." *Eat, Drink, and Be Merry: Poems about Food and Drink.* Ed. Peter Washington. New York: Knopf, 2003. 73–77.

Lockward, Diane. "Blueberry." *What Feeds Us.* Nicholasville, KY: Wind, 2006.

"Mark Twain Talks." *The Sunday (Portland) Oregonian.* August 9, 1895. Accessed July 2, 2009, http://etext.virginia.edu/railton/onstage/mttalks.html.

McPhee, John. *The Pine Barrens.* New York: Farrar, Straus, and Giroux, 1968.

Oliver, Mary. "Picking Blueberries, Austerlitz, New York, 1957." *New and Selected Poems.* Boston: Beacon Press, 1992. 12–13.

BLUE MOVIES

Blueberry. Directed by Jan Kounen. Sony, 2005.

My Blueberry Nights. Directed by Wong Kar-wai. Weinstein Co., 2008.

The Sound of Music. Directed by Robert Wise. 20th Century Fox, 2005.

BLUE SONGS

Armstrong, Louis. "Blueberry Hill." 1949. Accessed May 20, 2009, http://lyricsplayground. com/alpha/songs/b/blueberryhill.shtml.

Domino, Fats. "Blueberry Hill." 1956. Accessed May 20, 2009, http://lyricsplayground.com/ alpha/songs/b/blueberryhill.shtml.

Keith, Toby. "Huckleberry." 2002. Accessed July 2, 2009, http://new.music.yahoo.com/toby-keith/tracks/huckleberry–2027785.

L'auroel, Miria. "A Marshmallow Moon in a Blueberry Sky." 2004. Accessed July 2, 2009, http://lyrics.payplay.fm/Miria+L%27auroel/A+Marshmallow+Moon+in+a+Blueberry+Sky.

Ludacris. "Blueberry Yum Yum." n.d. Accessed July 2, 2009, http://www.lyricsdownload.com/ludacris-blueberry-yum-yum-lyrics.html.

The Mamas & the Papas. "Blueberries for Breakfast." 1971. Accessed July 2, 2009, http://www.allthelyrics.com/lyrics/mamas_and_the_papas/blueberries_for_breakfast-lyrics-397129.html.

Mercer, Johnny. "Moon River." 1961. Accessed July 2, 2009, http://johnnymercer.com/FAQ/Moon%20River.htm.

Midler, Bette. "Blueberry Pie." 1980. Accessed July 2, 2009, http://artists.letssingit.com/bette-midler-lyrics-blueberry-pie-6bpjksg.

THE BENEFITS OF BLUE

"Berry Good News." *Health*, June 2001, 30.

Foltz-Gray, Dorothy. "The Blueberry Breakthrough." *Health*, July/August 1998, 42, 44.

McCord, Holly. "The Miracle Berry." *Prevention*, June 1999, 122–27.

Upton, Roy. "Bilberry." *Great Life*, n.d., 16–17.

BLUES TODAY

Bolger, William C. "Elizabeth C. White (1871–1954): A Biographical Sketch." Presented to the National Organization of Women, Moorestown, NJ, March 12, 1997. Accessed February 3, 2007, http://www.whitesbog.org/elizabethwhite.html.

2008 *Blueberry Statistic*. USDA New Jersey Agricultural Statistics Service. February 2009.

United States Highbush Blueberry Council. n.d. Accessed June 18, 2009, www.blueberrycouncil.org.

White, Elizabeth. "The Development of Blueberry Culture." Address before the Philadelphia Society for Promoting Agriculture, April 17, 1934. Given to author from Mark Ehlenfeldt's personal collection, March 2009.

OUR PROBLEMS

"Census Finds Dramatic Loss of Virginia Farmland." *Virginia Farm Bureau News*. March 2009. 9.

"Farm Numbers." 2007 *Census of Agriculture*. USDA National Agriculture Statistics Service. n.d. Accessed June 18, 2009, www.agcensus.usda.gov.

Simmons, Andy. "Fat, Inc." *Reader's Digest*. August 2007. 112–15.

The works of Wendell Berry, Wes Jackson, and Michael Pollan have greatly influenced my thinking on these problems for many years. I strongly recommend their books.

LISTENING AT WHITESBOG

Hogan, Linda. *Dwellings*. New York: Norton, 1995.

Whitesbog Preservation Trust has a plethora of helpful resources including notices about their annual blueberry festival. Visit www.whitesbog.org.

ONE FINAL INTERLUDE

Rich, Louise Dickinson. *The Forest Years: Containing in One Volume: We Took to the Woods* and *My Neck of the Woods*. Philadelphia: Lippincott, 1963.

ACKNOWLEDGMENTS

✹⁄❧

Many, many people helped with this book and our field. Specifically, I want to acknowledge:

My grandparents who seeded this blueberry dream, and my parents, sister, aunts, uncles, and cousins who nurtured it. Also, to Kathryn and Karen, who tried out many of these recipes. And to Sarah's parents and brother and family for years of support and practical help with saws, sheds, outhouses, and such.

John Sutherland, for so many years of friendship and "advice." Rest in peace.

The editors and these publications where some chapters first appeared, often in radically different form: *Orion Magazine; The Land Report; The Roanoke Times New River Current; Rivendell; Appalachian Voice; Pilgrimage;* and *Now and Then Magazine.*

For help in the field, Melissa Lamb-Speed, Mark Shoenbeck, Doug Pfeiffer, Barbara Farmer, and many others. For patience and help with the irrigation system, Clinton Smith and Jack Spraker. For years of friendship and Web site guru-ship, John and Bonnie Dodson.

Dennis Anderson opened the door to historical photographs of our farm, and Hugh Dulaney, Maritha Lester, John Mumaw, and John Sutherland answered questions on this history as best they could.

All the berry growers and small farmers who provide us with good eats, and especially the Midkiffs, and Charlie O'Dell, and the many researchers who answer so many questions.

For time and expertise, Mark Ehlenfeldt and Susan Phillips provided terrific insight into the origins of our blueberry hero. Their work and that of the Whitesbog Preservation Trust is incredibly commendable and important in preserving the heritage of blueberry's humble beginnings. Nancy O'Mallon, with her filmmaking skills, also has contributed to this significant legacy.

At Radford University, Rosemary Guruswamy provided invaluable support, and Bethley Giles was researcher extraordinaire. For friendship, comments, and answers to too many questions, Ricky Cox and Grace Edwards. Gary Coté filled in my science-knowledge holes with generosity of spirit and good storytelling, and John Kell added insights into the world of Latin, cows, and flowers. With humor, Bud Bennett tracked down my too many obscure interlibrary loan requests. Cliff Dumais helped create a stunning Web site.

The many writers and friends at the Southern Appalachian Writers Cooperative and Hindman Settlement School's Appalachian Writers Workshop, especially Mike Mullins and Joyce Dyer. Sandy Ballard has provided good recipes, bad jokes, and years of kindness. Darnell Arnoult and our novel writing group have tolerated my nonfiction as I've tolerated the so-many prompts.

My agent, Paige Wheeler, didn't give up and found a home for this book despite several setbacks. And my editor Katie Gilligan asked the hard questions to make this a better book. The staff at Thomas Dunne/St. Martin's then made this a beautiful book.

The Virginia Center for the Creative Arts and the Woodhull Institute provided advice and periods of time that propelled this work forward. Thanks to these fine institutes' staffs, and to the writers and editors I met there, especially Laurie Lynn Drummond, Furaha Norton, Wende Jager-Hyman, and Naomi Wolf. Early on, Brettne Bloom also gave advice in shaping this manuscript, and Lee Wilson offered legal advice and good cheer. Henry Quesada helped with a quick question on names as well.

So many teachers have guided my growth with patience and skill—to all, much thanks. And teachers in the form of other writers have also shaped me. Some of these include: Wendell Berry, Michael Pollan, Wes Jackson, Terry Tempest Williams, Mark Kurlansky, Joyce Dyer, Larry Brown, Janisse Ray, Eric Schlosser, Barbara Kingsolver, and Steven Hopp.

I am fortunate to have friends willing to read parts or all of this manuscript. Their tolerance of my requests and their insightful comments have proven invaluable. They are: Theresa Burriss, Taryn Chase, Scott Christianson, Robert Gipe, Tempi Hale, Pam Hanson, Tim Poland, and Rick Van Noy.

And lastly, to Sarah, who has read every one of these words too many times, given pithy and timely comments, put up with being a subject in this project, and who still frames my day with hugs.

To all I missed, my apologies. To everyone, my gratitude.

ABOUT THE AUTHOR

In addition to *The Blueberry Years*, Jim Minick has written a collection of essays, *Finding a Clear Path*, two books of poetry, *Her Secret Song* and *Burning Heaven*, and he edited *All There Is to Keep* by Rita Riddle. In 2008, the Virginia College Bookstore Association awarded *Burning Heaven* the Jefferson Cup for best book of the year. He's garnered many other awards and grants, including from the Virginia Commission for the Arts, the Virginia Foundation for the Humanities, and the Virginia Center for the Creative Arts. Minick's work has appeared in many publications including *Shenandoah, Orion, San Francisco Chronicle, Encyclopedia of Appalachia, Conversations with Wendell Berry, The Sun, Appalachian Journal, Bay Journal News, Wind*, and *Roanoke Times*. He teaches at Radford University and lives in the mountains of Virginia.

Jim is a huge fan of book clubs and he is willing to speak—in person or via phone—with groups who have read one of his books. Book clubs should have at least ten members and a speaker phone, and they should be available to talk with the author on a weekday evening, from 7 to 10 P.M. EST.

To contact him, read excerpts, and hear audio interviews, visit www.jim-minick .com.